"GO QUICKER SOU SLOWER".

An actor's/voiceover's diary.
Part one: August to November.
by
Jonathan Kydd

The action is possibly set in 2007… ish.

Main characters:

JK. An actor and voice over.
Roop. JK's best mate. An actor.
Derek Fazakerly. An annoying actor friend.

JK's Mother.
The Girly. JK's fitness instructor girlfriend.
Iain. JK's acting agent at Iain's Agency.
Lynn. JK's voice agent at Diggerty Dawg.
Dexter D'Eath. A casting director.
Tom Curley. A top actor.
Mandy Fard. A stand-up-would-be-actor.
Nick Sweet. "Henry Hedgehog" producer.
Alan Thorpe. "Photographer to the Stars".
Sarah Maltby-Singh. An ad producer and JK's ex.

Maria. An actor. And voice over.
Tony Chorley. A voice over.
Lee Trinn. A voice over.
Seymour Simon. A voice over.

The story mostly takes place in and around London's Soho, Shepherd's Bush and Putney.

N.B. The author specifically explains a lot of voice over and acting technicalities that you would think, in a diary, would be abbreviated. But, such is his vanity, he was always expecting someone (not necessarily in the business) to read it.

Thanks to Joe Greco, Tim Rolls, James Byrne, Jonathan Coy, Jac

Cloake and Jonathan Tafler for their invaluable input. And to April Waters for her patience and understanding.

Tuesday 4th August

Suddenly remembered the dream I had last night. Something unlocked it, some ecclesiastical spokesperson or something, on the radio.

In the dream I was acting in a sort of "Whoops Matron I've Lost my Stethoscope" farce playing a Vicar. It was the first night.

It was being performed in a labyrinthine concrete regional theatre and having been in the dressing room - I was on a bit after the start - I walked briskly to the stage for my entrance, but found myself suddenly in the foyer wearing merely my dog collar, voluminous comedy Y-Fronts and socks held up by garters and panicked hugely and sprinted to get back into the theatre via the Stage Door but somehow missed it and instead was in a huge crowded Sainsbury's and asked for directions from a bloke behind the fish counter - I bought some sea-bass - and having exited via the car park was directed to a windy dual carriageway by a member of staff in evening dress, from where I was forced to hail a taxi - "The theatre? You're miles away mate!" - and the driver took me back via Worthing and I never paid him and I was chased down an alleyway by him - "oi come back 'ere you reverend" - and a group of pirates of whom he was obviously the leader - "arrrrh" - and he suddenly had a cutlass and I hid behind a Louisiana style hearse and wailing funeral cortège and crept back to the theatre to discover - inevitably - that I had missed my cue. I was "off". Which is unforgivable. In fact I'd missed the whole play. I remember tip-toeing my way back to the stage

- miraculously now in striped pyjamas, with ridiculously abundant poking out pubic hair and a clown wig - just as the play was ending and was correctly shunned by the whole cast. The Stage Manager had gone on for me with the book and she hurled it at me screaming

"Your selfish love of cake has had ridiculous repercussions!"

"But..but…but…why was there no carrot and walnut?" was all I could blurt.

William Shatner then appeared bellowing "I… have had…enough…of YOU" and kicked me down a crevasse that had opened up beneath me.

I had a feeling of immense bewilderment, joy and shame, all at the same time, while I was falling to my doom, thinking

"For fucks sake this bollocks is a dream isn't it?"

And woke up dying for a wee. What was all that about eh?

Wed 5th August

To the Beeb in White City. They like my dulcet tones there for their World News slot, I suppose, for my enunciation. I mean you can't have a promo about a news programme that's coming up being unintelligible to people around the world eg in Singapore. Or Hong Kong. Or Mumbai. Can you. So they tend not to want anything but a voice with a bit of articulation so I'd been told. I'd never worked with the producer before, a grinning willowy woman in specs called Steph, who said on shaking my hand

"Oh. You look nothing like your voice do you."

As if somehow I'd thought about this a lot and it was the norm and I'd instantly agree, or say

"No I don't. I do apologise for having misled you. I am of course, much uglier, presuming my voice is attractive of course."

She'd obviously only listened to my voice reel and not seen a photo.

The engineer Mick chimed in with

"You can't say that to the voice Steph! I mean come on! What do you mean?"

She was instantly uncomfortable realising she was possibly being quite rude and retorted confidently, but dug a hole quickly.

"Well I've not met him before and I've listened to his reel and he er doesn't look like he sounds."

I remained schtum. I was interested in seeing how this would pan out with Mick as my champion.

"What exactly do you mean Steph without being appallingly offensive?" He said.

They obviously knew each other well as this teasing was clearly allowed. And Mick wouldn't be reprimanded for cheek or insolence as there were only four engineers in the building and she and he must have worked together a lot.

"Well I mean obviously he er isn't as er….um..I mean he's er not er…" she looked at Mick.

"I'm not helping you out" said Mick.

"Ok…ok… He's…..much shorter than I thought he'd be." She blurted.

It was my turn now. I milked it.

"Ouch." I said. "How much taller should I be?" I asked. "I'm five eight as it is."

"Yes Steph." said Mick. "Six inches? A foot?"

The caption man (the man who puts the captions, the visible words, on the promos) seated at the end of the row in front of his computer had said nothing while all this was going on. Mick included him.

    "Nick. What do you think? Should JK be six three or even taller according to his voice?"

    He joined in. Very dead pan.

    "Well I've worked with JK quite a bit and yes this anomaly has always been uppermost in my thoughts."

    "Oh!" said Mick. "Interesting!"

    "Except I've always felt his voice made him about three foot six."

    Steph realised that they were acutely taking the piss and curtly changed the subject.

    "Can we do the script please? We've only got half an hour…twenty minutes now…Just the end line JK."

    I had merely to say

    "……On BBC World News."

    I did. We did two takes. Steph approved them.

    "Brilliant JK." said Mick. "And the first take was five foot nine. …..But the second was seven foot two!"

Thursday 6th August

Morning

    I scootered to Berwick Street to do a car ad at Slick. It's with a lovely helpful highly professional engineer who's called Ron. Ron gets it right on all levels. Charming and creative with the client, speedy with the equipment and technology and a friend and advisor to the actors. The perfect triple whammy hat trick. Consequently many people want to work with him. He's a friend. And who should be sitting in the reception area but the great actor, Tom Curley, who I have worked with before and who is wonderful fun if unbelievably eccentric. And frequently appallingly rude. He greets me all poshly and syrupy with

"Ah look it's JK. My day is complete. The lovely talented JK. Herrrrre's JK!" (this bit in a very loud not very good American accent). "You know dear boy you would be perfect casting for Uncle Vanya. Yes. Perfect."

"What Chekhov's "Uncle Vanya"?" I say knowing me Chekov. "But isn't he a manic depressive and suicidal?" I add.

"Yes he is."

And he cackles loudly, presumably meaning he's taking the mick. Or not. Who knows?

"You doing the car ad?" He asks.

"I am yes."

"Me too! Hee hee heeeee!" He squeaks maniacally for no apparent reason. "We're working together. Please don't show me up. Please! Ha ha ha ha!"

"They're ready for you. Studio 1 up the stairs first door." Says Jenna the receptionist in Estuary tones.

"Is it with Ron?" He asks. "Because he's such a sweet boy and I enjoy working with him."

"Yes!" Beams Jenna. The runners beam. Everyone beams. Everyone loves Tom.

We pass the open plan kitchen on the way. I ask for a tea. So does Tom. They will be delivered to the studio shortly.

"Oh you lovely man" trills Tom to the young runner in the snood.

The producer and client and copywriter are already there along with Kim Roberts a very talented VO with whom I've worked on several occasions who can do any accent under the sun and who's with my agent the Dawgs. She's terrific if a bit bossy. "Say it like this" she has been known to insist on several occasions which I grin and bear. Tom greets her warmly.

"Well we're in very safe hands if Kim's in this. She's brilliant. And delightful. And JK of course. And Ron! The dream team!"

He says to anybody who is listening.

We all enter the "booth", which is in this instance a room off the studio with a large glass sliding door and a series of tables and chairs with the mics and pop shields set up with all the cables wired through the walls. Tom sits in the second row on the right behind us. Kim and I share a mic. Tom's doing the end line. It's a kind of obvious stereotypical car sales commercial. Kim and I are the customers. It's something like:

"Oh darling look at all these great Voxfors at such good bargain prices. There are so many. I don't know what to choose." Says Kim.

"Well you can't go wrong with a Voxfor 47 it's such a great car." Sez I. "Shall we ask for a test drive?"

There are then FX (sound effects) of us getting into the car and driving. And the odd "wow" and "lovely drive" and "it's so comfy!".

Tom's deep thrusting car-ad MVO1 (Male Voice Over number one) then comes in with

"The Voxfor 47. £ 23000 on the road. It's a great car. Available in four different colours. Test drive one today. "

And we're back to me and Kim again. There's FX of getting out of the car and doors closing. Kim's character says

"That was great. Can we have another go?"

And my character says

"Well yeah! Let's buy it!"

And Tom says

"The Voxfor 47. Once you've driven it you'll want one."

Before we start Tom announces from the back of the room to all and sundry ie the engineer and client,

"Who wrote this shit?"

There is a beat until the copywriter says

"Well I did."

"Well it's terrible writing. It's ordure. None of these people is real."

The producer, who is running the session, hangs on before replying, expecting a laugh or snort or some sort of noise from Tom denoting he's mucking about. But none is forthcoming, because he actually does mean it. It's a regular event with him to make this announcement. It doesn't make for a good atmosphere. There's a sort of pause and then by way of getting on with it and ignoring Tom, Kim and I are asked to speed up the lines a "gnats" (short for "gnat's gusset". A gnat's gusset being a very small width indeed) as it's a 30 seconder but we were spot on really. Tom is ludicrously slow with his lines. Almost deliberately. In fact definitely deliberately.

"Could you speed up a tad, Tom?" Asks the producer.

"It won't make the ad any better" sneers Tom.

"If you could." Asks the producer ploughing on.

Tom does knuckle down though and regardless of what he thinks of the script, does it a bit quicker and very well. Is "spot on" in fact.

Kim and I don't make any errors and find a couple of Londoners, though we do one from Durham which the producer likes but prefers London.

"That's terrific everyone" says the producer after 6 takes.

"It's about 27 seconds and with the car sound FX that'll be a perfect 30. Isn't that right Ron?"

"Yup it'll fit perfectly."

He'll take a few breaths out of course to make it fit. The producer consults with the copywriter and continues:

"Could we swap round this time? Tom you play the customer and JK do MVO1?"

Tom pretends to retch derisively.

"Take 7" says Ron.

Kim does her bit.

"Oh darling look at all these great Voxfors at such good bargain prices. There are so many. I don't know what to choose."

"Don't you? Oh dear. That's a fucking shame." Improvises Tom in appalling growly comedy Glasgow.

"Well don't ever buy a Voxfor 47. It's such a shite car. If anyone tries to sell you one tell 'em to fuck off."

He is stopped in his tracks by the producer.

"Ha ha very funny Tom but can we do a normal one?"

"Take 8" says Ron. Kim starts it off again.

"Oh darling look at all these great Voxfors at such good bargain prices. There are so many. I don't know what to choose."

"I've just come down from the Isle of Skye and my penis is ablaze with joy that you and I are purchasing the worst fucking car in the world." rasps Tom Scottishly.

Once again the producer intervenes.

"Please try and do it properly Tom."

The engineer Ron, who has worked with Tom a lot and knows these antics - Tom basically only wants to do the MVO1. The Male Voice Over number one. The sell. He wants to be the "Voice of Voxfor", not the "turns" doing the acting the MVO2 and FVO (Female Voice Over) - decides to take matters into his own hands. He pulls the faders down, leaves the desk, opens the glass doors into the booth, closes them behind him again, marches up to Tom and within a few inches of his face says

"Tom. Fucking do it properly."

He turns on his heel, opens and closes the doors - no one in the studio proper has heard this exchange - returns to the mixing desk, says Take 9 and Tom reads the lines this time in a high pitched pantomime old toothless woman's voice, but there is clearly progress of a sort in that he's no longer using his dreadful Scottish accent. However when I do his MVO stuff he blows raspberries while I'm doing it, skilfully in the gaps.

Me: The Voxfor 47. (Small fart noise) Only £23000 on the road. (Slightly bigger fart noise) It's a great car. (Big fart noise) Available in four different colours.(Huge squelchy fart noise) Test drive one today". (Huge extended fart noise with lots of spit)

"Yes well I think this is a battle we're not going to win" says the producer. "Let's go with take 6."

"Before we go can we have a few getting into car "grunts" and some excited "isn't the car brilliant" wallas?" asks Ron. (a walla is a sound effect made by the mouth rather than one on an FX CD). Kim and I emit a few eees and oohs and aahs.

"That's great thanks" says Ron.

"Good I'm happy" says put upon weary producer who is clearly not.

We exit thanking him and the bewildered client and bemused copywriter who thanks me and Kim pointedly "for our professionalism" and a tight lipped hurt looking Tom exclaims "well I wish I could say I'd enjoyed it," as if it was all the ad agency's fault that he'd been subjected to such a difficult painful artistic struggle.

Despite the madness, it's a network radio ad so is "worth a few bob" as my father used to say. I leave the building into the market outside with Tom firing out goodbyes to all and sundry and immediately on his exit he's recognised and basks in the recognition. Which is fair enough. He's a very fine well known actor. Just barking.

Scootered languidly home. Avoided being scrunched by a white van on a mission but flashed him a discreet wanker sign that made his blood boil and he attempted to chase me down the Marylebone Road but failed miserably. Coz I'm on a scooter.

Lunched on tuna, sweetcorn and olives with a bit of pitta.

Voiced a video game in the afternoon for a couple of hours, in Guildford. Drove in the Mini. Too far for the scooter. I've signed an agreement so can't say what it is or even write it down for fear of huge legal repercussions (so they say) but it's the next one of one I've done before.

It's a bit of a drive from the Bush - across Putney Bridge to the A3 and up the always jammed Putney High Street - but rewarding, as it's a fun "gig". (Voice overs are called "gigs" by some voice overs which is quite cool and groovy apparently).

For the last one I was a ghost, and a series of non speaking wide tongued grunting goblins as well as a character from the film it's based on, who is played in the films by someone who is far too expensive for the game, so they use other actors who can replicate the voice and, more importantly, are much cheaper eg me.

The producer, a woman with a chin stud, wearing voluminous dungarees and a pair of Doc Marten's who has dyed her hair that interesting purple and white colour, gets me to do a series of high pitched noises because the goblin/monster has a very wide mouth and she doesn't think I'm quite capturing that quality.
After several minutes of contorting my face and larynx (I have a small mouth and it's not natural to be stretching it so wide) I come up with a noise that she feels corresponds with the picture of the nasty little dart blowing imp I am there for, and despite the discomfort, the contortion it's causing me, we progress for two hours with burping and shrilly crying out and shouting and expiring and giggling and all the things the little evil dweebos do when they are summoned by the person wot is playing said game. I even have a sweet song to sing with which she is finally pleased after about 27 gonad twisting takes.

My slight worry after all these attempts at finding the "right voice" for this creature is that he doesn't sound other worldly or magical. Just German. But I have learnt not to query these things.
    At the end of the session I am as a limp as a listing lily and have a throat resembling a brush that has been sweeping up thorns. I have littered the table and script with a pebble-dashed spaghetti of saliva. But I am content. The session has been rewarding. I have no idea whether they will use the character or not, (this is sometimes the case. You can voice an ad or game and when it comes out you hear it's someone else voicing it!) but I didn't disgrace myself. And I will be paid. I A3 it home and listen to "Steve McQueen" by 90s pop Gods, Prefab Sprout.

Friday 7th August

    "Crime Stoppers" audition. Disastrous. Ffs.
Crime Stoppers is a TV show where they recreate a crime for viewers to see if they can recognise or know anything about the criminal or crime and then ring in and say they have information about him or her.
    "Oh yeah…. He lives across the road….He seems such a nice man…. Washes his car every Sunday. Always has something pleasant to say. Wouldn't of thought he was a psychopath. Mind you sometimes he'd come out of his front door covered from head to toe in blood but I presumed he'd been slaughtering his pigs…" etc.
    I apparently looked like some criminal who had attacked a post office in Gateshead so had been asked to attend the interview. They'd seen my picture in "Spotlight", the big on-line actors' directory where

all actors have their photographs for all and sundry to peruse and contacted my agent Iain. On arrival, the producer, a "boy" of about 12 with a spikey gelled hairdo called Cosmo, handed me a rolled up newspaper and told me to go at him really angrily as if I had a pickaxe. He said, in badly hidden Public School tones

"Right...Now this guy right in Gateshead was a violent criminal. Ok? And you resemble him. Ok? But you've got to convince me right you can be as violent looking as him when he's being violent. Ok? So go on. Ok? Really show me your anger. Ok? Show me that violence lurking within you. Ok? Go for me and shout out in a Newcastle accent, "Give me the money". Ok?"

Oh God. What one has to go through as an artiste. Instantly on the back foot. No

"Hello how are you?"

No

"What have you been doing lately?"

No

"Well interestingly in the rich tapestry of my life I've been playing a hedgehog."

Straight in with the exertion.

I first of all didn't really bother. Limply hit him on the shoulder with the newspaper. I was offended really that he believed I couldn't beat the shit out of him if I'd really wanted to.

"No no no. That's not it at all" this person who was half my age informed me. No. A quarter my age.

"Go for me. Really go for me. Ok?" said the infant.

"I'm not convinced you've got what it takes. Go on. You're robbing a Post Office. Right? You've got a pickaxe. Ok? You're a Geordie. Really go for me. Ok? Lose your temper. Ok?"

"Got what it takes?" The dick. Questioning my acting cojones? Doubting my ability to be instantly angry? The steaming turdy.

"Got what it fucking takes?"

The red mist enveloped me. His patronising tone made me really go for him. I went for him so expertly, and with such feeling, that I bludgeoned him to the floor and under his desk where he hid as I trashed the office and tipped out the contents of his secretary's handbag and got him to lie face down on the carpet. Whereupon I tied his hands together with a rubber band and defecated in the corner. (Well not the defecate bit) (Or the tying up bit). (Or the lying face down bit) What made it even more scary was all I could say was "Alan Shearer" over and over again as I beat him over the shoulder (not the head. That wouldn't have been pleasant and might have caused me to be arrested). Naturally after such a display of idiocy…. I got offered the part. I naturally turned it down. I turned it down because

a) it's pretty much of a professional cul-de-sac being in those kind of programmes in the first place, (I mean it's not a high profile drama is it really? A casting person isn't likely to cast you from appearing as a looky-likey in a reconstruction of a crime scene) and

b) i know it's unlikely but I couldn't face the prospect of someone recognising me and mistaking me for the criminal and "having a go". Be great to be in a classy restaurant one night with a loved one just after the programme's been on the telly and have some courageous chap out to impress his girlfriend, make a citizen's arrest, pin you to a wall and duff you up while you try and explain to him and the maitre D you're just an actor who'd been playing a part.

"No (oof) that wasn't me (biff) I was impersonating someone (crack). I am an artiste (bleed). No not the face (stomp)."

c) I didn't really want to work with Cosmo (ridiculous name. I'd have been tempted to call him "ology" and would have done) having belittled him so much. I mean it wouldn't be fair would it? And might he not seek revenge?

My theatrical agent, a wiry pencil-thin bleached blonde-haired late forty something viper called Iain, was incensed with me. He's not my voice agent. That's Diggerty Dawg.

"I can't believe it. If you had these views and opinions why on earth did you waste everybody's time? Not to mention the mayhem you created in the office. Now he'll never employ you. And he might end up directing movies. You never know Mr Clever Clogs. And quite frankly the business is in such a limp state you should take anything that's offered to you."

Iain's just annoyed he won't be getting his commission.

"What happened to the whole concept of "building a career?" I asked him.

"Well in your case darling, I'd say you've got a series of small sheds. None of which is occupied. But we don't want to demolish them do we? There's hardly been any building work at all has there, since the kiddies series?"

("Windy the Witch". I played "Gnomey". "Henry Hedgehog" the animated series I do is through my voice agent). He persisted with his hackneyed building metaphor:

"I mean there's a plot of shedded land but none of the contractors have turned up to build any more have they? And several of the sheds look as if they're condemned."

Ooh he was loving it. He continued,

"Look. Next time tell me if you don't want to do something, rather than put a bomb under your edifice. That's someone else you've offended."

"What do you mean? Who else have I offended?"

"Well Michael Chiswick for a start. I tried to get him to see you for a commercial last week, but apparently you pratted about so much in the last casting he won't see you. You can't afford to fuck about in these pinched times. Must go. Other line going."

Can't understand what he's talking about. Michael Chiswick's casting was for a French commercial where I had to take something out of a cupboard and fall over with the effort. Highly comically taxing that one. Huge laughs all round. Name and agent and profile to video camera, no director present, just you and the casting director and a cameraman with a stick of toffee up his hooter, do the action several times (well mime it) and on my way thankyou. Can't think where I pratted about. Narr. He's just being spiteful.

Oh hang on. I remember now. I pretended to be French. He asked me on camera for my name and agent and I said

"Bonjour! Nom d'un chien! Je m'appelle Monsieur Jay Kay. I am wiv "l'agence d'Iain" that's Iain's Agency. I 'ave bin eatin masses of escargots and frog's legs to preparez myself mon petit chou! Allez les bleus!"

    I remember he didn't like that. And got me to do it again, "not in a stupid French accent. Just do it normally. you racist idiot."

Sat 8th

    Phoned by the ex, Sarah Maltby-Singh, who was clearly pissed. I got rid v quickly citing a headache. Not going down that route again. We've split. It's a no go area. Clean break. Get thee behind me Sarah. Will not see her again. A complete disaster. I will not be led by my willie. Standing at the end of the bed drunk and naked with a kitchen knife accusing me of having an affair with her gay friend Roxanne is something I will not put up with again.
    As mother says "darling it's here not here" pointing to her head and then her nether regions. I will be very disciplined. On yer bike Sarah. Anyway I'm seeing someone. The relationship I'm having with the person I'm seeing isn't working very well ("why are you going out with her?" Says Roop. Actually it's "what the fark has possessed you to go out with that sports obsessed money grabbing nincompoop emphasis on the poop?") and he is not wrong. But hey ho, the wind and the rain. First things first. Sarah. NO.

Sun 9th

    Mother phoned. Asked me whether I was using my mobile phone. As she was phoning me on it I was a bit confused.

"But you're phoning me on it" I spluttered.
"I haven't got it." She sang.
"What?"
"I haven't got your phone."
"No. I mean I'm on it."
"Well get off it."
"If I do we won't be speaking"
"What?"
"I mean I'll have to ring off."
"Why?"
"Coz I'm on it now."
"You've lost me darling… Are you using it a lot?"
"Well, off and on."
"Well be very careful."
"Of what? Thieves? People shouting? Angry callers?"
"Using it."
"Using it? But what else should I do with it?"
"You can get cancer. Especially in the car."
She's read an old article somewhere. She cuts them out and finds them years later in a drawer.
"Do you use it in the car?" she continues like a terrier trying to grab a pair of trousers just out of reach on a clothes line.
"Occasionally, yes."
"Well open the windows."
"Why?"
"The magnetic pulses reflect off the windows in the enclosed space."
"What?"
"And give you a tumour."
"Where?" I responded wearily.
"Here and there. You must hold it as far away from your head as possible."

I did so.
"Yes but you can't hear me if I do that."
"What?"
"If I hold the phone away from my ear you can't hear me as I'm not near the mouthpiece."
"I can't hear you."
"Proves my point really."
There was a weary exhalation. I continued with
"Mother this is old news. You've been reading some of those old newspaper clippings you keep in the drawer."
"And woe betide you should put it on your lap. Bye bye babies. Adieu heirs. Cheerio children."
"Oh for goodness sake."
"It's the rays emitted from the aerial."
"Mother you are talking out of your...."
"How's the garden?" she chipped in confusingly.
"It's very well thankyou."
"No. I'm not enquiring after its health. Is it tidy?"
"Er...I think so. Yes."
"It isn't, is it?"
"Er. No. It isn't." (She can tell when I'm fibbing)
"Darling, please tidy it for me."
"Ok".
"No really tidy it. Don't just say ok."
"Ok."
"Remember. You'll never get a girlfriend if you've got an untidy garden."
"Oh Mother. Please. I've got a girlfriend."
"Yes. But you don't like her much do you?"
"Well yes and no."
"Don't lie to me. I'm your Mother."
"Ok. I don't like her."
"Don't shout at me."

"I'm not."
"You are."
"I'm not." (I wasn't)
"You're just like your father. Never knew when he was shouting. I won't speak to you any longer if you shout. And stop using that bloody phone if you value your health......."

She hung up!

Monday 10th Aug

Scootered from Soho to do a "gig" at the basement Blue Bee studios at Channel Four in Victoria. The 4 in front of the building is a wonderful piece of iron sculpture. I could stand and admire it for hours. But then again I'd be moved on by security.

Drove stupidly quickly as I was late for the job having over-run at Jumble Studios in Wardour Street. I'd just voiced an ad for a Classic Car Jaguar Event doing a Pathé news 1940s voice, which I am frequently asked to do. I have no idea why I find it easy to do this voice. But I can. It's flat and very posh and goes like the clappers. Actually on reflection I know why I find it easy. I'm a bit posh and can sight read at speed. It's obviously on my "reel" as an example of my work. The "reel" is what would-be employers listen to at the suggestion of the agent, the file (or files) they can access on the agent's website so they hear if you're suitable for the job. It's examples of your work, your reads.

"I need a 1940s clipped posh Pathé read!" says the client and my agent at Diggerty Dawg Voices (how they arrived at that name Dawg knows) says "ah JK can do that!" And directs them to me and what I can do. And they choose me! I hope!

    I over-ran at the session at Jumble as the script kept changing even while I was doing the job. The client - not there in the studio - kept emailing in new versions, new wordings of the script mid voice over. Which of course irritated the copywriter as that's his job. The client then listened to the completed takes played to him live on his phone. Hardly ideal. He's not hearing it as it sounds in the studio. But this is not unusual. Some employers are ludicrously up themselves and boss everyone about. And lots of advertisers appear to "wing it", to make it up as they go along.
    "I'll know what I want when I hear it" being something I'm told a lot. Engineers and actors are rarely guilty of this. Though one deep voiced voicing legend could only work at eleven o'clock in the morning after several very black coffees. By lunchtime after a visit to the pub he could only slur. And after that he was unconscious. Still a great voice though. Possibly deepened by excess.
    The client liked my reading of the latest version of the script even though it sounded his end as if he was listening in a wind tunnel, but it was rumoured he was on board a boat in the Mediterranean. Well that's what the producer suggested.
    "He's on a fucking yacht" being his precise words.

    I'd gone to Channel 4 after the Soho job, to voice "tags" for "Film 4". That's when you just add a title and a time to a promo - which is a trailer for a programme or film. No repeats (residuals) here. One studio fee and that's it. They're the poor side of voicing. Good fun to do tho. And the programmes are interesting so you want to watch 'em when they're on the box or put them on your show reel. Eg

"The Shawshank Redemption. Next Thursday at 9. (PAUSE) On Film 4".

If I can get the pause in I do. It creates a nice effect. I then do the other tags: "Tomorrow at nine...." "Tonight at nine"...and occasionally you mention a programme the film is after eg "After Grand Designs". But that's usually for Channel 4 films and not Film 4.. They are different channels, obviously.

I tagged five films in a deep growly "film trailer" voice, matching the mood of the action movie and its hard hitting music. Though some producers nowadays go for the opposite and will use a weedy voice for a hard hitter. Sort of deliberately going for the opposite. Personally it doesn't make any sense. Why undermine all the work on making the promo? By naffly weeding it all up. But what do I know?

Took half an hour to do the tags on the five films. Can be longer if the tag is overwritten and won't fit the "end board" which is at the end of the promo where the title is. It might have "part of Fright Fest" or "part of our Adventure season". This can become a mouthful, and is then longer than the gap you've got available. So you have to put your foot on the gas which can ruin the drama of the read. The engineer can nudge the "read" back a few frames to make it fit, with the recording software, but frequently he or she is happier when it fits already and no trimming needs to be done. The engineer can always nick out a few breaths, but sometimes it's just too long and you really do need to get your skates on.

"Kingdom of Heaven part of our Ridley Scott season next Thursday at 10 on Film Four" has to get a lick on, but still sound intelligible and filmic. It's a skill that I believe I've mastered.

"Well done JK that's in" he says "and a nice read."

"I thought my "Thursday" was a bit squelchy" I said from the titchy cupboard-like recording booth where the mic and headphones are. "Flirsday it sounded like."

"Oh I didn't notice it but do go again if you want."

I do. Everyone's happy. I scoot home in a highly pleased and leisurely fashion ignoring the inevitable toots of the impatient many.

Student meal of pasta and tuna.

Tuesday 11th

No work. (Sob)

Got a fan letter. From being Henry Hedgehog, one of the characters I do on children's TV.

("Hooray it's Henry. Super Duper Henry. Henry the Her her her Hedddgehoggg!" goes the song)

The "fan", Mike from Sheffield, in very spidery slightly mad writing - all in capitals - on lined paper, offered me a small black cigarette holder "for my own personal use" were I to send him a signed photo. The problem is
a) This is the fourth letter he's sent this year (and I've replied to the other three)
b) I don't smoke.
c) He actually wants a picture of the cartoon hedgehog for which I do the voice. I am not who he

actually wrote to. He wrote to me sure. Via my agent. But he has put "Dear Henry" at the top of the letter and said

"I love the way you snuffle when you're collecting your haversack."

And

"I love our little song".

(Note he has worryingly put "our" song. He has possession of the song to some extent. He's sharing the song.) He has written to the hedgehog. To him, I am a hedgehog.

Anyway, the enticement for me to autograph this picture of the hedgehog (which I indeed possess, provided by the Production Company. Fifty of them in fact) this "small black cigarette holder for my personal use", will be appearing as soon as I find a picture and send it back signed. So he says. But oh dear. Mike from Sheffield has already received three signed pics of Henry Hedgehog. What does he do with them? Pin 'em to the wall and pleasure himself? Sell them on eBay? (This is probably what he does. My mate Roop has been in Medics and gets £2.49 for every signed pic. "It ticks over" he says.) And why does Mike from Sheffield never mention he's got three pics already? And where is my "small black cigarette holder for my personal use"? Nowhere to be seen. So... I have the letter here with me on the sofa…I've scrunched it up.....and...into the bin it goes……yesssss!… 1-0!......except I've missed.

Had a meeting in a Pretaminger in Putney about putting on a play. And then being in it. This is good. I'm all for actors grabbing their destiny by the scruff of the throat. Stir the pot and see what comes to the surface. Get out there and do something, rather than lie there and wait for nothing to happen. Don't be buffeted by fate. Make your own future. Control your destiny etc. etc. etc..

In this instance, Derek Fazakerley, a sweaty tub of a man with a flat nose and a very deep voice with an out of date penchant for tweed with whom I was at Derby Playhouse, in Wind in the Willows (I was Mole to his Badger) wants to form a theatre company to put on "the classics" in fringe theatres. And he wants me to be involved.

"I mean I just can't sit on my backside can I love?" he drones.

He calls me "love" because that's what actors do when they're with mates. They pretend to be unbearably camp. It's like being part of a secret society. "Hello love" we all say to stress our difference from other "normal" people. It's a load of old bollocks. But then we know it's a load of bollocks. And that makes it fun.

Derek hasn't worked all year.

"I'm skint old love" he tells me. "Had no interviews. Zilch. De nada me old fruitlet. Agent away with the fairies. Doesn't speak to me. And I don't speak to her. My life is falling into the abyss....Oh no. Tell a lie. She did. Once. I went up for a foreign commercial for insurance. Had to pretend to be a sausage. Didn't get it. Too tall apparently. Story of my miserable life. I was an average sausage in a pan. But there was a special sausage which was the better insurance premium. I was up for "un-special sausage". Clearly wasn't specially un-special. Bloody hell could have done with that."

Yes. Ads always get you a bit of dosh. You're "bought out" so the ad people don't have to pay you repeats. They used to pay out thousands. Some bloke who said "the drive of your life" on one ad, it was rumoured, recreated a Texan cotton grower's mansion in a field in Esher he had so much money. No longer. But it's still well worth it. Couple of grand not to be sniffed at.

Anyway Derek wittered on about the state of the business, the state of his business and then the state of the world. But there is a light at the end of the very very dim dank tunnel: his theatre company. He's decided the first offering for his "Proscenium Theatre Actors' Group" PTAG for short, "Pertag",

("What d'yer think of the name "Pertag" love?"

"Oh er …Great!" I lie, coz it stinks) will be his own translation of JD Suture's existentialist masterpiece "Closet Partitions" which unfortunately will be one of the most boring plays in the entire history of theatre and the universe and anywhere else, if done by him. He can be the gloomiest man I have ever met. Apparently, he confides, and not to tell a soul, but he's just been recovering from a nervous breakdown, after falling in love with one of those girls he "demonstrates items" with in supermarkets.

"Tesco. Met her there. Near the front of the store. I was dressed in a chicken costume selling stuffing old love. She was a banana. Selling kumquats. They didn't have a kumquat costume. Steaming affair. Dumped me. For the bloke I was working with. The other chicken. I still wonder if she made a mistake and thought she was with me when she was with him. I mean I did wear the costume a lot when I was with her. For God's sake don't tell the wife."

But he's better now and wants to put all this behind him and this play on, that was a big hit in France just after the Second World War, being an allegory of the Nazi occupation of France? (Oh God), or so he tells me.

"All the actors contribute fifty quid and my aunt's lending me some money which I can repay her whenever."

I feigned interest.

"Bloody good idea Derek. Create your own destiny. Grab your future by the lapel and give it a jolly good talking to, make your own er bits and pieces etc. etc."

But oi! Fancy having to pay fifty quid. You're out of pocket instantly with no prospect of getting it back. Coz let's be frank, no one will go to see his production. On reflection this philosophical gem is probably the perfect vehicle for a "serious artist" like him. And will undoubtedly be a big hit and I shall curse myself for not being involved. Not. Or "hem hem" as we used to say when I was eight. Which I prefer to "not".

Back home, faffed. Repeatedly lined up dots on the window pane with pigeons and machine gunned them. On a whim, went to the barber's in the High Street and had a number one haircut (ie v. v. short and stubbly). You've heard of comfort eating. Me, I have comfort hair-cuts. I think it suits me. (I hope it suits me). And it'll get me those tough parts perhaps. Those sneery thirty something tough guys that stand up to Sean Bean (mind you he's only five ten so it's not that difficult. If I'm standing on a stool) and get beaten to a pulp by the heroic Sean and his dynamite Sharpe skullduggery. Instead of the sad put upon sensitive comedy London characters I excel at.

The number one haircut also hides the bit of a bald patch I have on the top of my head. There I've said it. I'm a bit bald. But only a bit. Just a smidge ….ette …ish ….titchy …patch ..ish…ish. Which you can't see (much) if I have a stubbly head.
Girly came over.

"What the fuck have you done to your hair?" She said sensitively.

Wed 12th

Set alarm for 10.00. Girly had let herself out to run round the river with an aged client who was intending to take part in a marathon somewhere. Worked in the afternoon. Roop my actor mate, phoned. Chatted about castings. He and I were in the intriguing (wrong word. "Dreadful" is a better word) Edinburgh two man show "Tarts!" about two cannibal bakers stranded on a desert island in a dystopian world where every man was also a woman so I gave birth. It got one review:

"I was the only person in the audience. And I could see why. It was hopeless. I think there was an idea lurking there about an apocalyptic vision of an alternative universe but unfortunately it wasn't presented clearly and not helped by both actors being blind drunk."

This was true. By the end of the two week run in a very expensive cupboard in the Grassmarket we had done 13 of the shows (several to an audience of one who was frequently a friend) completely pissed which despite the view of the critic, I think improved the show no end. Roop's dad footed the bill thank goodness which was foolish of him. Roop's then girlfriend Tanga cast me in it (I was the the only one who applied, Roop said) and directed it so we rehearsed in her front room. Roop and I bonded amidst the lunacy of doing the show so he's stayed a mate. In the world of advertising he goes up for dog food. Or ads involving pets. He has that kind of look. The reliable happy pet owner. If only they could observe him after a bottle of Valpolicella they'd see him highly unreliable and likely to swing a cat around his head. He's been in a few films as well but seems to make a healthy living flitting about continental TV screens in a variety of pet food commercials and doing the odd bit of telly as an MP or accountant or smooth policeman.

"At the moment, I'm on in Germany for dogfood, Denmark for catfood, and in Holland I'm a vet dealing with a horse in a commercial for tyres," he told me without a hint of irony. Perhaps it's that he's got a reliable pet owner's jacket that he takes with him to castings. Whereas I am comedy bloke. Comedy dad, comedy swimming pool attendant, comedy narner - it's always comedy.

Scootered to Soho. All parking bays full. Parked miles away near the London Uni building in a bay which always has a space when I'm desperate.

I'm in town to voice a Christmas commercial for Kerry Mill Department Stores at Slick Studios. I know it's August but that's when they're made. It's for TV so I'm doing it "to picture" ie they show me the ad and tell me when to "come in" ie speak. In this instance it's after about ten seconds of an actor playing Santa and close ups of the store and I have to go like the clappers and cram the script in.

The engineer can offer you a "cue-light" if you want when it's your go to "come in" as he has the waveform in front of him, and you have a little red light in front of you, usually with a rather tasteful circular mahogany base that other voice overs have written "I woz ere" on; but I prefer to know what the timecode is and time it myself. (The ads or promos or whatever always have minutes and seconds ticking away on the screen. Or can be placed there by the engineer. The producer either writes the timecode on the script when your cue is, or tells you in the studio).

There is frequently a "guide" voice on the ad/promo either done by the producer him/her self, or the editor. In this instance there is no guide. During the action, I have to say

"14 shops and Father Christmas this Friday at 4.30. (pause for view of door) And we're open till late! (pause for pack shot) It's a Kerry Christmas!"

Inspiring stuff eh! There are 3 variations on the 20 second script outlined above, ("tomorrow" and "today" and a generic without the time) and there are two 10 second scripts. Eg "14 shops. Elves. A Grotto and good old Santa himself! And in the week, we're open late! Kerry Mill" etc. etc..

"We chose you because of your Father Christmas like quality" said a bright young thing in a business suit and the air of a brief case.

"Oh thankyou" I coyly responded slightly wounded as I'm a beardless slim man in his thirties and have come by scooter not sleigh.

"We're re waiting for someone but let's start. He'll be with us in a minute," I was informed by a bald man with a goatee and no chin. His face just became part of his shirt.

Now this starting before someone important is there, is normally disastrous, because no matter how far you get with the commercial, the late comer will scupper it. It doesn't matter how satisfied everyone is with it in the studio or how well it's gone, she/he who turns up late will be more senior and will create such doubt that the whole read is reappraised and redone. It is very rare for the new arrival to go "Oh that's great!" They feel the pressure to be critical. So they are. They say things like:

"Oh that's not how I imagined it at all" or

"Hmm. Not sure. Can we have another go?" and the engineer leaves the talkback on so you hear exactly what's being whispered.

"I thought he'd have a more Father Christmas like voice. He sounds like an elf" or "He sounds different on his showreel" or "Is this the same guy I heard before?" Or "He looks nothing like Santa."

It's actually more ominous when the engineer cuts off the talkback and you can't hear what they're saying at all. You know it's gonna be bad. And then they ask you to redo it all. What tends to happen is that you go round and round and return to the first read you did at the beginning. But she/he has to be seen to be leading you there, just to maintain his/her status as "grand fromage". It's pathetic really.

Anyway. He/she was coming later. I started well. Got it all in, in the twenty seconds. They liked 'em. Did the other 20. And the alts. (Alternative lines eg "tomorrow" "today" and the generic "all this week" which are "dropped in". You just read that bit and the engineer inserts it). Did a ten seconder. And the other one. Fitted all the lines, the copy, in. Did all of them in fact. Finished. They all listened back. Then someone asked if I could be a bit merrier.

"He could be merrier?"

"Yes. Can you be merrier?"

"But of course! Merry is on my CV!"

I cringe at my inane patter.

"I know this sounds contradictory but could we have a lighter less Santa like voice?" says another. I was giving it the full Werthers Original. We have another go - lighter less Santa. All over all of them. They're happy.

"Love it!" says a lanky bloke in a tweed jacket. "Cracked it!"

Then lo and behold in comes the latey. And there's twenty five minutes of the hour long session to go. It's classic. There is no explanation from the late one as to where he's been. It's clearly been something "important " e.g. he's been in the pub. Or shopping. Or dawdling.

"Can I hear the takes you've done?" he barks sternly. There is no confusing… he..is..THE BOSS.

We listen to what I did.

"Well "Kerry Mill" is much too hard" this thin lipped pterodactyl lisps. "And there's no "ding".

"No. There isn't" agrees the pusillanimous tweedy man who loved it moments ago. And what the fuck is "ding" anyway?

"Can we have more "ding" please....Er.. what's his name?"

"JK."

"More "ding" please JK."

"Ding?"

"Perzaz. Christmas. Joy. Lightness. Happiness. Cheer…. Ding."

Ah yes that fucking explains it.

"Oh ok. I'll have a go. Ding it is."

I am so cheerful it dismays me.

I do a 20.

"That's too husky "come to bed" for me. We don't want Santa coming across as if he's out to seduce you!"

They all laugh sycophantically.

"Aha ha ha ha! Haaaa! Noooo! Haaaaa!"

"There's no ding there," says the man who just turned up and is now putting pressure on me because we have less time to do it in coz he was so late.

"Oh sorry. I'll try to get more ding."

I have no idea what they want really so just try more energy. It's beginning to sound remarkably like it did earlier and we're on take fourteen.

"Ah that's getting there? What do we think of that?" says he who has taken over. There is silence. The others have no clue. Someone goes "Hmmm." Someone goes "Nnnnyessss!?!", in a doubting but positive tone, not wishing to commit either way for fear of being shot down in flames. The engineer Cam, who is my pal and who is thinking on the same lines as me that there's only 20 minutes left and he has to mix it before the next session, tries

"Well they're all to time and I think we've had several good reads there. I could always cobble a few and create a hybrid."

"A hybrid?"

"Bit from here. Bit from there."

Well said. Tactful. Not criticising. But reminding everyone there is a way to use what we've already done.

"A hybrid. That's a good idea" says the late man, seizing onto the word and rolling it around his mouth because he has heard a word he can add to his studio vocabulary for constant use.

"A hybrid. Yes. A hyyybrrriddd!"

"Yes" echo the others confused, as they quite liked everything really. I mean I'd read them all in time and hit the required words. "Father Christmas's Grotto" was all warm and cuddly and "Kerry Mill" was given attack but not hardness as was suggested. Someone chimed in with

"I'm worried "Father Christmas"s Grotto" is being rushed. It's very important you know."

I mean this was actually a rubbish opinion and utter bollocks coz it wasn't rushed but he's looking good in front of his superior.

"Good idea. Let's do a "Father Christmas's Grotto" without rushing it," says the man who was late.

"A slow "Father Christmas's Grotto"?" I ask slightly taking the piss.

"Yes. But not too slow or you'll run out of time and it'll all be too long."

"Of course. Slow but not laboured."

"Exactly."

What a load of poo.

I do another. I slightly slow the "Grotto" and speed up the rest a bit so it fits.

"No I thought we lost the "ding" there. One more."

The fucking ding again.

Cam catches my eye as he says "take 17".

"With more ding!" bawls the late one.

I try lightness and energy and happiness and Christmassy and all those dings while slowing "Father Christmas's Grotto" and giving "Kerry Mill" the right weight and it all fits.

"Perfetto let's do the alts. And then let's do the tens." says Latey. And I do. I do 'em all again.

"Do you think they're disjointed?" says a voice.

"Possibly" says Latey not having a clue.

"Remember I can do hybrids" the engineer reminds everyone. "The lines on the tens are the same as on the 20s with the odd different line."

"Ah yes. Let's do hyyyybridddds. We could take the Kerry Mill from take twelve and the Grotto from eleven".

"And there was ding in take six".

"Yes and the ten second commercials we can cobble from takes eight to eleven," says the man with no neck suddenly alive for the first time since Latey's arrival.

"Yes!"

They're all cooking now. They're all creating "Hybrids" and loving it.

"Yes! I thought the Elves and Grotto line for the ten second commercials was excellent in take 8."

"And we could use the Kerry Mill from 18 and the "Father Christmas's Grotto" from take 19."

"Yes we could."

"Excellent."

"Just to check" says Latey. "Can I listen to the first takes you did?"

"Ooh good idea!" Says Brief Case as if this was a game changer.

"Yes!" Everyone exults.

Cam plays all the versions of the takes we'd done at the beginning. We listen.

"Actually come to think of it I rather like them" says Latey. "It's more Santa."

"Yes me too!" says Lanky. Baldy and Brief Case are equally enthusiastic. It's laughable how sycophantic they are. And how ridiculous this is.

"I think we should use them. Can you do something with those Cam?"

"Yes of course!"

Latey has no shame or self awareness at all.

So five minutes to mix them. Which Cam manages to do brilliantly. Phew. He's really really good. Everyone is happy, especially Latey who has done nothing but fuck about self indulgently in the 25 minutes or so he was there. A nice wink from Cam on the way out, the irony of which the others in the studio miss completely.

Home and Tweeted. I'm @actorladdie. I have 278 friends most of whom are fans of Henry Hedgehog. I follow 649, mostly actors. Or casting people. Or strange facts eg "did you know that lobsters urinate out of their nostrils?" I have Tweeted today about the Kerry Mill job. "Worked @slickstudios today doing the VO on the Kerry Mill Xmas ad. Xmas has come early for me! No sign of mistletoe tho!" #santa. Slick very kindly retweeted it.

I find the whole idea of Tweeting what you've done during the day work-wise rather distasteful having been brought up by my mother not to "brag" or talk about yourself too much or point or stare at people coz it's rude, so consequently I have to gird the loins and pluck up the courage to show off when I Tweet and try not to embarrass myself. Iain my theatrical agent, not voice agent, likes his clients Tweeting. My voice agents the Dawgs are a bit rubbish at Tweeting and only Tweet about the stars they have on their books. Of which I am obviously not one. No they've got big film stars who weirdly are never available as they work in America doing films. But their pix look good on the website. And in the office. Henry Hedgehog doesn't make me a star. I'm a jobbing actor and V.O.. Stardom for me has galloped away into the stratosphere like manure off a supersonic gardening utensil.

Looked at Facebook. Posted about Kerry Mill. And the Voxfor. Took a thumbs up selfie. Got ten likes! And a heart! Though that was black cigarette holder man "Mike from Sheffield" who also put "Oi! Where's my photo?" who I have inadvertently befriended. He's now unfriended.

A lot of my "friends" most of whom once again are HH fans, appear to be in hospital after unfortunate accidents. "Here I am having an E.C.G." Or "Here I am having the last rites" or posting photos of their ginormous English breakfasts."Look at the black pudding on that." Which is probably the reason they're in hospital.

Thursday 13th August

Got up. Abluted. Checked Twitter. No one retweeted my Kerry Mill or Voxfor. Though a Henry Hedgehog fan hearted it. It was @ilovehenry so you know where you are with them.

Did an ad for some club place in Scotland at Jumble. Nicked the pens they encourage you to nick as they have "Stolen from Jumble" written on 'em.
In the ad they had converted a hospital into a country house. There you can eat cordon bleu food and use the fabulous gym facilities and go shooting, Do a bit of archery. Go for fabulous walks! Play croquet. Wank yourself off in the spa.
They wanted a straight slightly theatrical read. Think Simon Callow they said. All went fine till after about 6 takes the spotty youf who was overseeing the whole thing suddenly said I was pronouncing the word "Golf" wrongly. There is a phrase in the ad which says
"And of course the fabulous Golf Course."
He's been noncommittal about it all so far. In fact just said "fine" after every take. And "let's go again.

Slightly more up and down" which means light and shade. Suddenly he says

"The word golf. It's "golf". Not "golf."

Me and the engineer haven't a fucking clue what he's talking about. The engineer Pete is looking at me from behind the mixing desk with his back to the youf who's sitting on a sofa behind him and he mouths "For fuck's sake."

"How do you want him to pronounce it?" says Pete.

"Golf. Not Golf" he says making no apparent distinction. I chip in.

"Golf. Not golf?"

I make no attempt to differentiate the two.

"Exactly. Golf not golf," says the youf making them sound the same.

"Yes. Golf not golf. Got it." I repeat.

"Yes. Golf not golf. I see" says Pete taking the piss.

"Simple. Let's do it."

So I do "golf" exactly as before and he says "No it's not quite right it's golf".

I am by now going fucking mad. There is no discernible difference in the way he is pronouncing it from the way I am pronouncing it. Pete gets involved in favour of the client/producer whatever the fuck he is.

"I think Liam has a point." (What! You turncoat!) It should be "golf" not "golf". You're going "golf" when it should be "golf". Let's do another one taking care to say "golf" and not "golf".

But but but …What on earth is he talking about? He's just going "golf" and "golf". There's no difference! But aha… he grins at me. He thinks the client is from the planet Wibble just as I do.

"Let's go again JK. Remember it's "golf" not "golf" he says. "I'll drop you in."

And doesn't. He plays an earlier take. As I say the line I realise I'm not being recorded. And the nit-wit youf says

"Yes that's much better" and everyone goes home happy.

Ah the wonderful world of advertising.

Friday 14th August

Had a "pencil" put on for a VO Supermarket commercial playing a cauliflower. Named imaginatively, "Col".

"You can do cockney can't you?" says Lynn my agent at Diggerty Dawg voice agency somewhat ridiculously. Of course I fucking can. Just listen to my "character" reel ffs.

But it "went away" which is agent speak for when the ad agency don't want you and have only pencilled you in case their first choice can't make it. Or have changed their minds about the voice they want .Or occasionally they can't get the scripts finished. And then decide on a woman VO. No one says it's "rubbed out" which I presume is its origin. So if it's "inked in" it's a done deal. This wasn't. So pffff.

Didn't see Girly who is "busy". Though seeing her tomorrow. Lay about a lot playing the guitar.

Struggled with a lyric for a song called "Stupid stupid stupid" about a bloke seeing someone he doesn't get on with.

Sat 15th August

    Girly turned up at about 11.30 having been running somewhere exotic like Hampstead Heath at some ungodly hour. Then left having "borrowed" (I'll never see it again) forty quid as she was "skint".
    "I've lost my credit card" she said and disappeared claiming lunch with a client.
    Went to Mother's and mowed the lawn. She told me to grow my hair.
    "You'll only be cast as policemen darling. And you won't get the job as you're too small. Too short hair is not an attractive thing on a man unless he has a thin face and a delicate bone structure. You have neither. You have a large jaw and a head much bigger than the rest of your body. So have I. It runs in the Putney family."
    That's her surname. Bizarre. Her maiden name is Putney and she lives in Putney, in the family home which she rattles around in and in the garden of which she gardens, and shops in Sainsbury's and is up for a bargain.
    "Did you know darling that I got that quarter of a pound of mushrooms 6 pence cheaper in Sainsbury's than in Waitrose? You should watch what you pay for your food in Tesco. You just go in and buy and you never compare prices."
    "I can't be arsed Mother."
    "What?"

"I can't be arsed."

"Oh God what a terrible expression. Can't you come up with something else to express your discomfort than that? You had a decent education and I tried to impress the joy of the English language upon you. But oh God. "Can't be bothered" ."Couldn't care less" ."I'm not interested". Even "Can't be buggered" would be preferable to that. But not that ghastly word "arsed". Where's the poetry? Hmmm? I don't think you have enough poetry in your life. Let's do "How they brought the good news from Ghent to Aix" together. That was one of your favourites at school. Come on. Imagine you're a horse."

"I know mother. You don't need to tell me."
And she's off....

"I sprang to the stirrup and Joris and he,
  I galloped, Dirck galloped, we galloped all three".
I join in...
"Good speed cried the watch as the gate bolts undrew
"Speed!" Echoed the walls to us galloping through.
Behind shut the postern, the lights sank to rest...er...."
That's as far as I got... and she gets annoyed I can't remember more, and I go and finish off the lawn.

Sunday 16th August

Morning.

The Girly who'd stayed the night and snored and tossed and woken up several times screaming and punching coz of horrid dreams and ignored my best cuddling efforts to calm her, and was too tired for sex this morning, has departed at sparrow fart for some sort of huge two hour long endurance road race with a female chum built like a Russian weightlifter. We're supposed to be seeing each other tonight for a film. Oh yeah? A film in which she'll fall asleep and dribble? That'll be fun.

Mon 17th August

Pencil for "The Daily Terrygraph" from Lynn as she calls it.
Lynn my voice agent by the way is an abrasive potty mouthed sweetheart. A hugely loyal, tall, driven, dark haired leotard wearing exercise addicted ball of nervous energy with unfortunately the organisational skills and memory of a carp.
I hung about. Played the guitar a bit. Had a couple of boiled eggs. The job moved from nine to ten to mid-day to two to three and then five and then happened at 3.30. At Jumble in Wardour Street. Excellent facilities and friendly receptionists and engineers at Jumble. But then that's why everybody uses them. My father told me never to go out with a receptionist as they were friendly for a living and a lot of it is fake. They're like actors. If they're that personable all the time they're likely to be miserable at home. So I have never been out with a receptionist. (Other than an animal-actor obsessed girl at a gym when I was at Derby playing Mole who actually asked me out! And then chucked me after a week. Only to go out with the bloke playing Otter. He lasted a couple of days till she went out with Stoat).

Just to confirm my dad's theory, whenever I voiced a promo for Brian Slazenger in drug addicts' alley off Soho Square the receptionist was always an out of work actress! However one cannot but like all these receptionists at Jumble who are terrific. But probably horrid at home.

Anyway. Back to doing the "Daily Terrygraph" ad. The room is packed with agency people, creatives, account handlers, account directors, assistant account directors, assistants to the assistant account director's assistant, you name it, they were there. Eleven people by the mixing desk and me in the glass booth. Twelve if you include the Producer, who is an old actor chum of mine, Steve Needler from comedy duo Shunt and Needler. He produces ads occasionally and a jolly good job he does of it. This one is twenty seconds. We start off doing the usual kind of newspaper read that I've done before (and will do again I hope). It states the name of the paper, talks about what's in the paper and ends with the name of the paper again, as one would expect and one has no doubt heard before. Eg "In the Daily Telegraph this week, as always, we've got hard hitting opinion, forthright discussion and in-depth analysis from our top notch journalists. From politics to the Arts to sport etc etc". And it ends with

"That's this week. All in the Daily Telegraph."

We do a take. I don't make any errors. Hit some decent stresses. Fit it in perfectly. Steve asks for more "weight" on the name of the paper. And to make it slightly more "percussive". I do so. He then asks the "team" what they think of it so far. Only three people chip in.

"Yup. Sounds good to me" says a tall bespectacled woman in a sweater with a low neckline with a squeaky voice like a small marsupial.

"Yes very good. Excellent in fact," says a man in a suit that is too tight for him.

"Yes very very good. Hits all the points," says a balding man with a very full rucksack and a small moustache. No one else pipes up. Though there's a lot of nodding.

"Well I think we're all in agreement there," says Steve and adds

"You consummate professional JK. You've got it and we've hardly started! Let's do a couple more and see if you get anything else out of it but otherwise I'm happy."

This is always a dangerous moment. You can either try something totally different which encourages someone to see something else you could go for, in which case you're then off down a side alley of interpretation, or it's so bad you slightly lose the lustre you've obtained by doing it in two takes, or you take the easy way out and just redo what you've done in the first two, causing them to invariably choose takes one or two. Or even one of the two you've just done. I opted for the latter. I chickened out. I did it twice more very similarly to the way I had just done it. One was a bit long. But not by much.

"Choices everyone?" asks Steve. He tries to guide them.

"It's still take two for me."

"I agree" says low cut.

"Yes" says brief case.

"Yup" says too tight suit.

All eight others are as tight lipped as they always have been. Except a youngster in the corner pipes up.

"You could always go up at the end."

"What, as in "The Daily Telegraph!!!!" says Steve "going up at the end" and making it sound ridiculous as it goes against the energetic but laid back precision of the rest of the read.

"Yeah" she says a bit surlily.

The room is illuminated by this suggestion.

"Oh that's a good idea" says rucksack.

"Hmm why not?" says low cut.

"Yeah let's give it a go," says too tight.

"That's a very good idea" says a very small man in a baseball hat I hadn't even noticed before.

"I agree" says an invisible person tucked in at the back just out of vision.

"Absolutely!" says someone who hasn't taken their eyes off a copy of Grazia since they came in.

"Ah. Ok then" says Steve followed by "One moment."

And he leaves the studio and comes into the voice over booth to speak to me. He has tipped the wink to the engineer to pull the fader down on the mic so no one in the studio can hear us.

"I'm so sorry JK. That's the work experience girl they've asked. I do apologise. I admire her courage in a somewhat pressurised environment. But an intonation that goes up at the end is stupid, but that's what they've asked for so let's give it a go, but after we've done several takes I'll get em to go with take two. So sorry. Sheer idiocy."

"Ah thanks Steve."

"So do a few and I'll persuade 'em otherwise after you've gone."

"Ok."

So I "drop in" after "This week……" - they're happy with the rest of the read - and do several "All in the Daily Telegraph!!!!!" as if a locust had suddenly found its way into my underpants and was eating its dinner and I am "Surprised of Shepherd's Bush" and they all agree that that's what they want and I leave thanking everyone and the engineer grins at me and so does Steve and when I go home and hear it on the radio it's take two.

Tues 18th August

Squash club evening in Richmond. Played William from a division above me. He's a tall balding insect of a man with masses of jet black body hair. The type of bloke who shaves three times a day and after a week has a shoulder length stylie even though he'd just had a short back and sides. A total fitness fanatic. He's a solicitor. He runs to work with a backpack on, and he lives in Wandsworth and works in Lambeth. About a 300 mile round trip. Madness beyond belief. Lost feebly as he ran me all over the court like a novice and I became purple in the face with effort. He fucking loved it the bastard. Saving grace was he introduced me to a young woman in the bar called Hilary who was Irish. Nice boat. Lovely Irish lilting voice. Mind boggling "embonpoint", I think the Victorians called it. Works in a bank. Slight drawback was the white wine. She glugged it as if she'd been on a liquid free road trip to the Kalahari. She asked me what I did and when I said I was an actor, she didn't say "Oh a waiter" as most people say, as if I couldn't ever maintain a living as an artiste, and was lying and really worked in a restaurant. She seemed genuinely interested in the insurance ad where I was the Dad with the talking tortoise and the one with the crashed car where I was left in my underpants which I did about 6 years ago, and she flirted with me rather obviously! She went to the loo and William suggested I was "in there" and should take her out as he'd heard she was masterful in the bedroom (or a "demon in the sack" as he stereotypically called it).

"William" I confided, "I'm only interested in her mind for goodness sake. I'm after a life partner. And anyway I'm seeing someone."

He laughed as if I'd told him a very funny joke

Wed 19th Aug

No work. Played guitar. I have written a song about dating a spider. "Wrap those legs legs legs legs legs legs legs legs around me" goes the chorus. Went to the gym. Wednesday is intervals on the bike. Thirty second sprint followed by minute rest followed by thirty second sprint. Done seven times. Then a twenty minute jog.

Around me is the world of functional training where trainers persuade un-informed men and women to do the tiniest exercises over and over again with the consequence that after six months they have failed to be fit and have not altered the shape of their bodies one jot. But have altered the shape of the trainer's wallet. The swarthy instructor with a swirling rhunic black tattoo on his arm and up to his ear so it looks as if he's wearing a sort of roll neck sweater only on his left side, called Jeb, who'd shown me around when I first joined, has six people crawling across the floor and then doing an exercise that can only be described as "turning round quickly". You stand legs apart and turn 180 degrees then turn 180 degrees again. Then 180 degrees again. You have to do this really seriously. And they smugly do. As if it's something really really special. And worth a lot of money. And we all ought to be doing it. But only they are! They're the chosen ones! But in actual fact they're gullible planks.

    In the half hour I do my stuff, his trainees do this non-exercise over and over again and on his command then crawl. Slowly. He gets £40 a person for that. Ffs.

    Fascinating Nazi documentary on the History Channel. I don't know why but if I'm looking at the TV guide and I happen upon a title with Nazi in it I'm on it like a housefly. Everything is grotesque. This one was about gigantic Nazi bunkers. Is everyone who used them seven foot tall? I mentioned I'd watched it to my mother.

    "You're lucky we made the effort to save democracy all those years ago or you'd be marching about in a black uniform and speaking German" she says.

Thurs 20th Aug

Iain phoned. Casting tomorrow for some foreign commercial for Holland for cake or something.

"Now listen. They're going to show it off and on for two years so the money's good. Comedy man. Don't prat about. Just be funny. The casting director's Sally Carroll and don't go alienating her."

"Up yours you patronising git" I thought, whilst going "No of course I won't Iain. Thanks very much. How's business?"

"The usual. Slow for some. Quick for others. Must go. Someone's ringing the mobile."

I heard nothing ringing. He just wanted rid.

The skipper of my old school cricket team first XI, Damian Mackenzie, has emailed me attempting to get me to play in a Reunion cricket match which I have no desire to play in at all. Tho I suppose I could attend the party just to see several school mates who I haven't seen for an eternity.

From:
 "damian mackenzie"
damianmackenzie@hotmail.com
To: JK oohbanana87@yahoo.co.uk
Subject: Re: How's that?

Hello JK. Would you please play cricket for our old School first XI against a local team up here. If you come up on the Saturday Sept 19th there's a party and then we play on the Sunday. Would you keep wicket? My son said he heard you on the TV the other day playing a fruitbat. Is that right? Congratulations if this is the case.

    My reply as my occasional alter ego Cedric Trubshawe, a tailor who amongst other eccentric professions, makes garments for mice:
From: JK <oohbanana87@yahoo.co.uk>
To: "damian mackenzie" <damianmackenzie@hotmail.com >
Subject: Re: How's that?

ah MacKenzie. Your feeble attempts to weedle money out of me shall not succeed. I shall never purchase any of your vile hashish. I do not care who you show the risqué photographs of me and the snake to. I shall take whatever filth you dish out like a man. Warm regards Cedric Trubshawe. (Mrs)
Ps party yes. Cricket no.
Pps Any hamsters that need trousers?

Evening.

    Have joined Magma Running Club, where the Girly runs. I fear I have gone in completely out of my depth however as I have been roped in to run in a 5k at Wormwood Scrubs on Saturday. I Tweeted about it. No one "liked" it which was disappointing.
    The Girly is on Twitter as @OzFitgirl95 and she tweets about diet and pooh and generally uses it as an advertising medium. She's followed by other scary fitness trainers, like @traintillIdie666 and @bagsofsweatphil and tells me to Tweet more about my career and not re-tweet old pix of Pop stars or "did you know?" info. Or engage in discussions about

football or cricket. I suppose she has a point. Incidentally the fruitbat on that commercial is not me. Never been a fruitbat. Bizarre. Need to see the ad.

Fri 21st Aug

Went into town, near New Oxford Street, Coptic Street, for the casting for the Dutch ad for some sort of cake. Sally Carrol greeted me cheerily. I once went out with a friend of hers, of which she never ceases to remind me.
"Susie's just got engaged" she says as if I've missed out. "To a hedge fund manager!"
Perfect. He's got the dosh to indulge her shoe fetish. 130 pairs and counting.
"Ah well you win some you lose some" I say when in reality after a few dates I ran away from the acquisitive madness.
The character, the drawing of the actor, on the "storyboard", the story of the ad in pictures which will be the basis for the filming, which we are given to look at before we go in to the interview, along with the script, was about twenty years older than me with large hair, large body, and a beard. So I didn't feel hugely confident. And there was a large man with large hair, large body and a beard twenty years older than me in the waiting room of the casting suite. So the part's his then…..
This is nearly always an actor's reaction. The person in there before or after you is always much better suited for the part. It's utter paranoia but softens the blow when you don't get it.

The script was totally unintelligible having been translated by a man at the foreign advertising agency who has clearly said

"Oh yes. I am speaking good the language of the English, try it to me. Give! Yes! Give!"

It is utter pants. Eg it says:

"We are opening upon a car in the TV. It drived. It knock over and roll. Car man with over voice say

"Yes. This car not good. It not drive well. It roll. Not to have."

"We are returning to man with TV who watch who have the mouth wide. He has car! Yes the sames! We see in garage. Oh goodness goodness dearie! He has cakes in hand to him by wife who has come enter. He say "Oh well". He shrug shoulder! He now very happy. He smiler!"

What the fuckity fuck is that all about eh Man has bought a car which might kill him but doesn't care as he has a nice cake? And as for the script. Even Google translator does better than this!

Sally informs me I'm meeting the director Lucas, which is rare coz it's normally just a casting director and a camera. He bizarrely speaks English as well/badly as the script, and laughs loudly when I say "Oh well" and shrug to the imaginary wife when we act it out. I know he laughs loudly at everyone who comes in. The job was never mine and my lacklustre effort at looking nothing like anyone else at the casting or the storyboard means the job has run out of the window and round the block to escape me. But this happens at castings. The thing is not to be offended or unhinged by the madness of it all. It's a huge lottery. If your face fits in the cattle market, you get the holy cow.

     Tried to cry off the Wormwood Scrubs Magma run citing a bad ankle (imaginary of course), but the secretary was very insistent and persuasive. Flattering in fact. Suggested they needed runners of my "calibre", despite his never having seen me run. He said I could jog round if I wanted, just as long as I took part.

Saturday 22nd Aug

   Had a well deserved lie in to prepare for the run. Well when I say well deserved I always feel that any work you do during the week is draining and the batteries need to be recharged, so I made no effort at all to get up and in fact turned the mobile off the night before and tried to sleep as long as I possibly could as if I was a teenager when I could become dormant like a beetle and lie in my pit for sixteen hours, getting up at four in the afternoon before embarking on another night of attempted but frequently failed debauchery. Unless my mother came in and flung open the curtains screeching "the early bird catches the worm" as she was prone to do. But I was alone in my flat so no chance of that!
     Made it however till ten when the body clock clearly had had enough lying about so tick-tocked the eyes open and I stumbled into the loo for a huge wee. I actually managed to count up to one hundred and seventy five before I'd finished. Went back to bed to see if I could tack on an extra hour but to no avail. Showered and toyed with the idea of growing a

goatee but rejected it and close shaved so well I cut myself just below the lip. Staunched the flow with loo paper and reminded myself of my dad.

    Magma run on the Scrubs. Tip toed around like an elephant in ballet shoes. Though some around me were gorillas in hob nail boots. At the start the elite runners dash off into the distance and the not so elite i.e. rubbish runners i.e. me and several other misfits, stagger after. It was apparent that I was asked to run not because of my potential as a match winner but just as a body so that Magma might win the team cup, which they did clearly coz they had more runners than anyone else. I played my part! The fact I finished 278th was irrelevant.
    I found I had something in reserve and had a sprint in the last 100 yards and overtook a few!
    Annoyingly some bloke overtook me sprinting as I was sprinting and someone sprinted past him and me. And someone sprinted past him etc. etc.. For fuck's sake. I could have been 272nd.

Sunday 23rd August
And Monday 24th

    Bank holiday. Farted about. Watched far too much TV.

    Showing of the cop programme I went up for coz I looked like the bloke. They showed a picture of the bloke. I did look like him! The actor who was playing my part (I feel some kind of affinity with the character even tho I turned it down) looked vaguely like me. And was as Geordie as David Beckham. But I did resemble the real bloke quite a bit. Worryingly really.

That man in the newsagent/post office with the glass eye who used to be a military policeman who delivers the papers and occasionally helps out in the shop will be very suspicious of me if he saw the programme.

Girly out somewhere with some polevaulting/aromatherapy chum at some hen thing. Gawd knows.

Tuesday 25th Aug

Phoned by Lynn at Diggerty Dawg.

"How are yer darlin"? Ok? …Ooh one moment the other phone's goin…Hello….Diggerty Dawg…Can you hold? …Where were we?..Oh yeah I was askin' you how you were! Ha ha ha (this is a very dirty laugh) How are you? (she doesn't wait for an answer) Listen It's 'Enery 'Edge'og.' They want you again. You free?"

"When?" I ask.

"Oh yeah! Should 'a asked yer that in the first place! Ha ha ha. Week after next. It's to play er…"

"Henry."

"Yeah er course! You play 'Enery dontcha?"

"Yes."

"You free?"

"As a bird."

I mean I haven't told her I'm away anywhere have I? So I'm free!

"And it's off and on for the next three months. Ok?"

"Great!"

"I'll try and get you another few squids an episode but you know what they're like! Tight as Twizzle's chuff! (!) Right. Must go. Laters!"

Great energy. Slightly OTT. Twizzle? Not enough people in the office. More Henry Hedgehog eh? Wonder who the cast will be? Left a message for Bill who plays Simon Slug telling him we were on again.

Did some narratives for the agency Deeve Dove and Doove at Central Grandstand Studios. A narrative is where they haven't actually made the ad but it's been written and they need to have it all read out so it can be heard rather than merely seen on the page. It might take the form of:

"This ad takes place in a car on the motorway. We see a car driving at speed. We pan across to another car on the hard shoulder. There is steam coming out of the radiator. We cut to an attractive woman gazing at the driver. She puts her hand on his neck. Then it's clear she's about to throttle him. We cut to the driver's expression. He is crying. A voice over says

"Car broken down again? Girlfriend going to strangle you as a result? Death possibly imminent? Etc. etc. etc.".

I mean it obviously wouldn't be an ad like this. I have never heard the line "Girlfriend going to strangle you" in an ad and never shall, but you get the gist.

They get me to read out the ad with all its directions. Another actor might play one of the other characters. Or even the voice over. For example, if the "attractive woman" in our invented scenario were to say "'Ere pass me the crisps" they would get an actress to say the lines and I would say "The attractive woman says" before it.

In its finished recorded state, the completed narrative is then played to members of the public in research groups. Often the Copywriter's excellent/ crap idea is shot down in flames/lauded to the heavens by a group of men/women who find the subject "unreal" or "true to life" or "hilarious" or "not funny at all" or whatever.

I've been present at one of these research evenings which take place in special market research rooms with two way mirrors so the agency can look at the reaction from the research group. The agency people can be scathing.

"Oh bloody hell. She wouldn't know a good idea if it bit her in the leg" was one remark or

"Well that woman's only saying the opposite of that woman. They clearly don't like each other."

Or even

"That man is too bald to have his opinion taken seriously."

But they do get them heard by lots of different people in different demographics and different areas of the British Isles because indeed, the reaction of someone in London may not be that of someone in Liverpool. And if five lots of five people say your idea doesn't work then it's back to the drawing board.

The product of this narrative was "coffee". I had to read four different scripts. I could tell which was the best and funniest. It was one involving two sparring neighbours who were competing about everything. Kitchens. Cars. Their kids. Even their chest size! This was the gag! And of course they even competed over who had the classiest coffee. I mean it's not funny now me telling it but in the world of ads it's funny. But that wouldn't mean it would end up being made. Or if it was made, whether it would resemble the original idea at all.

The number of times I've done a good script at the narrative stage and then seen the ad on the box with the middle bit missing. Or the joke without the punch line. Or with an unintelligible voiceover and far too many mentions of the product. But that is because so many people interfere along the way.

The client puts their oar in. Obviously coz he's the wonga. He infests it with the name of the product causing important lines to be cut to fit it in. He frequently dislikes the agency's choice of library music or composer and wants a hugely expensive pop standard blowing the budget out of the water. He often has no sense of humour which is of course fatal. So never sees the joke. Or the ad is viewed by committee his end anyway and everyone has a say. The result is a complete dilution of the original idea.

The people who govern the content of ads have their say. They can find fault with the idea or script as being offensive. Or not explained well enough. Or misleading. "Legal decent honest and truthful" is their mantra. Sometimes their decency goes too far and they get possibly prudish as self styled guardians of the nation's morals.

The director of the commercial can nudge it his way as well. He has a funnier take on it (that frequently isn't funny) that is all about him. His insistent choice of concept and actors lets the script down and it becomes something else. The better directors can make it a success though. Often resembling the original not a jot.

    I always feel for the creative, the copywriter, when their idea has been butchered. Which it so regularly the norm. Sometimes by his own agency who fiddle with it, ceasing after a time to find it funny when it clearly was. Comedy can be like that. You hear the gag over and over again and go off it.

    So, the narratives I was reading were about people wanting classy coffee. I was on my own for the narrative and had to play all the characters, even the women. The agency were saving money I think.

    Everyone was very happy and I did it in half an hour which was nice as they'd booked me for two hours. I like it when it goes like that.

    Bill left a message. Has heard nothing about Henry Hedgehog. I hope I haven't put my foot in it and he's been replaced. You never can tell in this bloody business. I'll wait a bit before ringing him in the hope I get some info.

    I have got the Dutch commercial about the cakes where I say "Oh well". I was convinced it had thrown itself under a bus! Amsterdam in two or three weeks time. Iain my agent is overjoyed. According to Sally Carroll, the director thought my "Oh well" was by far the funniest. Bloody hell. £300 a day (it's a day plus travel and percentage buy-outs per country. It's going to three countries plus Holland, which is 200% of the studio fee. And on for two years. Yippee aye yay!)

Wed 26th Aug

Mother phoned:
"Darling. I've been listening to the radio. I want to talk about "Swing Low" Isn't it wonderful it's been adopted by rugby fans as a song. "Swing Low" the old Negro spiritual."

"Yes I know what it is. And I'm not sure you're allowed to call it a "negro" spiritual anymore."

"Mmmm?"

"And I know that it's sung mostly at England rugby matches" I added.

"Isn't it wonderfully spiritual." She persisted.

"Yes but it's also a song you can do rude actions to."

"What Swing Low. The N...?

"Ssh. Yes. Swing Low. The African American Spiritual. You can do rude actions to it."

"What? To Swing Low?"

"Yes Mother. To Swing Low."

"Are you sure?

"Of course I'm bloody sure"

"What kind of rude gestures?" (She is immensely dubious about my sanity at this stage).

"Well in the bar after rugby matches they "swing" their arms low down, then mime "sweet" which is a kiss to the lips, then "chariot" as if they're holding reins ie driving a chariot, then for "coming" they use a wank gesture."

"A what?"

(Oh God what have I said.)

"A wank gesture. Coming as in "coming" ie ejaculating."

"No. You're making this up."

"No I'm not. "For to carry me home" is then four fingers and two fingers, as in "four two" ,"carry" is a carrying motion, like rocking a baby, "me" is point to yourself, "home" is make a little roof with your hands and then it repeats. Every word is mimed."

"You're making this up. Why do you tease your mother so much in her old age? Why? You're trying to kill me aren't you."

"Mother. Why would I want to do that?"

"My God." She's shouting now. "Swing Low the religious Negro.."

"African American….."

"….Spiritual reduced to a song about masturbation. What is the world coming to. I despair of you, your friends and everything. Goodbye."

Thursday 27th

Don't fucking believe it. I mean ffs. I'm in a sweet shop buying a Snickers and some bloke comes up to me and taps me on the shoulder and says

"Excuse me. But you are very like the man who was on that Crime programme where they re-enact the crime the other night who committed the robbery in Gateshead."

And the girl with him says "Nar that bloke on the TV had more hair."

And he replies

"Well he could have had a hair cut."

And she says

"Yeah but this one's more of a baldy".

And he says "yes true."

And they wander off. I mean fucking hell. Rude or what. But you see! I was right! I knew I'd be spotted somewhere!

Shampoo test ad tomorrow. At T&H.

Fri 28th Aug

Shampoo test ad "gone away".

Iain phoned. He likes me now that I've got the cakes ad. Another casting this time via casting director Dexter D'Eath.
"Get this one too would you?" he ululates like a very pleased with itself wood pigeon.
"Get this one tooo ooo would you ooo!"
It's on Monday in Soho for some low fat meal for Norway. Bring my shorts. They want to look at the torso. No problem there. Did several hundred sit-ups to prepare. (Well, about thirty).

Sat 29th Aug

Last minute. Got a call. From Roop. Well actually he woke me up from my slumbers with several calls knowing I'd be gurgling in my pit.
Could I step in to do an "acted move-it-about-the-stage" reading of a play about Thomas Kyd the Jacobean playwright, at the Globe Studio? Playing an assassin! Now! Ooh yes! Bit of swordery. Hint of cockney cosh boy. Roop had had to back out. Change in the schedule of something he's in. Some veterinary ad thing. Has to fly out today or something. He's such a good friend so I'll help him out.
"Yes I'm free I'll do it", I enthuse.
"Thanks chum! I've bigged you up with the director."

There's no dosh of course. Just "experience". Or as some actors hope "it'll look good on the CV." I normally would avoid it like having a radish up my arse (a punishment for adultery in Ancient Greece apparently) but as I say it's for Roopy baby.

A director asked me to be in his short film recently. "You've been highly recommended" he wrote. When I queried what the fee was he said "everyone's working for the love of the project". And the cast were all staying together in a dormitory for his five day shoot. I bailed out gracefully. (Well I said "Love unfortunately doesn't pay the bills"). For this show today you can bet the audience were paying an entrance fee. Why is it jobs in the arts can be done for nothing, or "for a video of your performance"? Try doing that with your personal trainer.

"I'll pay you your tube fare for that weights session.":

Or local builder. "Can you build me an extension? No money! Just your passion for the work."

Or in a restaurant. "I'll video myself eating and put it on the net instead of paying you. Ok? You can be in the vid if you like! "

Someone always does do it for nothing and today it was me. But then again you might meet some nice people. Or that old chestnut - someone who might employ you in the future.

The director was an old actor friend of Roop, Jon Ladore - his son George had written the piece, nice chap - who was very unintrusive. Did naff all in fact. Could have occasionally done with being told where to stand. But in the end we all sort of gave in to milling about the bloke playing Kyd doing his "thang".

I think this is how some plays of the 19th century were done with stars. The star just turned up and everyone stood around him in a circle. Henry Irving I believe worked like that when he was giving his Dane. And his Thane. I did enjoy it though. Good to be in front of an audience. But naturally holding the scripts gets in the way a bit.

The bloke playing Kyd had actually learnt it, which was slightly unfair. He was very good and expressive, as you'd expect, wearing tights and a frilly shirt. I was ok as I'm a decent sight reader but he was giving a proper perf! I got to wear a sword. No other attempt at 16th century authenticity, just a sword in its scabbard round my waist. Oh. And a ruff. Otherwise jeans and a denim shirt.

There's always great potential with a large prop. Especially a sword. Got it tangled up between my legs on my first entrance and got a bit of a titter. As this was not a comedy but deadly serious stuff, perhaps this was not a good thing so I didn't do it again.

There was a small amount of fighting which naturally the Kyd actor did better than anyone else as he had no script to hinder his movement. I got scragged good and proper by him in an earlier scene which was what was supposed to happen but he was overdoing it. But we hadn't had much rehearsal so you just had to give in really. He did slap me once far too hard about the face but then I did kick him very eloquently in the shins in response, for which I got a whispered "what the fuck do you think you're doing?" I had enough time with my back to the audience to suggest quietly "Don't fucking hit me so fucking hard then."

The death became a sneaky affair with me "stabbing" him in the back with an imaginary knife. My "die die die you bastard" wasn't in the script but I felt he deserved it. And I was quite justified in saying it as I'd been at the butt end of his rough-house egomania. We all had a drink afterwards and he very obviously ignored me.
   Was complimented by an old lady on my performance.
   "You were marvellous as the boy" she wheezed.
   I thanked her profusely. Except I wasn't playing the boy. I was playing the assassin. The big butch assassin. The big butch smallish assassin with the comedy sword.
   The author George was very grateful which was nice and he loved my extemporised "die die die you bastard" line which he said he'd keep in when this was actually staged. Asked him when/where this was going on. "Possibly a fringe theatre somewhere?" He offered. I wished him every success. But I might steer clear if I'm asked to replicate my not enormous role "for a share of the profits" which is bound to be the case.

Sun 30th August

   Lunch with the aged parent. She got me to tidy the loft for her and dig up a rather unruly bush. And there's something wrong with the lever on the upstairs loo.
   "It won't flush darling. Don't know why. Could you have a look?"
   I wander in and pull the chain and it works immediately. I inform her.

"Oh fabulous. It's those fairy fingers of yours. Well done!"

"Mother. I did nothing other than give the chain a yank. I hardly feel it's "fairy fingers" as you put it. More "orc mitts" to add some Lord of the Rings imagery."

"What?"

"You just didn't pull the chain hard enough."

"Trust me darling I gave it a jolly good pull. No you've obviously been training well. But don't train too hard or you'll end up like my cousin Ted. Muscle bound. Trained so much he did himself a mischief. He's now a vegetable in Skegness."

"You're making that up. You've never mentioned him before."

"He's never come up in the conversation before. Now you're clearly on a roll so would you have a look at the boiler for me?"

Naturally when I look at the boiler I can't make head or tail of it other than I think the pilot light's blown out. I press some button and hold it in whilst trying to ignite something or other. There's a sort of whoosh and I think I've relit it. Mother is very pleased.

"Oh well done again. And as a reward you can mow the lawn for me." Luckily it began to rain so I was spared the tedium. .

My role now is clearly that of odd job person. But I do love her and she brought me up nicely so I don't mind occasionally filling this vacancy. As long as she doesn't get me to try to chop down any trees. Which she does. I refuse. She sulks. I go.

Girly phoned. Back from the half marathon she was doing. She apparently came third. I'd offered to watch but she was reluctant saying I'd put her off! But it was pissing down and miles away and I'd only have seen her once at the start. And once at the end. Then apparently they were all going to some unlikely "non partner" party or something being held for the competitors. Really? Hmmm.

Bill left a message again. No one's contacted him about Sid Slug. I phoned back and it went to voicemail and suggested that perhaps Sid wasn't in the first few episodes. Which could possibly be the case. Phoned Anne Wegerely who's Tricia Termite amongst others and asked her about Bill. She's been booked for next week. Doesn't know about Bill. Derek Fazakerly has phoned her too. She ran a mile.

Mon 31st August

Lynn phoned. Henry Hedgehog is Thursday. 11 till 3.

In Soho for the Norway casting: En route in Beak Street saw Chutney or Chesney or Chisney or something, in the street, a director friend of that old girlfriend Tricia who I was engaged to for a week during which time she took to wearing long ceremonial white robes and had nearly all her hair cut off, having previously looked rather fetching in mini skirt and long blonde locks, and suggested that as we were about to be married I should take her more seriously and stop playing/watching/thinking about, football, cricket, squash etc.. And possibly consider an alternative career to acting which wasn't earning me enough money, was it? How about house husband as she wanted a baby immediately and I could look after it while she got on with her very high flying career as a barrister? It slightly put a strain on the impending nuptials as you can guess, this revelation into the real her, and her coming clean about everything I did, which she had pretended to like originally, and we split up the following Thursday having had to return several congratulatory bottles of champagne and the gift of a weekend long fitness boot camp in Selsey.

Anyway, Luke or Les or Lenny Wotsit, or whoever he was, could never ever believe like her that I could possibly ever make a living from acting. He was always bemused at my non attempts to earn a crust from other means other than acting when I first started and said his Dad had been in the business and never worked and caused the family great misery. He saw me in an early fringe play at the beginning of my career ("Oedipuss in Chains" at the Tuffnell Park Tavern and I have to say I was very funny but it wasn't a comedy and he clearly thought this career was beyond me). He kept encouraging me to get a steady job that wasn't acting. Anyway. Here he was. Clearly pained at the encounter.

"How are you..er?" (He'd totally forgotten my name.)

"JK...." (I'd forgotten his too. He did that annoying thing of not mentioning his name after I'd mentioned mine and getting angry with me that I'd mentioned my name.)

"Yes yes. I know you're JK."

"Oh! Right! Well I'm fine. Really good," I replied.

"Really?"
"Yes. Fantastic."
"Why?"
"Well I just am."
"You're not still acting are you?"
"Yes."
"Oh God."
"What?"
"Getting any work?"
"Yes. All the time."
"Really?"
"Yes."
"Keeping your head above water then?"
"No. Working all the time."
"Are you sure?"
"What do you mean are you sure? I think I would know."

"Managing to keep the wolf from the door?"

"More than that. The wolf is lying dead in the street where I ran over it in my grotesquely powerful Mini. Working a lot. Lots of stuff I'm working on. Lots and lots. Henry Hedgehog for one. I play Henry."

"Well chin up."

"No not chin up. No I'm fine. Really fine. I'M REALLY FINE."

He's not listening to a fucking word is he. He throws me with

"How's your Mum?"

My Mum? Did he ever meet my Mother?

"Not great. All of her teeth have fallen out and she's turned into a bat."

"Oh good. Give her my love."

And he's off......Fnerhmweraaaargh.

Anyway. Back to the "Low fat meal for Norway" casting. When I got there, at the Casting Couch offices in Great Marlborough Street, all the men were podgy as fuck and nerdy looking. I was obviously in the wrong place.

"Low fat meal for Norway casting?" I said. "Is it next door?"

"No. This is it……Name!" says the spotty teenage receptionist practically inaudibly with shifty eyes giving the impression the last place she wants to be is here.

"Jay Kay."

She scans the list.

"No. Got a Jay…. Jensen."

"That's not me."

"No. That's him over there."

She indicates some bloke in an anorak with whom I think I auditioned for a yoghurt commercial once, who grins and says

"Hello love."

"What time were you expected?" she says.

"Now."

"When's that then?"

"Now. Two o"clock."

"No. You're not down here."

I am relieved. I am not to be amongst these looky-likees that I look nothing like. I must be in the wrong place. Or another casting is taking place and there's another room. There are a lot of women who look like models present as well so perhaps I'm with them in some way.

The strutting leather trousered pipe cleaner physiqued casting director Dexter D'Eath appears. We know each other well. He's put me up for a lot of things. I've got a lot of things that he's cast. Including the Dad with the talking tortoise and the one with the crashed car where I was left in my underpants. We're sort of friendly but he's very up himself so you can't ever really be his "mate" as he's aloof. Difficult to describe. You mustn't be too familiar I suppose. Coz in his world of cheese he's King Brie. And you're a piece of processed. He is very very fond of himself. But no doubt actually deeply unsure of himself underneath. (No. This is bollocks. He thinks the sun shines out of his wotsit. He doesn't have the intelligence to have any self doubt.)

"Oh hello JK. Is there a problem?" he rasps with flared prune nostrils as if you're somehow being difficult and he can really do without this as the casting is unbelievably important and hugely stressful. He has that "I'm very special and under pressure" look.

"Hello Dexter. I don't appear to be down on the list."

He's spikily annoyed with me.

"Oh for goodness sake. Of course you are. I phoned Iain myself. Let me look…"

Now he's annoyed with the receptionist..

"Look there he is…"

The girl gets both barrels of the pursed lipped irritated "there he is". Because there indeed I am!

"The J looks like a… T" she stutters.

"No it doesn't" says Dexter dripping with annoyance. "No one is called Tay, are they?"

She just stands there.

"There that's sorted" says Dexter sashaying off whilst shouting

"Right who's next? Dean Simpson. …..Dean Dean Dean. Ah there you are!"

And another tubster wanders off. Everyone here is a large.

The Reception girl, castigated, tersely speaks to me.

"Here are the forms to fill in Mr Ku*t".

"What?" I couldn't quite believe what she'd called me. "What?"

She ignored me

"Here's the script. Here's the storyboard. Go up against that wall and I'll take a photo. We're running behind. It'll be at least half an hour's wait." And I do so and she too was off.

Ah the forms. You always have to tediously fill in forms when you attend a commercial casting. They're always asking for your name and agent - despite them having that info anyway. And asking you whether you've done any ads in the last three years in that country that may conflict with this one. Or indeed any ads in the last three years in that country. I've never done a commercial in Norway so this wasn't a problem. Denmark yes. I was "amusing sneezing man in pharmacy". They also ask your sizes. Everyone here will be putting down "big". I always put down "petite". You can bet your bottom fjord that if you get the job, a person from wardrobe will be phoning you asking specifically what sizes you are so I've never understood why you're asked this. You're always asked your dress size too. Coz I suppose it's not gender specific. I always put down "buxom".

They also ask if you have an up to date passport which is pretty essential really if you're doing a commercial abroad. I bet there are actors who get the job and then realise they can't actually go to Vienna to play a strudel expert as their passport is out of date. Ooops. Their agent won't be pleased. Iain would dump me.

Jay Jensen talks to me.

"I've been here an hour" he says gleefully. He is in fact after me, but has turned up early just coz he can.

"I'm two fifteen. They're being very slow", he adds stating the bleeding obvious.

"As always." I venture empathetically. You always wait at castings.

"Do you remember? We auditioned for that yoghurt commercial where we had to pretend to be mice?"

"Yes I do. We had to squeak and run around on all fours didn't we."

"Yes. The mice who stole and ate the yoghurt as it was so delicious. I had a week in Milan. Fabulous money. We had these brilliant mice costumes. Marvellous time. (Aaaargh. I fucking hate him) Surprised you weren't there. You were very good. Remember we all had to go in and be the mice together?"

Yes I fucking remember. He did nothing at all. Just followed me about as I energetically mimed being a mouse. With big whiskers and a loud squeak. Shamelessly copied me in fact.

"Oh thankyou (I fucking hate him, I do)...."What are you up to?" I ask politely not giving a monkey"s doodah.

"Well I'm about to do "Closeted Partitions" for Pertag Theatre Co. Derek Fazakerly." He says "Derek Fazakerly" as if he's a top top director.

"Ha ha!..... Yes of course...... Superb play.....You'll love it... and Derek of course. Good luck. What a good choice. Ha ha ha. Send him my love."

Liar liar my pants are not only on fire they're burning my bits to a cinder. The poor poor bastard. He has no idea what he's let himself in for.

Dexter D'Eath meanwhile is buzzing like a striped hornet with a gerbil up its fundament, as he's in and out of the studio where the casting is happening, as he's not running the actual casting as he normally does, but there's a real live director present.

I wait an hour to be seen. I'm going into the interview room with one of the models (it all makes sense now) who is to be my wife, who won't give me eye contact. I am given a robe, and put on my rather snazzy dolphin covered swimming shorts in the loo, which I'd been asked to bring along.

We enter the casting room to meet the Director and be videoed (which is rare as it's normally not the director but the casting director. The director usually just looks through the takes and makes his choices miles away in his chateau or penthouse). The director asks us both to disrobe. I'm unprepared for the rather er attractive girl to get down to bra and knickers. Still. I'm a pro! (Gulp) I ignore her (Bigger gulp) and gaze at the director who looks like a less sane version of Lee Van Cleef in the Good the Bad and the Ugly (or "the Good the Bad and the rather Unattractive darling" as my friend Calvin amusingly calls it) with a huge walrus moustache and a sort of kaftan.

After the usual strained introductions where we tell the director what we've been doing, (she's recently been in a water biscuit commercial for Germany, I've been Henry…well last June) we both give the video camera a profile and show our hands (so we can prove we haven't any deformed fingers or strange lumps on our faces that he fails to see).

He explains:

"So you come bek from vork and she caress you. So caress him. (She does so. My neck that is. As if my neck is a dead vole that will leave her covered in fleas. Bloody hell) Und you feel perhaps you might make lerf."

"Make what?"

"Lerf"

"What, bread? Loaf? I'm a baker?"

"No. No. Lerf. Lerf."

"Oh. Ok. Love. I see."

"But as her hands vander down towards your underwire ..... she grab your big fat vobbly spare tyre, and you both laugh helplessly at how funny it all is. Ha ha ha ha ha.... And then you both eat the low fat meal."

I pointed out the drawback.

"Um..sorry to be difficult" (One always apologises as an actor. Force of habit really. It's the desire not to offend anyone in case they want to employ you again) "but I'm not a (don't say fat) spare tyre person. I have no vibbly vobbly...sorry, wibbly wobbly spare tyre. I have a er washboard stomach. I am in fact a fitboy. Look."

I grabbed at nothing. Not a single vibble to vobble.

"Never min'. Act fat," he spat rather too forcefully for my fragile ego.

I acted fat reluctantly but truthfully. Coz one thing I'm good at is "having a go". If some one says do something, I try my utmost, even if it's ultimately likely to be a complete load of poo. I have got many a job by "having a go". So many actors realise they're being humiliated and give up. Not me. Humiliation is my middle name. A load of poo can occasionally be rather lucrative darling. I remember playing an onion in an audition for a ludicrous soup commercial. The director cast me, so he told me later, because of my immense eagerness when he asked me to bounce round the room as if I was being chased by a cheese grater. (And my unique comedy talent of course.)

"I just loved your onion" is what he said.

So the casting seemed to go quite well! Well for me. The model had the comedic ability of a filing cabinet. But I mentioned the "anomaly" to Dexter D'Eath.

"Dexter. Sorry to bother you but I'm not very er big around my waist…er…."

"Well that's unlikely. Everyone has fat around their midriff. It goes with middle age" he said in his usual pursed lipped viper-like superior "I know everything" fashion.

I phoned Iain to complain.

"Oi. Mush features. Why did I go up for a casting where they were all porkers. It was a total waste of time. Oi."

Is what I thought. I said

"Iain. That Norway ad casting I've just been up for…."

"They thought you were very funny, and they've pencilled you for the job."

Oh fuck my old boots.

Tues 1st Sept

Pencil taken off the "fat" commercial. Ha!
"Too thin. Though they commended your comedic skills" said Iain.
"Still, you've got the cakes ad to look forward to".
I knew it was ridiculous.

Bloody Hell. It's not what you know it's who eh? Brian or Dave or Cyril Chutney or Leslie or something told a casting director about me who phoned up my agent Iain.
"The BBC want you for a "Docs" interview for "a put upon man" who used to be a bouncer but is not any more and has to have his leg amputated. Apparently the director met you in the street the other day and you were perfect for the part? Yes? (Yes?) Yes here's the brief. Small fattish put upon middle aged man who used to be a bouncer. Will lose his leg. Oh yes. He's now a crook. I omitted to say that. 17 lines. Not bad?"

He says the "not bad" knowing its not good, and knowing I won't like the "short fattish" bit but also waiting to see what I'm going to say. I say this:
"Are they long or short lines?"
"No idea darling. Do you want to go or not?"
He's gone rude with me.
"Yes I'll go," I reply slightly surlily.
"Elstree. You know how to get there don't you?"

"Yes."

He's slightly threatening. Oh dear.

Did a promo for CBeebies in White City produced by a handsome woman wearing a floppy grey seafarer's cardy and a brown full length skirt with orange swirls on it and her hair tied up as if to attract moths. She was looking for someone to play a tree and I had been recommended.

"Lozzer from Biff Films suggested you'd be a very good tree" she said.

"Oh that's nice! Give him my love if you see him," I replied on automatic pilot, not having any idea who "Lozzer" was, whether I'd ever worked for him or even met him, but it's better than saying "Err sorry. Who's he? And who the fuck are "Biff?"

Anyway. The tree said:

"Who's been inside me today?"

I tried to point out merrily that the whole thing could be misinterpreted but no one wanted to know. The spider says:

"Me! Me!"

Another actor was playing the spider who was turning up later. As is often the case. Consequently one gives one's tree alone (sob).

It's a nature programme about "What's in the Forest" for littluns and very commendable. The producer asked me to sound very brown and barky (!) and said after I'd made various rejected attempts showcasing the lexicon of my abilities

"Hmm. Not sure he's treey enough. More bark. More roots. More leaf."

Said without any irony.

And then after I'd done a voice very similar to the deep northern one I first started with and she'd rejected, she exclaimed

"Yes. That's it! That's our tree! Welcome!"

Wed 2nd September

Took the Girly out to dinner. Café Rouge. Had chicken and chips. Though they give you the ketchup in titchy dishes and you have to ask for about four to get not nearly enough and by then the waiter's patience has grown thin.

Naturally the Girly fell asleep during the pudding. She actually nodded off. Her head slumped forward and she managed to miss the tarte de pommes by inches. It's all this running she does. As you can imagine there wasn't much conversation amidst the yawning. Other than her wanting me to take her to the Maldives. Drove her home. I was vaguely hoping we might share my bed. But she's "feeling crook" and training someone at six thirty in the morning which is fair enough I suppose.

Having said that, I don't actually have anything in common with her. Other than the bedroom I suppose. And if that doesn't happen what is there? I mean I don't actually get the feeling we're actually having a relationship. I must be mature and adult and stop seeing her.

As we're on the subject of sleep, I had a vivid cheeseboard induced dream and had grown a foot taller, and was calling myself Denzil (clearly I was believing I was actor Denzil Washington). I actually remember speaking in an American accent to a dancing Janet Jackson. (she inconveniently ran away). I wasn't wearing any clothes, in Kensington High Street. That junction next to Church Street. Not far from the Royal Garden Hotel. No one took a blind bit of notice. A pair of stripey pyjama trousers was blown down the street at me in a freak whirlwind and I chased after them towards Holland Park. It began to hail. Huge hailstones. I unfurled my umbrella. They bounced off. The size of footballs. They became footballs. A woman screamed and I realised I now had a foot long penis. A talking tree said "Good wood!" Then Wayne Rooney in a curly ginger clown wig appeared in a doorway doing a bicycle kick.

"Wayne. What luxurious hair." I said. "Can I have some?"

Some exterior noise woke me up and as usual I stomped off to the loo, dying for a wee. Slightly disappointing as I'd have liked to have seen where this ended up. Not often you dream about having a foot long penis.

Phoned Roop. According to him, this nakedness means I'm very happy. Interesting eh? What about the penis? He thought this meant I was manically depressed. Make your bloody mind up then. What about Wayne Rooney? In a wig! Hmm said Roop.

"Possibly you fancy him?"

Thursday 3rd September

Did Henry Hedgehog today. It's every fortnight. And a four hour session. There is no Bill. They've dumped Sid Slug. Oops.

Being the Hedgehog is bloody good fun, though hard on the pins as I'm permanently standing up on mic. Nick Sweet, the producer, played us a few of the completed episodes from the last series to remind us of the flavour of the piece. The animation is excellent. Nick is a Spuds boy, and it's deeply important to him so I sympathetically remind him of my team Chelsea's best win over them.

"We won 6-1, at the Lane. We won 6-1, we won 6-1, we won 6-1 at the Lane" I sing to the tune of Rod Stewart's "Sailing." He is not amused. He cruelly finds constant fault with my snorting.

"Oh dear. What's the matter with you? What's happened to Henry? Where's he gone? Has he curled up and lapsed into hibernation? He's certainly not here with us in the studio today. Is he?" he laments for the whole of the session clearly getting at me for my 6-1 jibe and nothing to do with my perf. How petty is that?

In these eps there are fires being started in the woods and it's up to Henry to work out why. It's eventually discovered that a large magnifying glass has been focusing the sun's rays and it wasn't Gloria Grasshopper after all (played beautifully by Anne Shuff in a Brummie accent) who was the pyromaniac.

Bill left a message on my mobile asking me when the session was. I'll have to let him down gently. Or alternatively ignore him completely. No I'd better phone. Possibly.

Friday 4th September

A friend of Roop's has asked me to direct her play to put on at a fringe venue and then possibly Edinburgh next year. Roop has recommended me highly as I directed him ages ago in a one man show he did briefly downstairs at the Tuffnell Tavern about the comic Sid Field. It was funny! Got "an amusing piece with fine direction" in the Ham and High. And she's said yes! I think possibly she's chosen me as I said I'd do it for a tenner a rehearsal, cash in the hot little hand. A crisp note in me trouserpocket. She's pleaded poverty but I have to have some sort of fee don't I. Yes I do! It's directing. But with permission to rewrite. I like directing. And rewriting.

 I haven't directed since that show at Oval House where I asked out the writer and her boyfriend threatened to beat me up if I went anywhere near her again. As she was also in the show it was decided I would no longer direct it. Well I decided. The boyfriend was a big bloke. When I sneaked in to see it when it was on, they'd cut out all my added jokes. But I digress. I've been asked to do this comedy show about which I have no fucking clue. And if it turns out to be shite at least I haven't signed a contract so I can pootle off. I meet the author of the piece and who's also in it who is called Mandy, tomorrow.

Sat 5th September

 Morning. Met this Mandy who's a tall big boned posh person, to discuss her show. It's an ongoing project with no performance date as yet. Periodic rehearsals then when it's in a decent state, find a venue to try it out. Sort of workshopping. She drops a large bombshell when she tells me the show already has a director who she thinks is rubbish but she won't sack, so I have to direct when he's not looking, as it were, secretly. And she can only be directed by me in the evening coz she's working with him during the day.

"But what if I change all the moves and re-write it?" I ask.

"Ah well I'll say I did it" she replies.

It's all sounding a tadette complicated. She's given me a script. It's funny! It's about her coping with being large and posh. It's called "Throbbly!"

Sunday 6th September

Two hour bath. My wrinkles were wrinkled. Girly now farting all the sodding time. Is it her diet or the fact she doesn't care any more or she feels relaxed in the relationship?

Mon 7th

Slick Studios. Ron is the engineer. Who in spite of my overtures to get him to come over to dinner, always finds an excuse so I've given up asking him. Perhaps he thinks I'm looking for work and that's my motive for asking him over rather than the fact that I just like him,

Lots of people in the biz are like that. They think that any overture of friendship is transparently you asking for employment. That they would be beholden to cast you in their next piece/ad/film/jacuzzi/happening/whateverthefuckthey'redoing.

There's quite a well known director called Tom Flytit who visibly cringes when we meet although we were mates at school and becomes a monosyllabic "don't want to be here" creature and fark's orf very quickly. Perhaps he doesn't forgive me for bowling bouncers at his head during a House match when we were fourteen. People can be petty like that. I must admit I've still got it in for that bastard who stuck a drawing pin on my seat in Geography. You know who you are.

    Casting directors have the same problem. If you happen to meet one at a party, don't ever tell them you're an actor. They too don't want to talk to you coz they think you're going to be after a job and are going to try to impress them. They'll find any excuse to wander off. Unless they've heard of you of course. Then they're all over you like a cheap suit. So in fact pretend you're a producer. They'll think you might be able to give them work.Then give em a taste of their own medicine and wander off yourself. Make sure you give them a false name though. Don't choose Scorsese or Mendes as they're already taken.

    Anyway, I was at Slick to play a pair of socks and a cardigan for a radio ad for fabric conditioner for Saint Annie's agency.

    "Any tips on how I should play them? Accent? Attitude?" I asked the producer, a pretty young thing with no idea as she deferred instantly to the copywriter, an oldish shaven headed man in an ill fitting blue suit and peculiar pointy blue shoes and pointy nose to go with them.

    "The socks are in a drawer and the cardigan is on a hanger" the copywriter told me, as if this would help my characterisation.

    "And they're blue."

Blue is clearly a theme in his life.

"Oh I see," I said, sounding interested. As always you must sound interested, even if you think the directions you're being given are risibly useless.

"So they're blue, and not on anyone's feet." I ask actually taking the piss but of course sounding completely genuine.

"Oh no. They're fresh socks."

"Oh. Really. Great idea. Just out of the tumble drier then?" I said as if I knew what I was talking about.

"Exactly" said the keen rumpled pointy shoed copywriter.

How do you play a pair of socks for God's sake? And clean ones at that. And very importantly, in a drawer! And most important of all…. blue. But, as the words "in a boring nerdy voice" were written at the top of the script, I had a good idea of what was required. They naturally loved it, because I am good at nerds (aaargh), and they laughed uproariously at the line "it's all rather upsetting" which I did in an ultra nerdy voice. (One pair of socks is distressed that he hasn't used the Fabric Conditioner. The cardigan has used it tho). I suggested something.

"Why don't I record one pass through and then interject as myself in a slightly higher tone in the gaps I'll have left. Then I can be both socks!"

"What a great idea!" said the client. "Fabulous! Brilliant!" said the copywriter.

"Marvellous radio idea".

I did so, making one sock very tearful and the other indignant. I made the cardigan from Harrogate. A Northern voice is considered trustworthy you see. As he was on a hanger, I suggested he sound a bit in pain as he's stretched. They all liked that one as well. Hooray!

"Wow. Brilliant! Brought it to life! Superb!" (Utterly over the top but nice of them).

I did the end line in a straight voice as different as poss from the above garments. More like a pin striped suit. I'd been hoping to impress the young producer, but she had been on her mobile for the whole of the session and missed everything. She did say goodbye though. Ron grinned.

"Well done JK" he said which was nice. He gets the madness of it all.

Mandy arranged to meet me at the Actor's Hub in Seven Dials for "Throbbly" and I view her saying goodbye to the director, Jeff, leaving, walking round the block and then coming back to the main entrance again and then I greet her and we go in. I meet the cast who are in on the re-direction thing, though one of them surlyly gives me the fish eye for nearly the whole period I'm there. Mandy swears them all to secrecy. They run what they've got. The show's funny but in need of a lot of tweaking which I do with alacrity. (I mean for a start you can't hear a lot of the punch lines! And there's too much movement during jokes). And it waffles here and there so I tighten it up and write a few of my own bits. Which she and the cast like! And consequently warm to me. Including fish eye who now wants to be my pal which is of course annoying.

Tuesday 8th September

"Docs" interview at Elstree. I'd phoned Lynn to block the morning out so she wouldn't put me up for any jobs for the morning. Somehow managed to be slightly late even though I'd got the train and it was on time and ran to the casting session which is in a building they actually shoot the show in. Arrived a bit sweaty.

Didn't start off well. I greeted the casting director Enid Crimplene who I'd never met before, in the small waiting rooms where she picked me up to take me to meet the director and she says

"Thanks for coming in!"

"Thanks for asking me!" I reply enthusiastically. She blurts

"Oh my God, is that your voice? Oh dear, don't use that voice."

"What?" I squeak taken aback.

"Are you going to use that voice for the ex bouncer who is the amputee?"

"Well this is mine but I'll put a voice on. What would you like?" I respond annoyed and bewildered at the same time.

"Well not that one."

"Ok then."

"Can you roughen it up a bit? And make it deeper? And more masculine and a bit older? I thought you were a cockney. You won't be authentic now will you."

For fuck's sake. A great way to start. Be told off for using your own voice when you were going to try another one out at the interview. What has "acting" become. It's not "acting" any more. You've got to be "the real thing". I'm surprised she didn't say "oh my God I thought you were an amputee!" And I go in and as I said the director's fucking Chesney or Dave or Lionel from the other day and he's possibly got me in because he saw me the other day and taken pity on me. Or he knows nothing about it and it's a huge coincidence. Or he's taking the piss. I think it's the latter.

So I greet Brian or Dave or Lee who is in fact Leonard. Leonard Dobbard. Yes of course this was his name. Gawd knows why I thought it was Brian or Dave or Chidders, and I look cheerful because I know him. And he speaks to me as if he's never met me before. He's very distracted and I read it

"Doctor tell me will I have to have the other leg orf. Tell me. I can take it. Or is it worse? Is what I've got terminal? Tell me. I can take it." in deep old rough more masculine tones as required by the casting director which actually is by now a bit nerdy, and he says

"No. I don't like that at all. Use your normal voice. (For fuck's sake) But ….Make him more weasley".

So I contort myself into a kind of weasel and he says

"Yes but…ha…more real. Make it real."

So I try real weasel and he says

"That sounded like something out of "A Christmas Carol".

So I have another less Dickensian go and he says

"Ha!" Nothing else. Just "Ha!" and asks me how tall I am.

"5 eight" I say automatically.

"Ha!" he goes again. The casting director has, like me, seen the job flying vertically into the ether but adds

"JK's in "Small Craft Warnings" at Basingstoke."
I'm not of course. But I feel to contradict her would be foolish.
"Well…cheerio", says Leonard.
"Good to see you again" I suggest, lying my head off.
"Ha!" He says having switched off. For fuck's sake. He's done this deliberately. As I'm leaving the room Lynn phones.
"It's Lynn." She says.
"I know. It comes up on my phone."
Where are you?"
"In Elstree."
"What you doin' there?"
"I told you".
"No you didn't."
"I did I'm at the BBC interview ."
"How did it go?"
"Total effluent. What do you want?"
"Can you get into town? "Channel 5"?"
"Now?"
"Yeah."
I go straight to Mudchute on the Docklands Light Railway. Promo. "Worst Car Crashes". Metallic bliss. It made up for the arsegravy I'd just been put through.

Wed 9th September

Nuffink. BBC World News pencil never happened. "They want a bird now" Lynn said. Gymmed it. Did a forty minute bike ride as well as the intervals. Got to keep the fitness up to voice. Frank Sinatra used to swim lengths underwater to increase his lung capacity for those long notes. Knackered myself and spent the afternoon asleep on the sofa.

Evening

    Havelok Arms in The Bush with Roop for a quick glass of red wine and a chat about the world. He went to the loo and encountered someone en route, who apparently recognised him from a dog food commercial, and he then ominously pointed at me.
    I was confronted by a white haired double chinned woman of about sixty with a very plummy deep mannish voice and somewhat Victorian garb (long skirt and neck-high shirt/bodice thing) with a colourful choice of eye shadow who informed me that she'd recognised Roop from some ad on the box and he'd pointed me out as a voice over king ("voice over queen actually" I joked but she didn't get it) and as she wanted to do voice overs I was the perfect person to speak to.
    "Ah. What are you in at the moment?" I asked, knowing full well she wouldn't be "in" anything because of course she wouldn't be an actor because they never are these people who tell me they're going to do voice overs. They've been told by someone that "they have a nice voice" and "why have they never done voice overs?" These people who tell them this info rather than being in the biz, are frequently accountants or taxidermists or loo attendants or any other fucking job than actor or sound engineer or agent or producer or any other person who actually works in the correct milieu. So, armed with this completely crap advice and having done no research

into what becoming a voice over actually entails, the would-be voice boldly informs one that they are either wanting to do them or will in fact <u>be</u> doing them. Now I admire the positive thinking, but mostly all they know is that someone somewhere, be it their Mum or the man who just mended their car has said they have a nice voice and should do voice overs. Then they meet me. And air their wish. And I don't put them off. I just find out what they know of voice overs and inform them of several essentials for being a voice over eg "Can you read?" This very obvious one stumps a lot of would-bes. They answer "yes of course," slightly indignantly.

"Yes but can you read well?" I probe.

"Yes of course," they continue, slightly offended because I'm possibly accusing them of being illiterate.

"Out loud? A script you've never seen before? In thirty seconds without making mistakes? A script which probably has too many words? Some of them tongue twisters? And will be rewritten in front of you? So no time to scrutinise it? And you need to fit all the words in in the thirty second script in thirty seconds, because that is what you're being paid for? And the studio costs £350 an hour and they want you to do the job as quickly as possible so they can mix the ad/documentary/promo/animation/corporate/whateverthefuckitis and don't want you doing lots of takes and nancing about and costing them more money?"

This normally lets the doubt creep in as they realise that perhaps they haven't quite thought it through. And when I inform them they have to get an agent and (God forbid!) make a show reel ("A what?" they ask) and that it should be professional standard and will cost them over £300 to make, and then you have to make copies of the cd and send them out or send links to a website with it on or send files with a photo so you need to possibly do a photo shoot and you need to buy a book called "Contacts" to find the addresses to send the cd or links to, they normally gulp and thank me for my help before reconsidering their position vis a vis the new career and decide that perhaps being a bee keeper/morgue attendant/ wankstain examiner is possibly the job for them after all. But in this instance the Victorian garbed wanna-be would not be diverted from her task of extracting information from me. And said in rich unemployable gruff masculine tones

"I read and use my voice every day and am constantly informed by members of the public that I should be a voice over. I read cold and perform in front of large numbers. It's what I do. I would have no problem in a studio."

"Why, what do you do?" I found myself asking, irritated.

"I'm a celebrant in the crematorium at the services." She replies proudly.

"Oh really! Good for you!" I said for no apparent reason, imagining her declaiming a psalm or telling an amusing story next to the deceased and the captive audience. I mean they're unlikely to tell you you're rubbish when they're burying a loved one are they? Anything vaguely emotional and enunciated and they'll praise you. Forgive my cynicism, but it's not the most critical of "crowds". But I don't voice my thoughts as usual and just hear myself saying

"Ah well that's different of course. You must make a voice reel and send it off to an agent immediately," despite my misgivings that as she's not a "youf" the best way for her to get work in this somewhat shallow environment that can still cast according to looks and celebrity, is to do it down a link on the computer so her age can't be seen or send mp3s in to producers. But the words "reel" and "agent" fox her.

"Oh I have to make a reel do I?"

I want to say

"No. A CEO from a top ad agency will hear your deep dulcet tones whilst burying a relative and immediately offer you the latest Sugar Puffs commercial playing the part of a small round cartoon character and you'll earn about two grand and you'll give your job in the crem up and play small round cartoon characters probably never again!"

But I don't say this. I say

"Yes you need to show your diversity on the reel as to what different types of read you can do so you need versions of ads/promos/documentaries/corporates/cartoons/trailers etc. and you then send them to an agent. Mind you they do like you to be in something do the agents as then they have a hook to hang you on when they try and sell you. It helps if you're in a soap or a series or an ad or are a stand up because you're easier to sell. But then you're not an actress or stand up so that avenue isn't open to you. (And then I fan the flames). And as you're one of thousands of people doing this you'll be lucky if they actually listen to the cd or link they get so many. So appearing in a soap or series or ad means they're more likely to listen to it. But you're not are you. You're in the crem. It'll be difficult I'm afraid. Particularly if you look like something out of Wuthering Heights as you do."

    Obviously I didn't say this last bit as it's cruel. Overburdened with info she thanked me and wandered off. Roop returned from his wee and giggled uproariously and bought me a glass of Rioja to make up for having dumped me in it which of course made me a bit pissed.

Thursday 10th

    Iain phoned. As he does which is good. Despite him talking bollocks which is bad. But being put up for work is good. Even if it's bad work.
    "There's a casting for an Italian biscuit and I've put you up for it." He burps. "Red faced man".
    "But I'm not."
    "Yes you are. When we've met you've been red faced."
    "Well occasionally possibly but not all the time."
    "What?"
    "I'm not always a red faced man."
    "What do you mean?"
    "I'm sometimes red-faced."
    "Either you are or you're not."
    "No I sometimes have eczemic flare ups that make me red faced but I'm not a big drinker who gets a red face."
    "Well I've put you up."
    "But I'm not red faced at the moment."
    "Will you be on Wednesday?"

"I don't think so, no."
"Well I'll phone the casting director shall I and pull you out?"
"I suppose I could wait till Wednesday and see if I've had a flare up and you could cancel me then if I haven't."
"No I'm not going to do that. They'll be even more pissed off than they will be when I pull you out today."
"Ah ok. Sorry."
And he rings off. And I've apologised because he got it wrong that I don't have a red face. Well occasionally. Due to an illness. Ye fucking gods.

Did the test ad for shampoo which had come back. It's for "L'Ory". That'd be a nice gig. A test is when they haven't decided you've got the job, and it could be someone else who they think suits it better and also the ad may be going nowhere anyway. It could be one that works abroad but they're not sure if it will ever be aired in England. Or it could be an ad that is for a foreign country but they want an English version to play in-house to English speakers.
Apparently they like my voice as I sound like an authoritative scientist in a white lab coat. Interesting eh, as I tend to wear jeans, trainers, T shirts and jean jackets. I just did my straight informative read.
"Great read great read!" Said a beardy Frenchman. "You act sincerity real well!"

Bill phoned. I'd forgotten to phone him. He wasn't happy with me because he heard from Anne that we'd done an ep and why hadn't I been in touch? He thought we were mates etc.. I came clean and apologised but still said that Sid hadn't been in any of the eps so he still had a chance. Sort of redeemed the situation I think.

Friday 11th September

Did the cat and mouse stupidity at the Actor's Hub again with Mandy and Jeff. I was primed by Mandy's email coz she's told me Jeff hates all my additions and she's agreed to cut em all. But she only agreed to placate him and she wants me to take over the whole thing now so she's decided from tomorrow to pretend to be ill and cancel it when in fact she isn't ill at all and won't cancel it. I emailed her back saying this was silly and why didn't she just tell him. But no he was so sensitive and had just recovered from a nervous breakdown and his boyfriend leaving him, and he'd fall apart if he was told he was being replaced but he was actually a terrible director. No she'd work with me tomorrow evening after her rehearsal with him, and put back the bits that I'd written that he'd cut. And tell him at the weekend. For fuck's sake.

Phoned by Anne. Nick has asked her to play Sid Slug who has made a re-appearance and hadn't had salt thrown over him at all. Fuck. I must phone Bill and tell him. No I won't. Surely he can ask his agent?

Saturday 12th

Girly turned up unannounced with a girlfriend from Minsk who spoke no English and had the build of Vlad the Impaler, drank a bottle of Zinfandel from the fridge with her "pal" and borrowed my bike and buggered off somewhere on it. She didn't return it and wasn't answering her phone. She's either in the pub or training someone or just can't be arsed to speak to me.

Sunday 13th

    Roop had a spare away ticket for Palace v Chelsea. Arranged to go and meet him there and he'd give me a lift back. Went on the train. Had that annoying thing of being in the middle of the crowded carriage by the doors without any over head handholds, so kept bumping into a woman next to me, who clearly thought that this was some kind of sexual harassment. I was so anxious to dissuade her that I blurted out "I'm so sorry but I haven't got anything to hang onto" which sounded as if I was using this as an excuse for attempting to hang onto something on her. Luckily she disappeared behind a very tall chap who was ineptly bellowing a Chelsea song ('Carefree, wherever you may be. We are the famous CFC' to the tune of "Lord of the Dance") as some supporters do in these circumstances. He's saying "look at me! I'm a true blue! I sing songs about my team in public places!" (In what other context can you suddenly burst into song in a crowded train? If you were commuting they'd call the guard. But just because he's on the way to football we accept his tuneless efforts).
    Met Roop and a pal Jude just outside the away entrance as agreed. Our seats at Selhurst Park weren't far from the home supporters who were on the other side of a line of blocked off seats and

stewards and not far from one of them whose hatred for us was off the scale and was unfortunately near enough to be irritating. He did that weird thing of creating a huge penis for himself and masturbating it while pointing at us. What his ten year old son next to him must have thought was beyond me. I caught his eye and he slit his throat and gestured outside.

"See you after mate. I've got your number you Chelsea whore." He shouted. Whore. Can't work that one out. He never ever watched the football just looked for eye contact with opposition fans. Disturbing. Wonder what he does for a living? Solicitor probably.

Roop was at his most belligerent best.

"You're not very good. You're not very good. You're not very, you're not very, you're not very good" he sang far too beautifully on his own to the tune of "Knees up Mother Brown," getting a few odd looks in the process. He's a classically trained singer. The man with the large knob went mad. "C*nt! You're a c*nt. C*nt!" His ten year old joined in. I realised now he was his accomplice. Foolish of me to have thought he despaired of his father's behaviour. Then Chelsea scored and everyone began bouncing up and down like demented goblins - I got grabbed and bounced by a couple of strangers but felt good I'd be chosen to share their joy - and Palace fans attempted to climb over the blocked off seats and surge past the stewards to "get" us. A group of stewards dressed like a SWAT team appeared and surrounded them pushing them back. They were impressively big and persuasive. A Palace fan was led away much to the glee and goading of the Chelsea fans who burst into

a glorious raucous triumphant rendition of "We love you Chelsea."
("We love you Chelsea we do. We love you Chelsea we do. We love you Chelsea we do! Oh Chelsea we love you.") Marvellous.

    We left early which I hate. I mean either team could score and you miss it. But that meant an unhindered exit. Roop had parked not too far away and as there was no traffic due to our early exodus we got off very very swiftly. However on leaving Roop almost collided with a man on a bicycle who harangued him for being "a blind twat." Roop had been at fault and had come straight out in front of him at a junction. Roop's winding the window down and screaming "Look just fuck off" was out of character and badly timed as we sped away straight into a jam at a traffic light which allowed the indignant cyclist to catch up with us. I didn't help much by giving him a vee sign in support of my pal, even though the cyclist was completely in the right. Roop still had his window open from his last verbal volley and just as he was attempting another one, or possibly an apology, or even a polite discussion, the cyclist, spurred on by my evil thrusting hand signals, emptied the contents of his water bottle all over Roop's head before uppercutting him viciously on the nose with it, with a hollow plastic sound.

    "Look before pulling out next time, arseole" (my mother wouldn't have approved) he throatily suggested, and then weaved off cackling.

    "Oh fuck" wailed Roop holding his nose which had begun to bleed profusely. I hastily hid my guilty fingers. The liquid turned out to be orangeade, so everything was a bit sticky, as well as a bit bloody, though he did manage to stench the flow before any blood got on his fleece. But his Chelsea scarf had a red stain on it.

"They have got red in their colours though!" I said somewhat tactlessly.

"Yes! The 1994 side had red on their blue I remember! A big red bit on the neck!" said Jude.

Needless to say we hung about until he felt better and could drive, and got stuck in traffic thus undoing any of the good of leaving early.

Monday 14th September

Did the Argot Christmas ad at Ostrich. But it was no big deal as it was just a guide. i.e. they would voice it with someone else who was a star or celeb but they wanted someone to do all the groundwork so they could fiddle about with the script and storyboard or casting ideas or music or whatever bits they've actually shot or animated. And try the voice over script out for time. So I was just a sort of donkey doing the work in progress. Good idea though.

Based on a book - the catalogue - being opened and a kid walking into the book into a world of gifts kind of thing. I actually had to start with "Once upon a time there was a boy who read a book". With gifts flying into a magical universe where the original boy actor had become part of the cartoon and a cartoon character himself who finds himself in the Argot universe. Apparently it's on air in November. So possibly some work on it till then. I just read a few versions of a script over a sketchy animation. I was in and out. Fairy tale kids' read. Slightly spooky but

whispery story-telling. Producer called Leon very complimentary.
 "Well done mate. Excellent."
 Nice.

 Back to Jumble for the "L'Ory" shampoo test ad. It's far longer than before. Beardy Frenchman said "we 'ave added a few words". It wasn't a few. It was an orgy. Masses of undulating adjectives about hair. "Wavy." "Glossy". "Voluminous". "Shiny" "Epic" "Curvaceous" "Thrusting". "Elephantine". "Corpulent." Well obviously not all those but you get the gist.
 I was voicing around a film of an American model I'd never heard of talking animatedly about how uplifting it all was and how gorgeous her hair and her life were as a consequence of using it. I fitted my bits in with all their anti frizz intensity as lab coat science boffin but unfortunately also as if my scrotum was ablaze. Sheer madness. And would you believe Beardy received a phone call and added another sentence. The engineer Graham piped up with "it doesn't fit". No poop Poirot. I made it fit. It wasn't worth it as It sounded utterly unintelligible. A ridiculous dash through syrup from start to finish. Beardy and his colleague Francoise were strangely 'appy though.
 He commented "Good job. You 'ave a vairy fine voice fir thees product. We will see you again."
 Francoise said "Yes. Parfait. Till zer next time."
 That's the kiss of death then.

 Iain phoned. Cakes ad now 21st. Phoned Lynn to book the day out with Diggerty Dawg.
 "What you doin' then?" She asks.

"A cake ad in Holland."

"Ooh I like cake! Bring me some back!"

"Ha ha! I'll try!" I say. It'll never happen. I won't have time. And they won't give me any samples. They never do.

"And take some condoms. They're mad for it over there" she adds bewilderingly. And then "must go other phone's going" and she's off before I can ask her if I'm working tomorrow or what secret knowledge she has of the sex lives of the Dutch.

Mandy hasn't told Jeff she's ill and Jeff has put his foot down. He can't work out when this new dialogue is being written/rehearsed and is getting suspicious. He's said either the new dialogue and moves go or he goes. So she's taken them all out again. The cast are very pissed off.

She almost told him what was happening but didn't coz she can't bear to upset him so we have to go through the silly rigmarole of her saying goodbye to him again and her walking round the block as I observe from the other side of the road. However this time Jeff sees an old friend and hangs around outside the Hub chatting. She does her circumnavigation of the square and reappears. She sees him, re-greets him, lies to him about forgetting something, goes back in, and phones me. I then have to tell her when he's gone and she comes back out and fetches me. I insist she reinstates all my moves and dialogue. And add more. She agrees with me. The cast who are hanging around the café sneak into the rehearsal room again and we do it. Badly. Unfocused. All over the place. This is beginning to do my head in.

Tues 15th

Wandered into Soho in the afternoon to do a narrative for a supermarket. Had one line in the narrative. Was playing a "champagne bottle" who says "Oh I don't like that." The champagne bottle had specs and was "a bit of a jobsworth" according to the Producer. I used the nerdy voice. "Perfect" I was told.

Lynn phoned and said could I go to Ostrich again and redo the Argot ad. Few more line tweaks.
"Well done JK " says Leon. In and out again.

Wed 16th

Morning.

More Argot. The animation is progressing. Lots of the kid flying and a few alien and fairy tale worlds and football stadia and he gets gifts at each of them. A copywriter I'd never seen before came with a different script which of course didn't fit time-wise. Or correspond to the animation. So they cut a lot out and moved it about and it began to resemble the other script which was pointless. He left and we went back to the first script they'd been animating to.

Evening

Gymmed. Thighs strangely weedy.

Thursday 17th

More Argot at Ostrich. They've changed the gifts - a rather large plush cushion sneaked in as well as a microwave - so consequently the script is different. In and out again. No one there from the agency. Just me and the engineer, Scott. Five mins.

"See you tomorrow!" He says.

"I haven't been booked" I say.

"Oh you will be" says Scott. The end line which was "Have an Argot Christmas" is now "Argot…..It's a completely different universe."

Henry Hedgehog: Anne Chuff is good as Sid Slug. Very drawly and crawly. Slightly creepy. We won't be seeing Bill again. Nick is harsh with me about my interpretation and suggests I should listen to a few old eps to re-discover Henry because I'm much deeper and he wants more child like. Though still the good snuffliness that is Henry's hallmark. But slightly more high pitched.

"If I didn't know better I'd say you were a forty a day man. Ha ha ha ha ha!"

He plays me the old Henry stuff from last time. And guess what! I am doing it exactly the same. I do not need to be highpitched at all.

"Ah well this is a mystery" he says, backtracking.

"Because the criticism of your performance is not coming from me, but from the Canadian producer, who I had on the phone this morning, and she specifically told me to tell you that you need to be higher as you were before. So, I'm afraid JK old boy, that regardless of how you sounded in the last series, my directive is to get you to do it higher now. So if you please, do it higher now."

And he puts me through the hoops and I sound like a squeaky git and am immensely fed up.

"Oooh! The hedgehog's got a snit on!" says Nick irritatingly. And he's right. I do have a "snit on" whatever that means. I am very not pleased, and no amount of ribbing and teasing from the abundantly noxious Jack Taylor who plays Willie Worm can placate me.

"You've got the biggest snit-on I've ever seen. I can see it through yer trousers!" he hoots.

One of the four episodes we did in the three hour session (it's divided into four fifteen minute eps each one of which we take about 45 mins to do what with retakes and farting about) was called "Henry learns to Waltz" and was an amusing story about Henry wanting more self esteem and not constantly rolling up into a ball at the drop of a hat when he felt frightened, so Sid Slug encouraged him to go and learn how to be more assertive if he learnt how to dance, with all the predictable amusing consequences (gets literally kicked out of the class by eager tap dancing ants, injures Alex Aaardvark who is tangoing who knocks into him and is spiked, punctures his partner Tina Terrier whilst trying to do the Pasa Doble etc.) But he finally learns to waltz and hooray everything is super! I suggested the ep should be called "Prickly Come Dancing". Got a titter.

Fri 18th

Argot. Ostrich. More new products. A bike. An X Box. Phones. A chip thing. Been told to give it awe and wonder. As it's not me ultimately doing it I don't know why they're being so thorough, but I do and they like it. But the new items are rushed when they're added. And awe and wonder is difficult at speed. And of course there's no animation for them. But they replace the trouser press (well-weird Christmas gift or what!) and the electric massager (ditto) and the backpack that plays hits from kids cartoons. (!!!!)

    Game of squash against an unbelievably smelly bloke. Old calf stiffness a problem early doors but held up but ye gods the BO. It's how he wins I think. People just give him the points to get out of the court. Luckily though his squash was pretty average and a few decent serves followed by some timely nicked drop shots had him panting and I eased through. Which is just as well as I was gagging on a couple of occasions from the stench. I wanted to tell him but you just can't can you. Mother would say it was glandular.

Sat 19th September

    Drove to York for the evening to meet up with the school undefeated cricket XI for the reunion thing. But not to play. Calf still a bit dodgy. I duly left the Girly, who had come over post training with two rucksacks of washing, to her "things to do". I didn't quite tell her the truth about where I was going. I mean actually I said I was going to Ealing to see some contemporaries from school and she wouldn't enjoy it and it was all boys anyway.
    "Ah mate. I'll stay here. (Phew! Right response!) I'll use your washing machine, make myself

something to eat (that'll be the smoked salmon then) an' I'll watch a couple er DVDs and just chill. Ok? You're not gonna be too late are you?"

"No of course not" I replied knowing full well I wouldn't be back until four o'clock in the morning if I was lucky, as I was clearly madly driving to York and it was half four and I might make it by half eight.

And gawd knows what was going to happen to me with my insane "prank-playing, semolina pudding down your undies, cricket bag full of beer and flattened road kill squirrel waved in yer face" cricketing school chums!

I sped up the motorway for four hours expecting fireworks! And took my water pistol, sausage floating in a bowl of lemonade kit and spare set of car keys and complete change of clothes just in case!

However. Everyone hadn't been pissed and raucous and setting fire to each other's trousers and pouring custard all over their cars. They'd been doing all the usual things oil magnets and solicitors and advertising moguls and heads of industry (which they were on their way to becoming) are used to doing when with their families, like orgies of table tennis, and disgusting acts like Twister and croquet and darts and obscene French cricket and perverse acts of rounders in Damian's house and then moved onto the local where they'd guzzled debauched grub like vols aux vents and egg and cress sandwiches which the pub served in a room upstairs.

And being the only actor there, far from being asked to sing infantile songs and tell filthy jokes, and regale them with stories of seducing the leading lady, I was ignored by my team mates and grilled by their' offspring as to whom I had worked with who was famous. Everyone had heard the Hedgehog series and was most enthusiastic. And had noticed me as the fruitbat which as I've said however wasn't actually me. I've never been a fruitbat in anything. It's a telly ad apparently. I must look out for it.

    I had expected to be debagged, have my car keys thrown out of the window and my genitals smeared with embrocation. But no. Everyone was very charming; the men all stood on one side of the room regaling each other with stories about their cricketing youth, several involving me and situations I have no memory of (eg I once apparently ran across the cricket square at an old boys' game just wearing a jock strap, vaulted the stumps, waved my bottom at the umpire, and ran back again in a plastic Ronald Reagan mask, but that was actually Damian. And I'd sung "Hey Big Spender" standing on a table at the Weyfleet cricket dinner whilst steaming drunk. Yes in fact that was me but I hadn't touched a drop and it was "I Enjoy being a Girl") and the women and kids stood on the other side.

    After my grilling by the kids had finished (they were annoyed I wasn't in Peppa Pig. Or couldn't do the fruitbat voice. (Wtf) And they were most miffed I couldn't remember any of the Buzz the Bee lines from that cereal commercial I did. In fact they recited them to me.

    "Hi I'm Buzz! I'm buzzing about the honey in this crunchy breakfast snack!" (Which was a tad scary.)

    I chatted to the women. Mostly about why I wasn't married.

    "Are you by any chance "gay"?" said Peter Armstrong's wife Sonia who I'd never met before. She said the word "gay" with a pause and enunciation as if it was a species of tropical plant.

"Most actors are "gay" aren't they. And waiters coz they rarely act. Is this you?"

"All waiters are gay?"

"No silly. All actors are "gay" or "waiters."

"All gay waiters are actors?"

I feigned confusion and then told her I was a lady boy and would be attempting to pull her husband before the evening was out. She laughed a little too hysterically for my liking.

Don Trebilcock said his kids had a video of the "Tripe and Onions" cartoon about the monkeys, and he always pointed out a TV appearance or ad or voice he recognised me on, especially the fruitbat recently (Ffs) and he was very disappointed we wouldn't be able to renew our great batting feat when we held out against Highmere School and preserved the unbeaten record!

When the pub closed and we were chucked out, I was offered several beds and told I was mad to drive back and why wasn't I going to play now that I was there and I was too pissed anyway.

"Look at you, you're roaring!" said Sonia Armstrong incorrectly. "Come and spend the night with us!"

I politely declined. I had the feeling she half believed I actually was a lady boy and wanted to have a look.

"You're not really injured are you? Stay and play! Stay! You're a hypochondriac, Damian said you were!" she said.

But I would not wilt under the pressure of such badly argued abuse. Very nice of them and all that, but "I was ok and had only had one glass of wine. See them all next time possibly?"

I made it back in about three and a half hours and played Stevie Wonder, Prefab Sprout, The Beatles, David Bowie, The Rolling Stones, Jacques Brel and Buddy Holly at huge volume. One of driving's great joys. Loud music aligned with speed. Ahhh luvverley.

Returned at about four. Did quite well! Possibly occasionally illegally over the speed limit. There dribbling on the sofa in front of the TV wrapped in a duvet from the airing cupboard with a bottle and a half of red wine inside her, was the Girly who had slept in situ and had to be cajoled to go to the bedroom she was so comfortable. Well. Pissed. She insisted we make love! But she still got up at seven thirty and bashed about the bathroom eager for her personal training assignment.

"Mate. Where's the Neurofen?" she selfishly enquired as I hid under the pillow to escape her thrashing and loud pungent urinating.

"Phwor mate. Smell that!"
Ffs.

Sunday Sept 20th.

Slept in. Faffed. Drank far too much coffee. I have a cafetière and indulge myself with exotic sorts from Tesco. Guatemalan. Java Sumatra. Colombian. Mind you not too exotic obviously as they're from Tesco. I mean you won't see any of them going through the digestive system of a civet. And to be frank I can't tell the difference between any of 'em.

Am in the middle of a rather thrilling Le Carre.

Mon 21st

    Argot at Ostrich. Animation and real life/live footage still not done and will cost a fair few pennies but the ad is coming together and they've almost finalised the script and items to feature. It strikes me they've set up some interesting environments that will be CGI'd. Emphasis on space and a bit of teleportation and the odd magician. According to Leon though they're casting the actors this week and then shooting next. They were trying out music tracks today and delving into a lot of library music. They wanted me to read the almost finalised script differently according to the track. Coz you do of course. A rock track requires a more rocky harder read. Soft strings something intimate. The client is quite keen on a pop standard and the agency is convinced this will wreck the sentimental kids' Christmas aspect of it. I have to say I agree with the agency so they're likely to get a music company like Mick Casso to pitch for it. Something warm and squishy switching to slightly cosmic or fairy tale would be my take on it. Having said that the number of times the client gets their way and blithely destroys it with some completely inappropriate pop ditty.

    The broadcast date is a few weeks away so it's all not that tense yet. The agency are aware I'm away tomorrow but back on Wednesday. Might consequently lose it. Would rather not as it's fun regular work. But as I'm not going to be the voice on the finished product if I get replaced I get replaced. That's the actor's life I'm afraid. Lynn of course is annoyed.

"Why the fuck do you have to fuck off and do a sodding ad in the middle of this one?" She spits charmingly at me sounding as if she's in the gym in the middle of an aerobics class. Which she then says she is.

"Well Leon the copywriter has said they don't need me tomorrow so fret not."

"We'll fuckin' see about that won't we."

Cycled in to meet Mandy at the Actor's Hub again with all the usual flummery and subterfuge. She'd told the rest of the cast to leave and not come back till she phoned. I presumed they were somewhere round the corner. I arrived and hid outside, she faked her exit, but again he didn't leave and hung about outside. She came back and seeing him again said she'd lost something. Again. She phoned me, I observed him still hanging about and then he went back in. She then spoke to him and left.

Apparently he said he was staying and having something to eat so we went to a pub for about three quarters of an hour. She re-entered the Actor's Hub to see if he'd gone and saw him in the Café so met me behind a Renault van and we went back to the pub and tried to look at the script amidst massive shouting and hubbub from a rather competent sound system and people bellowing in each other's ears. As you do in pubs. We then thought up a plan. I would go in and sit in the rehearsal room and wait for her and she would pop in. But she was waylaid by him and she had to pretend that she'd lost her watch and had worked out she must have left it in the café, so she got all the people in the Actor's Hub café looking on the floor for her non-existent watch. He insisted on walking her to the Tube. She phoned me and we decided to give up for the day and she's going to tell him she's ill again on Wednesday when she's next rehearsing and then I'll rehearse her if I'm free. A member of the cast then phoned me to say they were still waiting in a pub in Old Compton Street and what should they do? I suggested they all go home. For… fuck's… sake….

    Went to see Mother. Having the scooter is great coz I can just whizz over to Putney from Shepherd's Bush in minutes. I have a key of course. On my entering I found her at the kitchen table, reading. I went in for a kiss. She lifted her head up I thought to receive said smooch but instead sniffed the air somewhat cruelly and said whilst recoiling
    "Your breath smells like a decomposing rodent that prior to death swam in its own faeces. Go to the Nescafé jar and take some coffee granules to munch. You have to mask that smell or not one single member of the female sex will ever want to kiss you. I'm surprised the one you have actually does."
    I retorted with
    "I'm not sure the Girly and I need to mother coz when we have sex I normally do it from behind."
    Which I thought was quite good in the circumstances. She played the "old" card.
    "Oh my God. Far too much information for an old woman to take. You're going to kill me you know that don't you? Or is that what you want? What an image you have thrust into my mind. What makes you say things like that? Have I brought you up badly? Have I? It's all those people you used to go to Scouts with isn't it. I knew I should have prevented you from

mixing with them. And the result is I have to put up with such filth. Oh my God! I thought my old age would be a pleasant amble towards the twilight. Instead it's a staggering rush towards a black hole filled with sewerage and mayhem and images of you having doggy style sex with strange Australian women. If you're going to be horrible to me please go. Now!"

I did nothing. There would be more. I went to make myself a cuppa. I wasn't disappointed.

"Are you still playing squash?"

Yup. Here it goes.

"You know I am" I replied.

"Well don't. I've heard on the radio it's bad for you."

I said

"Only if you don't have exercise at all, surely." (A little bit of doubt begins to creep in such is her power. Suddenly she knows everything. For she is my Mother).

"Well you're not a man of twenty. All that twisting and turning. It's not good for you."

She is of course correct. How dare I presume to be able to do anything without her approval. After all, she brought me up and looked after me when I was poorly and puking, she prevented that nasty surgeon from operating on my penis (a story for another time I feel) so she should be allowed to run my life now that I am an adult. Should she fuck. I deflect her with a subtle

"Unfortunately Mother, your advice is going in one ear and out the other. Whoosh! There it goes."

I mowed the lawn for her again. She likes the lawn mown as much as possible. My father was wheeled out regularly to mow the lawn. Until he moved on to mowing a celestial one. Sigh.

Tues 22nd

Went to Amsterdam for the ad for which I said "Yes" so amusingly. For the cakes. Flown out at ten o'clock from Heathrow on KLM to which I tubed immensely early. Picked up by a solemn cabby at the airport which is a boon as I can kip nicely in the cab. Arrive at the studio at lunch time. In wardrobe, am dressed in clothes similar to mine. I am greeted on the set by the strangely speaking director, Luke.

"Greetings Jakey! You fly well?"

"Yes yes. Flapped the arms a bit and here I am" is what I'd liked to have said. I just say

"Yes thankyou. Hostess poured coffee over me and I've lost all feeling in my nether regions, but otherwise fine."

I didn't say that either.

The script is completely different. The set is completely different. It's a park bench. In a park setting. In the studio. There is a dog in the scene I know nothing about which is now the star of the show. But it's not arriving till tomorrow. So I act with the imaginary dog.

"We put dog tomorrow!"

We do a run through. I thought it went quite well. I am supposed first to throw a stick. I throw with gusto and intent. Then a ball. I hurl it adroitly. Then beckon the dog. My fingers are a blur with energy. Then hand him a bone. My precision is remarkable. Then pet him. Even though he's not there I rub his imaginary coat with joy. Then eat cake with him. I eagerly cram it in. Then laugh uproariously. Ah ha ha I go.

"I halt you……I not get feeling there dog" says the director.

"Oh sorry" I grovel, typically playing lower status.

But of course there isn't actually a fucking dog there. I'm imagining the dog. The dog arrives tomorrow. I'm not here tomorrow. We try again. I am realer. He doesn't like it.

"I no feel there is dog in your acting."

"Ooh sorry", I mumble.

He decides to direct me as if it's a silent film, shouting orders while the camera is turning over

"Imagine dog big in mind. You have him? Yes? There! He be. Big dog. He friend. You love. He have doggy face. Doggy skin. Doggy teeth. Ruff ruff. (He's barking at me) You have, yes? …Now throw him a wood…… But no. He no fetching…..Now ball…but no no no… You are surprise…. Now bone bone bone… You indicate him round with fingers…. You make him a fuss….fuss fuss fuss… You a very smiling man…..fuss fuss fuss fuss.. You laugh and laugh and laugh….Ho Ho hee ha ha ha….But he not fetch ball…..He not eat bone….. Sad sad sad. You fetch ball. Fetch! Fetch!... But he eat cake! Ha ha ho hee ha ha. Now you eat cake….More…more….yes. You love cake. YOU LOVE CAKE….(bloody hell) You laugh….Hahaha ha ha. So…CUT….."

It's like a work out.

"….Dog better. …..but…..Again…..we go…. again…"

Clearly to him I am very dense indeed. He simplifies it. Angrily.

"Hear….. Concentrating Jakey. Throw wood. He do nothing. You throwing ball. He do nothing. You handy him bone. You indicate with fingers. You fuss. You go ball. When you not there he eat cake. And you come here and worry where cake go? But he eat it! You happy! You have more. You eat too! Very very very funny. You be funny."

Gulp. I have never been ordered to be funny. Ever. I'm not sure it's possible. It's like a torture technique. I go again with his silent movie directions. And again. I am a manic marionette. I am a mechanical toy. I don't think I've improved. From time to time he cuts early and screams "I NOT SEE DOG." It is hellish. And what happened to my highly amusing "Oh well" and shrug? I am doing something completely different. What's happened to the car? And the wife?

In a tea break I am introduced to a woman (a producer? The client?) who smilingly congratulates me on how well it's going (?) and reiterates the mantra that the dog is in tomorrow and is a German Short Haired Pointer called Bart (well that's good to know but I have no idea what that breed looks like so derr) And she says the other English actor doing the other commercial is arriving in the afternoon. And he's Bill Masbro. And do I know him? Apparently he knows me and says hello. Nope. Haven't got a scooby. Surlily pretend I do of course.

It suddenly all makes sense. No one bothered to tell me. I am doing the "other" commercial. The other commercial about cakes but involving a cake loving dog. Who is, I'm being constantly informed as if I'm a plank, given a ball and a stick to fetch and a bone to gnaw but would rather have a cake. Ffs.

We do it 46 times. Comedy by bullying. Finally Luke is pleased. Or exhausted. (I know I am). Who knows? I certainly wasn't funny. Though he did do a mass of cut-aways of me laughing and grinning uncontrollably. Which he loved. ("I love!") And there were two cameras one of which appeared to be shooting my hands and feet. Or my face. Or my perplexed moments after he'd shouted "CUT". Who knows. Perhaps it will all work wonderfully in the edit. I actually reached a stage where I didn't give a monkey's doodah.

I am finished by about four - "Thankyou. You funnyman" says Luke - and taxi'd to the airport and flown home. What a bizarre life I lead. Lynn left a barely audible shouty voice mail.

"Chippa Choc at Jumble Studios at ten. Ok JK boy? And Argot at Octopus at twelve. So you haven't fucked up with your little jaunt. Must go. I'm in the wine bar."

Little jaunt. Ffs.

Wed 23rd

At Clearcat for this Chippa Choc ad. I had to say
"Beware. It's a new Chippa Choc bar. It's got more choclatey chocolate chips than ever!"
There's a copywriter there who I've worked with before who just reads how he wants the line to be read. Normally I'm not in love with having lines read to me, as frequently the person reading it is absolute dipshit at reading and insists on reciting the whole thing from start to finish as if somehow you'll pick up some of his classy non intonation when in fact he's

reading it like a man with a dinner plate and cutlery and a fish starter involving broccoli in his mouth. But this chap knows what he wants and it's only a short line. He says "I want it like this". And he does it his way and I copy him and he says

"Yup perfect. One take wonder".

"One for Lloyds?" says Mick the engineer who is a good lad. He means "one for insurance" (Lloyds you see) in case somehow we'd all suddenly got struck deaf and had all heard the ad as if it was excellent when in fact it was terrible, or the equipment had blown up or something and we missed it or there's a noise on the first take that no one noticed, or I said "livestock" instead of Chippa Choc. So I do another exactly the same way and the copywriter says "Yeah great." The producer, a nice giggly girl, asks, as they always do,

"Well we've got JK for another hour. Shall we get him to do it another way?"

This is often met by "Ok!" and once again the usual happens as you embark on a hellride to oblivion because you try various voices and accents and different stresses and pitches and they don't like any of them and then go back to take one and you somehow feel you've let them down. But in this instance the copywriter says

"No I'm happy."

"Money for old rope" says the producer somewhat churlishly and I go off her completely.

"Yes but what charming old rope. This rope has silken strands." I retort.

Everyone giggles but it wasn't very funny.

Argot at Octopus. Would you credit it they had another VO in yesterday doing their script tweaks. Scott the engineer wasn't on the job today and it was one I didn't know who played me the new script that I hadn't voiced, all the way through thinking it was me who'd voiced it. No awe or wonder. Very matter of fact. Said "Once upon a time" as if ordering a sandwich.

"Oh isn't that you?" Asked the engineer annoyingly who is Mo. It was fucking obvious it didn't sound like me but I let Leon sort it.

"Do you want me to do it like that?" I asked Leon, to give him the option but thinking "ffs what Eeyore has voiced this"?

"Definitely not. That's why you're back. Usual awe and wonder please."

"Oh thanks. Who is that?" I asked.

"Pierce Sark."

"Oh ok." I replied. Never having heard of him. I didn't want to diss a fellow VO but he was fucking awful. Well, completely different from me. Narrow mouthed and lispy. Pert even. Pert and bland. Monotonous. Dull as a ditch full of dull dung. Where on earth did they find him? We added a mountain bike to the list of products.

Mandy at the Actor's Hub again. Had them all for the afternoon which was rare. I reassembled my scattered bits and pieces and got them to stagger through it. As you'd expect it's all over the place. She's written some clever sketches though. And her self deprecating monologues on her poshness and tallness and how clumsily she copes with it are really good. But the cast is all too quiet and still ruin gags by upstaging each other and hiding props that need to be seen and of course forget my lines and blocking and lurch into his. It's a dog's dinner.

    In the middle of my attempt at reassembling it he turns up. Well, bursts in. He isn't a fool and has realised what is happening. And the cast had told him anyway. He bursts into tears in front of us all. It's weirdly like being in the middle of a clandestine affair without any of the fun. He is deeply hurt so he says. She says she loves his work (!) but needs another eye. He pathetically says he'd like a compromise. Can we share the piece? So I say yes, wondering how the fuck this will pan out but all he does is sit there sullenly as I undo his work and far from contributing, he shakes his head theatrically, argues with me about reinserting my stuff he's cut and flounces out. I tell Mandy I obviously can't work this way. She agrees to sack him. Then amazingly he waits for me at the end of the rehearsal, and says he can see from the stuff I've cut out or added he likes the way I work and I'm really good and he can't compete and he'd like to be my assistant. And can we go for a drink! And we go for a drink and he asks me out. His name is Ben! What the fuck! I decline but am of course flattered.

    Lynn rings. Chippa Choc ad redo tomorrow. ("Those c*nts at Chippa Choc want you back! Must go, got a call coming in and I'm on the bus.")
    Wot no Argot? Bloody hell.

Thursday 24th

Lynn phoned.

"Don't worry about Argot. They're shooting it. And then animating. They'll be in touch."

So that'll be the end of that then. That's what happens.

Lunch time: Worked on a redo of the Chippa Choc ad I voiced yesterday. They needed to change an "a" to a "the", as in "Beware it's "The" new Chippa Choc bar etc." As opposed to "Beware it's "A" new Chippa Choc bar etc." And I had to be more enthusiastic. There were a whole new lot of people there. The giggly girl from last time wasn't there and instead there was some girl in a bright sweater who had her head in "OK Magazine" and another bloke in a suit and some others who were very junior. The copywriter was there in the same jeans and shirt and jacket as yesterday, but was engrossed in a conversation on the phone and when I'd done the change, left. The new girl producer stopped reading "OK" and told me there might be a different line so could I not go until they'd sorted it out? Got paid for hanging about. (Ha ha ha hee hee hee). Even got offered food which is really rare!

The actor or "voice artiste" in a voice session is never offered anything! Normally at lunch time all the ad agency lot are guzzling and stuffing and reading "Hello" and Tweeting, or chatting to some mate or texting or playing some computer game and never actually listening or paying attention to anything else around them and generally having a stonking good time of it. (Whenever you hear anyone say "Can I hear that again?" it means they were paying absolutely no attention the first time). The poor old runner is rushed off their feet going out getting Lattes and Skinny Cappuccinos, "not too much froth oh and with maple syrup" and "Oh yeah. I'll have some Sushi and some seafood balls. And a Bud. Nar hang on. Make that a craft beer. Anything will do. You choose. And get me twenty Rothman's as well. And the Standard. And some Strepsils, coz I got a sore throat."

And the actor is just wheeled in, does his/her job, and wheeled out again. And never offered anything! But today it was:

"Er JK. We appear to be having a bit of a problem as the script might change. We can't let you go until it's okayed so can you hang around?"

"Yup. Of course."

"Have you got anything later?"

"No no! I'm all yours!"

"So while you're waiting, if you'd like some grub, that's ok."

"Oh great!"

"What would you like?"

"Oh nothing much….errr…..Tuna neapolitana in some Ciabatta no butter with rocket and cress and a small fat Americano no sugar and a piece of chocolate chip cake. Yes. That would be great".

"Great".

"And a banana".

"Oh ok".

"No hang on. Jacket potato with coleslaw and baked beans."

"Right"

"And a banana."

"Oh ok."

"No no no. I'm being ridiculous. Coronation Chicken. With some grapes. In a baguette from Pretaminger. If they do that."

"Great".

"And a banana."

"Right"

"No actually I won't have anything. Just the banana."

"Oh ok"

"And a hot chocolate"

"Right"

"No no no. I"m being sooo stupid. I'll have some crayfish in a filo parcel."

"And a banana?"

"Nope. No banana."

"You sure?

I look across at the table in front of the engineer Gary which in turn is in front of the voice booth. The creatives are tucking into Pizza, Salade Nicoise and Crab something and huge Sausages.

"No it's ok I'll have what you lot are having.

"Right."

This is the problem with suddenly being offered a free lunch in an environment where you've never been offered it before. Somehow the fact you've never been offered food where everyone else is always stuffing themselves, makes you want to order the earth to make up for all those times when you've been ignored, in an environment where your hunger has never been taken into consideration. It becomes a huge scoff opportunity. And actors must never pass up a scoff opportunity. They never know if they'll ever eat again. They need to maintain those fat levels to see them through the winter. Like Eskimos. Or is it Inuits? And whales. (And camels? Or possibly not any of them and I'm talking bollocks?) So free food must be devoured as quickly as possible and in as large a quantity as possible.

On film shoots, the actors are constantly at the trough consuming every available morsel. And because the competition to be film caterers is very very competitive, the food is invariably extra tasty. And this is another reason to be constantly scoffing. It tastes excellent and is the kind of grub you never ever get to eat in your own kitchen. Coq au vin. Duck a l'orange. Boar en croute. Fox en mustard. L'Otter avec hog de hedge. You don't know what to have it's so abundant. And there are snacks all through the day to truly maintain that gut. Ooh. Film shoots can be the most calorific experience you'll ever have.

Script change never happened.

"JK. You can go! We're staying with the line. Thankyou very much."

"Thanks for the grub!"

Left the studio having eaten half a restaurant. Fantastic. More fantastic coz it was all free. And I got an extra hour's dosh! For hanging about eating!

Fri 25th

Did a bizarre job today for cat food with the lovely engineer Bill Greaves. He's one of the best and is rewarded accordingly as he's used a lot. On entering the studio, at T&H, the producer greeted me with

"Ah JK. It's a "Preena" cat food ad that you've voiced before. They've changed the end line so you just need to revoice it".

"Ok!" I enthused. I had no recollection of ever doing a "Preena" ad, but then some ads are infinitely instantly forgettable so just stood and watched this ad featuring a dancing mouse unfold. A music track started.

"Shake it to the left. Shake it to the right" it went. The singer sounded familiar. We heard the voice over. A smug smoothly up its fundament cheesy cocky toothpasty sing song smarmy voice with very little tone change.

"There you are JK. That read with these words."

"Ah" I grunted, noticing that the voice wasn't mine. I paused. Bill confirmed it. I awaited the explosion.

"That's not JK" said Bill.

"What?" stuttered the girl, showering the desk with prosciutto.

"It's not me" I owned up.

"It's Tony Chorley" said Bill.

"Yes" I agreed.

"Tony Chorley? But it says here that you did it."

"No it's not but it is JK singing!" said Bill.

He played it. He was right! It was me doing the "Shake it to the left etc.." Yes I had a vague recollection of having sung it for a narrative and someone must have "recycled" it - used it hoping no one would notice. It happens. That's why my name was on the job.

"What shall we do?" said the young lady despairingly.

Bill chipped in.

"Look Chorley's such a pain. Let JK do it. He can read much better than Chorley anyway. Chorley's reads are just awful. The cheese is dripping from that." (Ah Bill. I love him).

"Yes I agree. He's a preening cock. Always so bloody fond of himself" said the producer in an unexpected gush of hatred. "JK you do it."

Blimey! Must be some previous there.

"And JK can be the mouse at the end as well" said Bill.

"What mouse?" squeaked the girl slightly hysterically. (who was Jill by the way).

"The mouse has a line here on this script" said Bill.

"Oh shit so he does" said Jill.

"Don't worry. JK can do a mouse voice and I'll put an effect on it" said the marvellous Bill.

And I did. It's a network TV ad! And all me! Hurrah!

"Well done, you fuckin' well nailed that and then took the nails out and hammered them in again! Then made that wardrobe!" Said Lynn peculiarly after I'd told her. She's been at her local B&Q hasn't she.

"Ha ha ha ha that'll serve Chorley right. Unpleasant fucker....Oops phone's goin'. I'm on me own. Well done pigeon. Laters!"

Pigeon?

Sat 26th

Mother phoned. "Hello!" I said clearly.

"Oh dear. You're in a bad mood." She stated abruptly. Where did that come from?

"Mother. I am not in a bad mood. I am in a good mood."

"If that's your good mood, I'd hate to hear your bad mood."

"I am not in a bad mood," I say calmly, but slightly irritated. She spots it with her irritation radar.

"Oh yes you are! It's that girl isn't it? You must stop seeing her. She's so not good for you. Deep breaths darling. That's excellent for excess anger."

"I am not fucking angry" I suddenly explode, slamming my ludicrously expensive Mickey Mouse novelty phone down and breaking it into two separate pieces. I am actually fed up with the Girly and she can hear it. She knows me too well. Twenty minutes later I phoned Mother back on the badly glued phone and apologised.

"I don't know where you get your anger from. Your father was never angry. A little lamb he was. "Manners maketh man" is the saying I would use for your father. Whereas you have an Irish temper he never had. And he was more Irish than you, having been born there. Whereas you were born in Hammersmith. But no. You'll have to control that temper or you'll never have any friends. Or a girlfriend. Because I fear for you if you don't. It won't be a great life with no friends and no girlfriend."

I took a deep breath and claimed an imminent bowel movement.

Sunday 27th

Bit bored. Replied to a spam mail.

----- Original Message -----
From: "Taylor M. Danso Esq."
<taylor.d@endowmentclaims.co.uk>

Subject: This Is Our Last Notice To You

We wish to notify you again that you are a beneficiary to the sum of US$8,500,000.00 Dollars in the intent of your relative the deceased (name now withheld since this is our second letter to you)

We contacted you because you bear the surname identity and therefore can present you as the beneficiary to the inheritance since there is no written will.

In your acceptance of this deal, we request that you kindly forward to us your letter of acceptance, your current telephone number and a forwarding address to enable us file necessary documents at our high court probate division for the release of this sum of money in your favor. There is a US$250 fee to process the deal. Yours faithfully,

Taylor M. Danso Esq.

My reply

Taylor.
How are you? Good I hope in these difficult times for those of us with pets and good wholesome values.

"Again" you say? Slightly rudely if I may be picky. Look. I have received nothing from you before. This is the first I have heard of it. Where in God's earth did you send the first one? Or perhaps my boisterous impulsive spotty son has got to it first? That is always likely as he's constantly on the computer looking at porn. Eagerly spanking his monkey. He has a hairy palmed haggard sunken eyed look I can't quite describe. But I suppose it's a learning curve. I myself did the same as him and I'm a fit healthy chicken farmer with one lung and a pronounced limp due to a shooting accident.

You say I have inherited some money? Why is there a time limit on this? Either I am the beneficiary or I am not? I was also not aware I had any relatives left alive. The whole of my nearest and dearest were wiped out at a family reunion in Australia by a freak flash flood. Thanks to the Almighty I was down the road at the liquor store getting some beers and visiting a prostitute when the flood struck and 27 Mortensen Ramsbottom Pickilings were slain. Other than my son Tickler. My dear wife Doxycycline was unfortunately one of the drowned but we'd not been in a physical relationship for years - she lived in Friern Barnet - so there was a kind of inevitability about it all. But you're saying I have another relative I knew nothing about? Well that's a great wonderful surprise! Especially as he's so well minted. Deduct the $250 from my winnings why doncha!!!
Here's my address.
Tinto Mortensen Ramsbottom Pickiling the 3rd (known as Pimples) (Mrs)
The Pig and Horsemeat Farm
27B Larchbay Crescent,
WC1 1AA

Phone: No!
Send me the moolah NOW
Not very Sincerely
Tinto Mortensen Ramsbottom Pickiling (know as Egbert) (Mrs)

I await a reply

Mon 28th

    Faffed. Gymmed. Am doing rather good squats aided by a young trainer who seems to know his stuff.
    "The squat is the gem of all the exercises. You can't do betterer than that" he tells me. Well that's good to know.

    Went to see "Woyzeck" that my mate Sid was in at a pub in Clapham. (We were in a strange production of Aristophanes' the Frogs in which, funnily enough, I played a Frog, years ago at college. Strange how I'm still playing frogs, metaphorically and literally). Utterly tedious. Understandably sparsely attended. It's an "unfinished" play. Buchner never completed it so most directors add their own endings. Woyzeck kills his wife after she's had an affair with an army captain and then drowns himself. Very merry stuff. But the director made the ending into a Rock and Roll musical and set it in the 50s and after their deaths they had a reconciliation in heaven and jived to "That's Alright Mama" by Elvis. Bewilderingly incomprehensible and a stilted translation (done by the director of course).
    Met Sid for a drink in the bar after and we discussed football and cricket whilst the Girly dizzily

sipped a Merlot. Not a word was said about the play. We both knew that it was best not mentioned. I greeted him with "You old dog!" And a noisy hug. And "Bloody hell bloody hell bloody hell!" And that seemed to suffice. He talked about his impending nuptials to a waitress he'd met in a restaurant in Seville who it turned out had a father who owned a vineyard.

"He's offered me a job! Better than doing this self indulgent tosh!" So another of my mates bites the thespic dust.

I escorted the once again brain dead dribbling snoozing Girly out of the bar and into the car and back to bed where she lay gibbering and moaning and evil breathed, and I found a small part of the bed that her noisiness didn't inhabit and slept fitfully.

Tuesday 29th

Iain phoned. Continental traffic warden ad tomorrow. Nerdy man. Wasn't overjoyed to be going to the nerdy interview, which he picked up on.

"Oh do cheer up. You can be so miserable," he said before adding "Must go. Other line's going."

"Fuck you. FUCK YOU." I said…… after he'd put the phone down.

Gym. Upper body. Possibly too soon after yesterday but it was lower body yesterday. Beautiful blond girl training who I'd never seen before, wearing a short top and showing her midriff. All the blokes were surreptitiously peeking at her but pretending not to. Snatching glimpses in the mirror. Looking at two mirrors to look at her reflection and thus not catching her eye. Looking at her reflection in the window!

Great coz it looks as if you're gazing out of the window! I was doing all of this. How shallow we all are.

Wed 30th September

Was phoned on my mobile by Maria. I was about to go in for the interview for the foreign commercial at the Oratory casting suite in Soho as the (dohh) nerdy traffic warden who gives a girl motorist a ticket and she tries to get him to tear it up by showing him her cleavage. Slightly dubious from a political correctness point of view but then it was a bra commercial. As usual it was nerd city in the waiting room. Everyone's got strange noses and weird teeth. Or is very large. Or ultra thin. Or wearing silly glasses. Or ultra short trousers with luminous socks. And I'm there amongst them. Not wearing a silly tie or day-glo shirt or upturned green shoes. Just jeans and trainers and a polo shirt and a jacket. I wasn't asked to "dress weird" just "show us your personality". I'm sitting in the waiting room and I'm next to go in. I've looked at the script and had my picture taken and my mobile plays "Life of Surprises" by Prefab Sprout and I answer and it's Maria.
"I'm naked." she oozes.
What do I say? I'm surrounded by actors. Nerdy ones at that but they're possibly all listening. I bizarrely and creatively pretend I'm speaking to a cold caller selling me cut price gardening equipment. Gawd knows where this came from. But I was inspired.
"Good timing. I'm thinking of buying something for my plums."

"I'm lying on the bed". She groans.

"A raised bed eh? My sprinkler could certainly do with an upgrade."

"I'm thinking of you."

"I see. Do you have a bush trimmer?"

I hear a hum.

"I'm thinking of you and ohhhhhhhhhh."

"Ah is that an electric dibber I can hear?"

I try to keep calm and in control. I am obviously in fact, fascinated.

"I want you".

"Yes I could certainly do with a fork, but I'm about to go into a commercial casting."

(Yes. Clever. And good control.)

"Oh what for?"

Her "sexy voice" changes to a business one. Maria is an actress so castings interest her. I can still hear a hum.

"It's a bra commercial and I'm a sort of dickhead traffic warden who isn't enticed by this girl's chest and so gives her a parking ticket. Which he sticks on her bosom and runs away. It's a bit non PC. But then it is abroad."

"Who's casting it?"

She's in actor mode now.

"Valerie Vin Eeze."

"Oh yes. I went up for "woman rained on while running for a bus but is comfortable" for her. It was for Spain. It was a sanitary towel ad."

"Did you get it?"

"No."

"Oh."

"By the way..... I'm very very wet for you. Ohhhhhhh."

"Oh. Thanks very much! " I respond uselessly but politely. "Ooh it's me. I'm on!" I lie. "Bye! Speak soon!"

"Break a leg" I hear her utter amidst gasps.

Why did I say "Thanks very much?" What is the matter with me? The problem is, I find it rather disturbing, in an exciting way, to have someone tell you they're that pleased to speak to you. Went in. Was nerdy. Was pencilled for the nerdy traffic warden. Oh dear God no. Iain was over the moon.

Did a voice with that rude bastard, Lee Trinn. Weird surname. Weird bloke. He's with the Hoodoo agency. We were both playing comedy sheep in a radio commercial for a car window replacement firm. The sheep throw stones and have baaing cockney accents. His sheep bleated twice as stupidly as mine and all over my dialogue. He got told off. He hated that. What an arse. (Sorry mother). His sheep were good though. Funny even. Good bleating when throwing the stones to crack the windscreen. Perhaps I was being too competitive. Am I possibly jealous of his abilities? He is good…. Narr. But possibly yes.

Thursday 1st October

Pencil off for nerdy traffic warden. Complimented for comedy ability but not eccentric looking enough. Oi! I can play eccentric! You didn't ask me! Should have worn the comedy teeth and trousers and taken a fart cushion! Hem hem.

I am slightly sad. Why? Coz I can't stand not working. Aaaaaargh. This competitive streak does my head in. Iain was not pleased and spat the information out as if he had a woodpecker in his troos and someone was badly massaging his leg.

   Mandy phoned. She's agreed to work only with Jeff and thanks very much for everything but he's changed his mind and having thought it over he's now threatened to kill himself if he's replaced. And he doesn't want to be my assistant. So that's that. And he's back with his boyfriend. I feel strangely unattractive.

   Iain phoned back and is less spiky as I have a rubber glove ad casting tomorrow for Germany that he put me up for and they've approved my selection.
   "Comedy man" says Iain.
   Keeshie Casting suite is the venue, which is in that alleyway where people clearly shit and inject themselves. It is desperate. The casting suite is peculiarly colourful, perhaps overcompensating for the filth outside.
   "Don't muck about" says Iain.
   "But I'm a comedy man. I've got to muck about a tad." I reply.
   "You know what I mean" says Iain slightly witheringly and rings off. He's beginning to get on my nerves, though I'm beginning to think it's the other way round.

Friday Oct 2nd

   Had the casting for the rubber glove commercial for Germany. Everyone in the waiting room is bald. Not nerdy. Just bald. (Ing). There is no director there.

Just the casting director, who is a jolly old stick called Sooz who knew an old girlfriend of mine called Jo who handcuffed me to the bed till I "came to my senses" when I suggested we split up as she spent most of the time telling me I was useless at everything I did. I came to my senses when she uncuffed me and we split up.

In the ad casting, which was videoed to be shown to the director in Germany, I just had to act out putting a pair of rubber gloves on, then being slapped on the head by the other actor. Then whilst the other actor put his pair on I slapped him on the head. Coz these were not the right gloves. We had the not very good gloves. Our reward for having the wrong gloves was us slapping each other. The right gloves were worn by the third actor. We didn't slap him. He slapped us. So we had two lots of slapping. I mean obviously we didn't actually have any gloves. We mimed them. I mimed huge dangly plastic gloves. The slaps weren't mimed unfortunately.

I went in with a very tall actor called Max who was the bloke with the right gloves and a small sweet bloke called Jimmy with whom I'd done a Horse of Troy type ad for a chocolate bar a few years ago where we'd been soldiers in a wooden horse sent into Troy not to raise the city to the ground but to steal a bar of chocolate in the possession of Helen of Troy. Yes not sounding good is it. It was as shite as it sounds. One of those unfunny ones that should never have been made.

I somewhat put my foot in it by slapping my fellow actor Jimmy too hard on the head (all that playing squash has given me an extra hard whipped slap I suppose) and he needed a minute or two to recover. I was very apologetic. Sooz was not pleased and gave me the fish eye. We had to go again, this time with me "not behaving idiotically" as Sooz put it. And "don't mime the gloves as if you're Marcel Marceau because you're not."

    Mandy phoned again. She doesn't care if he kills himself. She can't stand his useless unfunny script ideas and directions and she wants the show to be a success and not to be put on as a psychotherapy for him. So she's sacked him and when can I start? Again. And his boyfriend's left him again. I tell her life is too short and I'm no longer interested. She shouts at me for wasting her time. She owes me 50 quid.

    Some new girl on the phones at Digerty Dawg - a temp I think - phoned and told me I had a newspaper ad at Jumble at midday on monday and was I available.
    "Of course I'm available!" I spat back slightly paranoiacally. "Are there occasions when you don't phone me because you don't think I am?" I asked.
    "Pardon?" said the girl clearly not coping with my syntax. Come to think of it it was quite a complicated sentence with two negatives in it. I gave up.
    "Yup no problem I'll be there." I replied.

Sat 3rd

    Lay about mostly in bed doing absolutely naff all other than watching DVDs. Watched Godfathers 1&2 again which are sublime. Love the "hits".The revenge is addictive. Plus some StarTrek of course. Enterprise this time. Very good time-travel eps. I'm fond of sci-fi time travel. Could do with some time travel in my life. Muck up the space time continuum and undo some of the gaffes in my past. Eg Sarah Maltby-Singh.

Girly joined me at some stage, shared the bed, and the DVDs, shared the Chinese I'd ordered and later went off for a run. I declined to join her as it's always humiliating. Then she returned for further beddery and DVDery..

Sun 4th October
More of the same. Plus some footy on the box. I'm almost ashamed by my gluttony. A weekend of sybaritic indulgence. Wrote a song about how uncomfortable it must be wearing a thong.

Mon 5th

Had lunch at the Actor's Hub after doing the newspaper ad (which was an in and out end line) and round the corner. And of course bumped into Mandy. I mean it was inevitable wasn't it. Would you believe she is now going out with Jeff who is bi-sexual. Well he wasn't but now is, as she's allowed him to discover "another side to his sexuality" apparently. They're an interesting pairing. She looks like a Giant Panda. And he's a diminutive camp skeleton with a quiff. Incidentally did you know that Pandas give birth to minuscule babies? That then grow at an alarming rate? Got a tenner off her. Was all she had she said.

Went for a casting for Italy in Denmark Street, the Casting Hut as it's quaintly called. It's not a Hut or Cabin, merely the basement of a block in Soho.

"You're playing a very boring man" says Iain. "I'm sorry, but there it is. A very boring man. The casting director Anna Fascione, has deliberately asked that you be boring."

"Oh God Iain"…

He interrupts me.

"Look there's not much work about. Play boring. And don't prat about. I know you're not boring. (That's nice!) Just make an effort. Act boring. 10.30."

"Oh alright. But it will be a struggle. No actually it won't! It'll be easy! Well easy but difficult. A challenge definitely. As usual I'll try try try. What's it for?"

He has already rung off.

On arrival I am confused of Shepherds Bush coz everyone crammed into the titchy waiting area isn't particularly boring looking. Just very old. At least thirty years older than me. All grey haired and grizzled. Why the fuck am I there? And why have we all been called for the same time?

"Oh hello" wheezes one. "We worked together at Sulgarve House didn't we?"

I am convinced I have never seen this old bloke in my life, especially not at the venue he has suggested, which I think is an old people's home for actors, but I agree readily with him.

"Oh yes. Of course. How are you? Phew that was a long time ago! What a good memory you've got! But then you would have. You're an actor like me!"

His eyes have glazed over.

"I remember you being very good," I added trying to be liked. There was a flicker of a smile and then he unfolded a newspaper.

The casting assistant, Eva, a tall attractive woman in camel-toe creating troos and a vest which allows us to see the barbed wire (!) tat on her bum, hands us a script and takes the usual snap against a white door. I still have no idea what the product is. We have to "rap" the following:

"Just take me to the river and check my face
Don't expect me to like you just change my place...
Uhuh."

Or something like that. There is a worried debate about the "Uhuh" from the assembled wrinklies. (There are about twenty wrinklies and me (why am I here? Why?) in this small room). For example. How is "Uhuh" pronounced. I say it's pronounced "Erhoo ha".

"What's wrong with "Aha?" says Sulgarve man who has taken a dislike to my eagerness to please.

The casting director Anna Fascione enters and is a woman on a mission if a bit flustered. She catches sight of me and slightly gives me a curly lip! She is a lady thrusting out from the unforgiving tapered jeans and tight top and small blazer she is wearing.

She explains we are all supposed to mimic the rappers she is about to show us and the result is obviously unbelievably amusing because we are all far too old to be rappers, aren't we ha ha ha ha!!!! No one laughs. All are daunted by the fact they have to impersonate and possibly move like these youths. (Apart from me that is. I'm still the youngest one there by several decades and utterly bemused as to why I'm in the company of these septuagenarians none of whom look boring. Just old). There is a low anxious murmur. Some of them are undoubtedly worried about their hearts/hips/blood pressure/recent stroke/

prosthetic limbs/etc.. Anna assembles us and plays a DVD of all the "rappers" she wants us to attempt to be. We watch the Beastie Boys (why them?) deliver similar lines to the ones we've been given, leaping about and pointing and doing that attitudinal rap stance and gesticulation that rappers do. The camera is at a low angle and the Beasties are v confrontational as you'd expect. They "spit" the lines out. There is dismay amongst the actors. We return to the room. There is great perturbed banter.

"I'm not fucking doing that" says an indignant bloke in what looks like a pinkish wig….. and he exits!

"Do they want us to behave like that?" says a wrinklie with a broad Yorkshire accent.

"Just imagine you're trying to fend off a wasp" says a totally bald actor who I think I last saw playing Bardolph at the RSC. What's a fine actor like him doing here? He needs the money like us all. A very old man with a stick chips in.

"I can't do any of that bloody dancing."

"I think that's stating the bloody obvious," says the man from Yorkshire.

"Oh well darling just do yer best" shouts out a very red faced corpulent man who was that bloke in the classic ad for Jammy Dodgers. We're going in in threes. It is my turn. I go in with a wiry man of about 80 with a fake tan, and a very unsmiling sort who's with quite a high powered agent (we have to state who our agent is to camera). Anna plays us the track and asks us to move about Beastie like. There is no director. The video of us will be shown to the director who is in Belgium. I'm not bad at this and do the rapper thing rather well. I think it's because I'm not seventy five. The thing is I don't think I'm supposed to do it well. But perhaps I'm there to do it well. I dunno. Fake tan man is quite lithe. Unsmiling man with the good agent, moves as if he's got a hanger up his 'ole. I suddenly realise he'll get the part. He is so bad he's perfect casting.

We rap.

"Justa takea me to the river hmm and checka my face

Doan expect me toa like yer justa changer mah place... Arooha!"

I am a groover. I begin to sound exactly like the Beasties or whoever they are! We do the track over and over again. Fake tan man is good. And consequently funny coz he's an old bloke doing it. Unsmiling man manages to cock it up. It is bollocks. No rhythm or idea. It spews out. What a goof. He's now a cert to get it. Anna looks daggers at me. I'm confused as to why. I leave slightly out of breath having attitudinised like a loon and rapped like 50 Cent but what the fuck was I doing with this lot? No fucking way have I stood a chance getting this. I phone Iain and tell him.

"You're very lucky to be going up for anything at all" he tells me sharply. "And did you do it in a boring way? She wanted you to be boring. The other line's going."

Fuck. No. I wasn't boring. Or crap. I was good at it. I showed off. Fuck. And Iain has put me in my place. I still have no idea what the product was. Or what I was doing there. And no one has told me. And never will. For I will never get the job in a million trillion years. Of course that's why the casting director was so po-faced with me. I wasn't boring enough. Or was that it? Perhaps she thought I was 70? Then as I clearly wasn't, why didn't she ask me to leave? Or perhaps she was hedging her bets and wanted a younger not very good person as well as the oldies? Or even a younger good one? Or a younger good boring one. But actually why was I the only young one there? Why weren't there more younger ones? Who cares? Of course, I do. Very much.

Tues 6th Oct

No work. Dohhh. I hate having no work. Phoned Lynn to see how the week was going.
"Oh it's you. Where you bin? On the nest? Shaggin'? Dippin' yer wick? 'Avin' a wank??""
"What?"
"I fuckin' phoned you about a job this mornin'. It fucked off about an hour ago. I even left a fuckin' message."
I have had no calls from anyone. Or messages. I tell her this.
"I fuckin' phoned. You check!" She squawks. And rings off. I check. She hasn't. Nothing on lists of calls. No Diggerty Dawg anywhere. No message. Nothing. I phone her back. Despite her having clearly cocked up I am apologetic.
"Lynn I'm so sorry but there's no message or anything."
"Your phone's fucked. You can't have a fucked phone in this business. Other lines goin'."
And she's off again. I phone her back once more. I have to hold.
"It's me JK again. Sorry. What have I missed?"
"Workin'".

"Yes I know that. What job. Who was it?"

I am slightly in despair. Especially as it's not my fault. Missing work means you miss working with people who probably don't know you, who might use you again. And the dosh of course. I prepared myself for a Telly ad with a huge buy out. But no.

"Pete Fee at TorkSport."

"Oh ok!"

Radio. Studio fee and a repeat. And I know him already. What a relief.

"Sort your fuckin' phone out."

And she's off again. Blimey. She's got a big snit on. I get Roop to phone me. And Mother. Nothing wrong with the phone. Fuck knows what happened. Lynn probably phoned someone else. Oh well that's a pain and I fucking hate that….but phew I know Peter Fee anyway. And he'll be back for me. He's an amusing very tall Irish guy with a growly voice like a damp sock. He gets me to do aggressive slightly laddish sports reads and silly ass types. I'll ring him myself to apologise and explain the situation. I won't diss Lynn but he's aware it's frequently just her in the office and he calls her "Lynn can you hold". And tells me to "get a new agent she's shite". But double phew that it's him.

Wed 7th

No work. Is my career over? Faffed. Replied to a ludicrous spam mail

----- Original Message -----
From: "Frank Bank" lyndonbjohnson@gmail.com
To: zolaisgod@yahoo.co.uk

Subject: Chelsea FC

Goodday to you.

We received your informations From The Board of Directors of the CHELSEA FOOTBALL CLUB PROMOTION, stating that you are a winner of the accredited sum of £1,000,000.00(ONE MILLION POUND STERLING).

We would like you to send to us your personal information as well as your direct phone number, so that we can go through the files we have with our bank, before any form of payment can be made out to you. There is a fee for our handling of £350 Sterling payable prior to the transaction .
(THAT'S WHERE THEY GET YOU. THE FEE)

Best Regards
Mr. Frank Bank
(Foreign Remittance Department)
Tel: +44-702-401-3483

I replied:

    Dear Mr Bank. How appropriate that you work in a bank and are called Mr Bank! Amazing coincidence. But then again I have a friend called Johnny Carr and he's a mechanic! And another pal who's Alec Toothy and he's a dentist! And another chum called Brian Horsemedicine-Cowpat and he's a vet! But another mate, Jed Combine-Harvester is a greengrocer so it can disappoint you.

Anyway I'm so so happy to have been given money by Chelsea for no apparent reason under the sun that consequently I have fallen hook line and sinker for your deceit and obviously give you my details and the 350 quid scam fee. Which I shall pay in used loo paper. Feel free to phone whenever and the phone will be answered by my handsome busty assistant Tallulah who will be me putting on a silly voice. Here's my number: +44444 23786 4445556667771112223339876540987650 98765 386426186447789632. I may have left a number out.possibly a 3. Please insert at your own convenience. Ask for Cyril Drainpipe.
Here are my bank details. It's Twoey Bank. Number 2 Two Street, Twoville. Twocester. TW0222 Sort code 22-22-22. Acct number 22222222

Wishing you all God's bounty and I am the happiest man in my garden. Villa for the cup!
All the Bust
Liam Mousetrousers. (Mrs)

No reply as yet

Thursday 8th October

No work. Ffs. FOR FUCKS SAKE. But I do have HH tomorrow.

Turned up at the squash club in the afternoon and played against some bloke from a lower league with the thickest specs I have ever seen and one of those big mechanical brace things on his leg and a very bulky bandage on his arm. He kept squealing in pain and after a bit I was sure I was taking part in a

Reality TV show and someone was filming my reaction to his being the most injured opponent I have ever played against. Normally I'd say that I took pity on him and gave him points or was put off by his squealing antics. But no I wiped the floor with him because he was total rubbish. And then felt upset that I enjoyed beating him so easily.

Yippee. I have a Film 4 domani. As well as HH

Fri 9th Oct

Ah work. Job job job job jobs. Jobbity jobs!

Did the Film4 at Station. "Great work JK!" said Sam Brook the producer. It's for a "Fright Fest" season. For upcoming Hallowe'en. Deeply deep and thrown away as if I'm not interested and growly and scary. The engineer was the fabulous Ian Chrottam who is such good fun. There was a lot of dialogue ("grabs") I was interspersed with, eg "Doom is on your doorstep. Don't let it in" or some such scaredy stuff. And then I tagged it.
"Fright fest starts with The Insects. Thursday at 9.00. (Pause) on Film Fearrrrrrr."
Did two takes. "Don't need to do any more" said Ian. "Fits like a gobstopper. Love it. You are so good!"
I like that.

Henry Hedgehog. A new character has been introduced. Mick Mole. Played by the actor Cliff Jones who is basically a film star. He'd been suggested as the next Bond but Daniel Craigy got it. Gawd knows why he agreed to do this. He doesn't need the moolah.

"A coup! A veritable coup!" trills Nick.

For a character with all the lines Cliff is rather a taciturn individual. Mick Mole is the heart-throb who tries to take Henry's new girlfriend Vicky Vole away from him (played with exactly the same voice as she does Tricia Termite by Anne Wedgerley. I'm surprised Nick said nothing). They've made the usual casting mistake in believing that just because he looks good they think he'll sound good. He doesn't. He sounds a bit fey.

From a writing point of view, "Mick Mole" with "Vicky Vole" goes well together and I suspect they'll run with this for a bit. In the meantime Henry will spend several episodes moping and everyone has to try and cheer him up. "You're very good at moping!" says Nick. "It's like having a snit on, but more whiney. Very good! We must get you to mope more often."

Cliff Jones is annoyingly monosyllabic until the coffee break when he charmingly informs me he's a bit nervous coz he's never done any cartoons before, he's sorry he's being so quiet but he's
a bit intimidated, and could I give him a few tips. Him? Nervous? He who might have been the next James Bond? He who was down to a loin cloth in that black and white sci-fi film whose name escapes me. He had a big ray gun and a ripply six pack if I remember correctly. Tips? From me? Bloody hell!

Naturally I try desperately to become his pal and over-advise him, even explaining how to avoid rustling your script, subtly bending to leave a page you've just done on the floor while the other actor is speaking and how not to "pop" (the mic "pops" if you say a P too loudly. The mic's diaphragm moves with the air the plosive generates) by turning away slightly from the mic on plosives, and even give him some pointers on acting animals. (When in doubt pitch it up). Jack Taylor who is Willy Worm whispers in my ear

"I see the Hedgehog is a star fucking Hedgehog with a brown nose so far up Cliff's posterior he's coming out of his ears isn't he?"

The jealous bastard. Even Anne gives me a funny look. Nick commented somewhat queenily.

"So you and Cliff are mates now are you?"

What does he expect? I'm the Hedgehog, it's called Henry Hedgehog, I have the most to do, he acted with me a lot, especially in the scene where he told me he loved Vicky and they were going to go to the Frog Dance at Hogweed Hall together and I challenged him to a toadstool hurling competition (whoever writes this must be on drugs) which Mick won, and we got on well. I am a friendly helpful sort. Aren't I? Yes I am. I got his email address.

Evening

Lynn phoned. Video game on Monday.

Emailed Cliff. Said
"Hi! It's JK from the cartoon! Just touching base! Hope all is good!"

It came right back to me. I must have written it down wrongly. I shall ask him again when we next "cartoon" together.

Lynn phoned again really late from a party somewhere to ask if I was free tomorrow, Saturday, as the announcer on the Bitty Cake show was sick and they needed a replacement and they wanted some funny voices and something like the lottery bloke and was I up for it? She had difficulty hearing "Does a bear shit in the woods?" so I gave up any attempted mirth and shouted "Yes".

"I'll mail you the details then. It's Mountain studios in Harrow. Must go! It's the Bees Gees!"

I presumed that this was a track at a party she was about to dance to, rather than her stumbling into the remaining members in the street.

Sat 10th October

Turned up at 3 as Lynn said in her email. Three till nine. My phone went en route whilst I was on my scooter at about half two. I pulled over and answered.

"Where was I?" asked the Bitty Cake production company who had clearly been given my phone number. They'd had to start the run without me coz I was late! The run had started at 2.30 and a P.A. had had to read the intro I was supposed to do. They insisted they'd told Lynn it was a 2.30 start (they hadn't. I phoned Lynn there and then and despite sounding unbelievably hung over she had the book with her and it said 3.00). Consequently once there, I was stampeded by an assistant via the gallery where all the screens are and the director and vision mixer and sound etc. sit (the director Joe Southern was an old acquaintance having directed me in children's TV when I played opposite DJ Squirrel at Sky) and after a small kiss on the cheek from him and a slightly too full on embrace, I was positioned on the floor of the studio at a tiny "sound-table" with a mic and switches on it and big cables off it next to a busy entry point surrounded by huge drapes, and also next to the bald man handling Bitty's autocue (and there was a lot of it. Every question, thought, aside and fart was scripted) and handed a lip mic, as used by football commentators when there's a lot of windy weather and crowd noise about them. Don't know why I had that but there you go. Mind you there was so much hubbub around me it began to make sense.

The floor manager greeted me cheerily.

"I'm sorry I was told three o'clock" I bleated, as I'd similarly apologised profusely to the other assistant who'd shown me to my "place". (I hate being late. You should never be late as a VO. Everyone's pissed off).

A sound man wandered up and showed me how to press a button that made me "live". I had to write directions to myself on the script to remember to turn the button on and off. (Always take a pen with you) I found that "Button on" and "Button off" sufficed. They started the whole show again. For me!

After my first burst of voice-over (Button on!)

"Prepare yourselves...it's the woman who put the S into sausage (?) it's Bitty Cake!"

(Button off!)....the sound man came up and said

"Can you be louder? You're very quiet".

I couldn't actually hear myself at all but thought I'd bellowed anyway.

I said

"Yes. But I can't actually hear myself."

He added

"We'll get some more level off you in the break and sort the volume out".

No one ever did.

I leafed through the words, alarmed by the loud comings and goings from technicians and passers-by and props men around me and the fact that it was hugely difficult to see the script, there bizarrely being no light for me. There was a bit of spill from the autocue man's light, and some from the grid above, (which was soon turned off) but it was very inadequate. I asked a floor person for a light. I was told there'd "be one along in a minute", (like a bus). None was forthcoming.

I had five sections of VO, the first at the beginning of the show, two at the end of a couple of ad breaks, a fake lottery (called the "Bittyombola-lala". For which they supposedly wanted my lottery voice.) and a "goodbye see you next week" bit. Not much really. But requiring concentration. And also requiring a light to see by. I mean derrr. I got my phone out and used the torch on that, but ye gods surely the voice over has a light? What did the guy I was replacing do? I asked the autocue guy.

"Well he was normally in vision in a booth next to Bitty. But he's ill and they're not using you that way this week I suppose coz he's a regular character and it might be confusing."

Well for them possibly, but I could have made it work.

I heavily marked up my script with notes for myself eg "me next in 17 pages" or "me over. Button on!"

We ran through the whole show at break neck speed, all around me a bustle of noise and activity. "Quiet please" was a regular annoyed shout from the floor manager. Bitty was practicing reading every question to stand ins for "celeb" Kimmy Kisser and singer Buggy from White Courgettes who would be there for the recording but weren't needed for this accelerated facsimile of the show.

"Has he ever got his tadger out?" Bitty was supposed to ask on one occasion as she was reading through her questions to be delivered to her guests. This one, to be posed to Kimmy Kisser, was about a "well hung" pop celebrity apparently.

"Oh I don't fucking like that word" she moaned. "The word "out" I mean! ….ha ha ha….nar, but really. Can we have another word for tadger?"

Winkle was suggested in her earpiece. One eyed trouser snake someone else shouted to giggles. Manhood was another one

They cut the question. The autocue man next to me expunged it on his screen so she wouldn't be encouraged to read it.

I could hardly hear the director in my cans (headphones) it was so noisy and the volume so low.

"Any chance I could have the volume up?" I asked the gallery sound person.

"No that's as loud as it gets" I was told.

I was promised I'd be cued every time. On two occasions the director forgot to cue me but I knew the cue on the end of one of Bitty's lines so did it anyway.

The line "And now the moment you've all been waiting for where Bitty gets the balls out… it's the Bittyombola-lala!" they said they'd pre-record in the break. I asked the assistant floor manager.

"Oh yes we'll find you and do it". They never did. So I never did the "Bittyombola-lala" at all. And that was why I'd been hired in the first place, to sound like the "Voice of the Balls" National Lottery bloke, Lynn had told me. In fact come to think of it, no one gave me any directions. Was I supposed to be funny? Northern? Welsh? (the guy I was standing in for was Welsh) French? Louder? Quicker? Big? Small? Not a jot was forthcoming. Not a single suggestion of direction.

Reading off the small amount of light from the autocue bloke next to me and using my phone torch was proving slightly ridiculous so I chanced my arm again and in the break I once more asked the floor manager for a light. This opened up a huge can of worms. The stage manager was summoned and said she didn't have one. The lighting designer was called in! He said he'd rig one up for me from the grid but it would take ages and would make the area illuminated which they didn't want, so in fact no they couldn't do it, sorry.

I reiterated firmly that I had to have a light to see the script! I was told in no uncertain terms they couldn't. For fuck's sake! I was getting a bit panicky. I mean you're doing a show and you're unable to read the script properly!

The autocueman Johnnie was sympathetic and said I could share his light! He moved it onto the end of his table. And moved his table next to mine. Hardly ideal. I still used the light on my phone.

I managed to attract Joe the director's attention via my "button on" switch and asked him to please cue me as he said he would. He apologised profusely, said it was maniacal in the gallery and they were all under huge pressure and bear with him and assured me he would and it was essential I wait for his cue. When we did the recording I never ever got one. I asked him about a light.

"Oh I'm so sorry. Don't worry we'll get you one. Bear with us."

It never happened. I mentioned the "Bittyombola-lala".

"We'll find you in the break", he said. No one did.

He also said he'd come to see me in my dressing room before the show. Nope. He didn't. I spent 5.30 till 7 in the dressing room watching repeats of "All in the Family" on UKTV and returned to my position to await the beginning of the show. At 7.35, having listened to a very funny warm up man and a hugely raucous audience, the show began.

I was a bit nervous but after the first burst and several stops for technical reasons (problems with Bitty's mike) and a redo of the start, all nerves evaporated. As I said, I was never cued, couldn't hear myself at all so just shouted, (it's obviously so important to be able to hear yourself as a voice) and no one said anything and that was that. All the while using the light on my phone.

When it came to the actual VO lines, I waited - it's normally "We're coming to you in five…four-three-two-one and cue" - and it didn't happen so I just dived in, every time. I mean the cues were all written down in the script. Eg after the break the band played and I had to say:

"We're back. And here she is, the girl with the curl …ooh, crumbs, the tastiest morsel on the plate,… the star of the show tonight… all the way from the kitchen…the icing on her is pink and delicious… here's ….Bitty Cake!" so it was pretty obvious. I mean on reflection, perhaps I should have just sat there doing nothing. They'd have had to retake it anyway.

When the show was over ("you've been watching the Bitty Cake extravaganza. See you next week for a slice, Cake lovers…") and we'd sat through Kimmy Kisser yattering on about her gargantuan sex life and Buggy of the White Courgettes singing a song and monosyllabically discussing her solo career, I shook the autocue man's hand, thanking him for the use of his light, (we did a thumbs up selfie) and wandered onto the set to see if anyone would say something or even acknowledge my existence. Fat chance. No one knew who I was! Why would they? I found the director though who was doing the rounds, who kissed me on a cheek, gave me another far too chummy embrace, told me they'd cut the "Bittyombola-la" as they'd over run so it didn't matter, shook hands with an assistant who I'd never seen before who congratulated me and said he thought the show had been a pile of shit and he knew that no one had cued me and everything was amateur night out and he couldn't wait to get off the programme, and I fucked off home. Oh I forgot. I did introduce myself to Bitty as a temporary VO replacement and she said "Hello."

I left thinking of the money. And the fact I'd read it without making a mistake.

Sun 11th

Derek Fazakerly phoned. His name came up on my mobile and I let it ring onto the voicemail. In his voice message he rather eagerly informed me that he has an idea for his next project for Pertag. (What happened to "Closet Partitions" then? I am intrigued. Or perhaps "Closet Partitions" isn't on yet and he's planning ahead!) He wants to do an improvised "two hander" based on the life of the acclaimed philosopher/playwright/homosexual Jean Genet, who he says "deliberately set out to live a life of awfulness and degradation suggested by his book "The Thief"s Journal"."

"We'll deal with that period of his life and research and rehearse for about six weeks and make the play out of that and I want to put it on in a room or pub somewhere near the French Lycée in South Ken to attract the audience and you are perfect casting for Jean himself love. I'll be playing all the other characters. And directing and producing it. Obviously there's nudity, and gay sexual simulation and a lot of violence. Would you audition love? There's a small amount of money as my aunt left me a bit when she died the other week. Possibly £15 a week for expenses and a cut of the profit? Get you out to do some proper acting instead of all this self indulgent onanistic commercial bollocks you do. I've got a room in the Church Hall in the Earls Court Road for the audition? Could you make two o'clock tomorrow? You'll have to strip off. I think you might be a bit fat. If so you'll need to diet. He was a very effete emaciated bloke. But no you'd be perfect casting. Expecting to hear back pronto love! Ciao."

Ye Gods. He sounded decidedly perky for him. So let's get this straight. Jean Genet. Derek's in it and directing it. Two hander. No script. Improvised and researched over six weeks. Violence. Nudity. Sexual simulation. All with Derek. 15 quid a week. I do onanistic commercial bollocks? And I'm too fat? And the fact I'm not gay hasn't entered his head so I shouldn't actually do it anyway. And I'm perfect casting? FUCK RIGHT OFF

Mon 12th October

The Bitty Cake people phoned Lynn saying I was late, had been difficult asking for a light, couldn't be heard, had missed my cues, had jumped in doing the cues when I hadn't been cued, had been rude to the sound man and autocue guy, and hadn't done part of the script as couldn't be found to do it as I'd gone out of the studio just prior to the show and consequently they weren't going to pay me. Anything.
    I told Lynn what really happened and she said
    "The c*nts. Don't worry I'll get the money. Fuckin' 'ell."

Video game playing a Viking axe man troll at Suede.
    "He's like a sort of Arnold Schwarzenegger without the German accent. Massively muscular. Massive weaponry. Massive. He's Norwegian. With a serrated axe." Said the producer. An Oz girl with a butterfly tattoo on her ankle and black lace gloves.
    "Ok".

"And then we'd like you to play his Scottish victims. Though the Viking dies as well, so we'll have some of that. Yes?"

So I do the statements eg

"You will die soon….horribly".

"Stand still it will be quicker".

"You puny Scottish fool, you are wearing a skirt and are therefore a girl" etc., in my deep slightly accented growly Scandinavian voice. And then do the fisticuffs and sword wielding.

"Yah! Pah! Oof! Eeeya! Neraaaaaaaaaaah! Eeeearrrrahhhya!" Etc..

You need gallons of honey and lemon during this which the Suede studios provide.

I tried the Scottish peasants.

"Aaaaaaaaaargh!"

"Nyaaaaaaaaaaaaaarghhhhh".

"Warrrrrrrrrrryahhhgh!" Etc..

"Yeah. Not bad. But could you put some Scots into their screaming?" asked Ozzie. "They are Scottish?"

Now this is hard to do. I mean screaming is screaming isn't it? Unless you go "Och..aaargh" or "Mc..Aieeee," it's unlikely to be terrifically accented is it? But I knew what she meant so gave it a kind of Highland lilt.

"Ach noooooooo ergh" was Scots running away and being beheaded, and then

"Ohh Nerarrgherrrrder. Aaaaaierrrrwahhh." was a painful run-through-the-guts Scottish scream.

As usual the whole thing was totally knackering. I mean you have to pretend you're slicing people with an enormous battle axe. (Aaaaaaaaaagrrrrrrreeeeee) And fighting. (Errrooooeeeugg) And even having a blade lop your own arm off.(Aieeeeeeee). And then die in excruciating pain. Which is exhausting. I am in a muck sweat after a few moments and then drip all over the table. The pleading for your life and then being slaughtered bit caused the pretty Oz director to get all weepy.

"Oh mate that was heart wrenching" she said.

"Yes I was imagining family and friends having their throats cut and then being disembowelled and bits of them being displayed on poles," I replied sadly.

She went silent and a little tear rolled down her cheek.

Really enjoyable but voice-losing (all that primal scream shrieking stuff) and you need a shower, a lie down and a coffee afterwards. And possibly some counselling after seeing (and being) all your relatives butchered, even if it's only in your head.

Evening:

Despite being exhausted I decided to go to the gym. So typical of me. Unwind through exercise. Exhausted myself even more.

Mama phoned. She's accidentally killed the neighbour's cat and wants me to discreetly get rid of it.

"How the fuck did you do that? This is serious," I said, worried in case she would be arrested. I had this vision of her little face pressed up against the bars. But then you can't be arrested over cat death, can you? But I suspect the police would be called. It'd be a civil liberty or something.

"Oh I left some poison out on the lawn," she replied nonchalantly.

"Poison? Where did you get that?"

"Oh it was something left over for when your father and I weren't getting on."

"You what?"

"We had a vermin infestation a few years ago and I kept the bottle I bought from that man on the corner with the wife who had a stroke. I was trying to kill the wretched mangy fox that sneaks into the kitchen and sprays.

"Not dad then."

"That was of course a joke. I mixed a little with some bread and milk and left it out. The other day it ran upstairs and peed all over the bed and actually got in."

"The fox actually got in the bed?"

"I found it with one of its legs tucked in, smoking a small cheroot."

"What?"

"Darling where's your sense of humour?"

"With the dead cat."

"Well it was making itself at home all curled up and flea ridden. When it saw me it clearly got very scared as it pooed itself and jumped out of the window. The stench was appalling. I had to wash all the linen and drench the bed in rose water."

"How did it jump out of the window without hurting itself? That's almost Olympian!"

"I think it shinned down the drainpipe. I don't know. Anyway that's irrelevant. What do we do about the cat?"

"Where is it?"

"It's in a Sainsbury's bag in the shed."

"Oh bloody hell. Let me deal with it."

"It's a bit whiffy."

"I'll bury it in the garden."

"No don't do that. Next door's dog Blooper will exhume it and leave it strewn all over the lawn. Bury it in your garden."

"Ok. I'll come over tonight and bring it here and do that."

"You are a treasure. Loves yer."

"I love you too. I'll try not to wake you up."

Was pencilled for the Daily Thingamerjig and they'll ring and tell Lynn tomorrow if I'm needed. I've called it the Daily Thingamerjig coz that's what Lynn called it on the phone. I don't know what paper it is.

Tuesday 13th October

No one phoned about the Daily Thingamerjig. Had to phone up Lynn to find out if I was needed, which is a bit crap really. I mean she should ring to say "Oh it's cancelled" or "I still don't know I'll ring again" or "they're ringing back in half an hour they haven't got the scripts yet" (frequently an excuse when actually they've gone with someone else) or whatever.

"Is it on?" I asked.

"Is what on?" she replied.

"The Daily Thingamerjig."
"The what?"
"Well you told me I was pencilled yesterday."
"Who is this?"
"Who is this? Don't you recognise me? It's JK!"
Silence.
………"It's JK!"
"Oh sorry babe. There's a lot of din outside the window. Drilling. And banging. Drains or something….……Who did you say it was again?………"
What the fuck. I mean. What the fuckity fuck?
"Nar just kiddin". What were you pencilled for?"
"The Daily Thingamerjig."
"The what?"
"The Daily Thingamerjig. I don't know what Thingamerjig is because you didn't tell me. Express? Mirror? Parrot? Trousers?"
"Nar. Nothin" in the book. I've rubbed it out. They must of cancelled it last night."
"Well you could have rung me and told me."
"I did didn't I?"
"No you didn't."
"Ah well must of forgot then."
The other line goes.
"Whoops. Other line's goin'. It's only me in the office. Laters!"
So I'm no longer pencilled. Therefore today is "clear" from a voicing point of view. I decide to go for a run. Brush off the cobwebs, expand the lungs as you do. Or something. I'm just getting to Hammersmith Broadway when my mobile phone rings. It's in the bum bag I wear in case I'm phoned urgently (or just phoned really). It's Lynn.
"Where are you?"

"I'm in Hammersmith."

"Whacha doin' there? You're the Bush incha?"

"Runnin'. Sorry. Running. Obviously not at the moment as I've stopped to talk to you."

"You're supposed to be at the Complex."

"In Covent Garden? Doing what?"

"The Daily Thingamerjig."

"But you told me the job was off!"

"I've made a mistake didn't I. I've told 'em that your bike won't start."

"What?"

"An' you'll be there in twenny minutes."

"Twenty minutes? It'll take me ten minutes to get home, five minutes to change and twenty minutes to get there if I drive like a madman."

"Change? What cha doin'? Fittin' in a shag?"

"I'm running. I'm having a run. I'm at Hammersmith Broadway!"

"Blimey you'd better get a fuckin' move on then!"

"Fuckin' right! (the "fuck" felt a bit contrived in my mouth) How late am I already?"

"Fifteen minutes. I'll tell them you're on your way."

"Ye fucking Gods and a stuffed marmoset!"

"Dunno wot 'appened. It wasn't in the book. I'll phone 'em. You get there ASAP!"

I turned round and sprinted back panicking, (fear gave me wings) putting pressure on my dodgy calf which didn't like it at all but held up. I dressed like a loon throwing on a hoodie and jean jacket and jeans and obviously didn't shower and smellilly scootered down to Piccadilly Circus in unbelievably record time annoying everyone especially a man in a grey Fiat Uno who gave me the finger as I undertook him rather spectacularly and had about fifteen minutes left on the clock for the hour long session.

Arrived with the adrenaline flowing somewhat. I was greeted by a Producer for whom I'd worked before, one Kate who was immensely lovely and hugely concerned but then she would be as she's like that. We'd discussed the world on a few occasions. I'd have liked her to have fancied me.

"You poor poor chap." She cooed. "An accident! Are you well enough to do the job? Thanks so much for making the effort to come in. We've got someone standing by. Lee Trinn. He's round the corner doing another job and can step in if need be. Do you know him?"

(Fuck my old boots. Lynn never warned me she'd set up an elaborate accident scenario. And would you fucking believe it the peculiar mouthy Trinn was standing by!)

"Quickly into the studio. You've got seven minutes but it's only one line so it'll be no problem as it's you (aw sweet). And you've hurt your leg Lynn tells me?"

My leg? Ffs. I immediately put on a fake limp while walking with her from reception and looked suitably pained.

"I'm fine thanks. Only a small fall. The bike's a bit dented though but rideable."

"Oh Lynn said it had been written off!"

Written off? Fucking hell.

"Oh did she? Well I'll have to check how much major damage there is when I get home, but it's still moving in a straight line."

"Did you repair the puncture yourself then?" Asked a man in a denim shirt and specs sipping a beer. Puncture? PUNCTURE!!!!

"No I er the tyre went a bit flat but was rideable."

"And we hear you've gashed your knee" said a voice hugging a cushion.

"Hanky used as a bandage. I'm a trooper though. Ha ha ha! ……..Let's do it!"

Laughs all round. I pulled focus rather beautifully and limped into the booth.

"Yes. No more chat. Let's do it." Echoed Kate.

I had to say "All this and more in your Daily Thingamerjig tomorrow." And "All this in your Daily Thingamerjig today."

I did three takes on each. One to get my bearings (it was spot-on actually) and then two more just honing, in the time available.

"That's the one" said Billy the engineer. All agreed. Estuary. Energetic. Assertive. Loud. Coz it's a tabloid. Then I copied that intonation for the "today" version. One take for that. Then it was played down the phone to the client/editor/bloke at the paper who loved it! (Phew).

"He loves your voice" said Kate.

That's why they'd hung on for me.

Billy the engineer is a sweet cuddly amusing chap and he was as usual, totally on my side.

"Great stuff JK! The consummate professional as always" he said joyfully, and he told us all a story about having a motor bike accident where he then spent nine months in hospital and still had a metal pin in his right leg. And how the other person in the accident had died.

"Oh dear." I said.

"Ah." Said Kate.

Bedenimed Specs made a gurgling noise. Cushion didn't utter. It deflected from me excellently. There was a silent beat. Then another. I broke the ice.

"Anyway. Sorry for my lateness. Huge apologies. Thanks for waiting. I appreciate it:"

"No no no. Great job" said Denimmy Specs.

"Yes" said Cushion.

"Great job JK" repeated Billy. "Heal well!" Which was nice of him. As he clearly hadn't.

"Well done JK I knew you'd do it. I'll phone Lynn and tell her everything's ok!" Purred Kate.

"Thanks. I'll phone her as well!" I said enthusiastically.

And I did. Loudly. In the street.

"What the fuck did you tell them I'd had an accident for? They almost replaced me. With that self obsessed plonker Lee Trinn! And you never phoned me to tell me what you'd told them! Thank God I didn't run into the studio! Apparently I smashed my leg up. And had a flat tyre! And the bike was a write off. And I should have been bleeding! And it wasn't the Daily Thingamajig. It was the Daily Star!"

"Was the only thing I could think of to give you more time. Worked though didn't it!"

"Yes ok but bloody hell Lynn!"

"Shuddup. You just earned a grand plus."

"Ah. Ok. Yeah. Right. Good. Yes. All's well that ends well. Thanks. Er….great. Byeee!"

"Yeah. Laters!…. Oh hang on. Don't go home. You've got three more."

"What the fuck?"

"Yeah dunno what happened. Factotum at 1.00, corporate Yamaha. Slick at 3.00, radio ad for Leeds Castle. Central Grandstand at 5.00, TV ad for Iceland."

"Fucking hell Lynn. Have they just come in?"

"No."

"What?"

"Yeah. Sorry. Had 'em in the book all along. Dunno what happened."

Utter mayhem. Flying by the seat of your giblets.

Mother phoned. Why haven't I picked the cat up? It's truly humming and she's dousing the Sainsbury's bag with Airwick Freshner. Tonight I'll do it. Oh ok. Tomorrow.

Wed 14th October

Morning

Pathé read for a Sky History thingie promo. Fun.

Evening

Decided to cycle over to the parent rather than drive or scoot. It fitted the whole clandestine nature of the thing. And there's no registration number of course in case a security camera were to spot you to connect you if someone from Neighbourhood Watch saw you taking the "cat out of the bag". Or something. Bloody hell my imagination. Felt I should be in all black with a bag marked "swag". So cycled over and put the bag into another bag and then another bag and then into a rucksack. Now would be the time to be stopped by the police wouldn't it. But these things only happen in films I kept reminding myself. Mind you I could always say it was my cat and I was burying it on the common despite cycling in the wrong direction. If they pulled me up on that I could say I was distraught and had got lost. To be frank I'm not even convincing myself with that story. Made sure I had lights that worked. Didn't want to be stopped under any pretext. But having said that I don't think legally they could have done anything. I mean a cat's not licensed is it, like a dog? But then they could have asked questions couldn't they. About where I'd picked it up. And done tests and found out it was poisoned. And then the neighbour could have had me arrested or something. Or sued. Oh bloody hell I've freaked myself out now thinking about what could happen……..

Luckily though and possibly anti-climactically it was an uneventful journey. Which on reflection was always on the cards. Buried the poor thing in the plastic bag in the garden at about two o'clock in the morning hoping neither neighbour nor anyone in the flats above could see what I was doing.

Thursday 15th

Lynn phoned. I have to write my version of the Bitty Cake saga and send it to her. Dohh. Tedious or what. But essential. I'll send her the diary entry.

Documentary for Moonshine and Grape agency about skiing at a studio I'd never been to before in Hammersmith.

All went swimmingly with a well written script. I do like 'em when it's like that. Two hours, and a bit of a strain as it's constant concentrated reading and about twenty pages in a small font but that's why they get me in to do it: coz I can make it flow and not have many retakes. Woman engineer Petrina fantastic.

Slight problem over some of the French names which the producer insisted on giving an English twist to, but it was his baby so I quietly concurred. When I say "OK then" I'm agreeing because to disagree leaves a nasty feeling in the studio and you don't want to alienate the man who might employ you again. So when he corrected me over the pronunciation of Chamonix (he wanted it pronounced with an x rather than Charmonee. "No no no. It's Tchamonix".) and a bloke called Jean Dubois (he wanted Do-boys rather than Du-bwar. "No no it's Do-boys"), and Jean as in the girls' name not Jarn as is the French I said "OK then!" And Benoit Blendier was Benny Blender. But as I say he was the boss.

Mother phoned to say a sign with a sweet picture has gone up on the lamppost outside asking for anyone who's seen "Tweedledee" the cat to ring the following number and they will receive a reward. She is keeping her head down.

Fri 16th October

Lynn says Bitty Cake have a witness to my unprofessional behaviour. The autocue guy. Ffs! My supposed chum. Who now says I insisted on using his light, was ridiculously loud and all over the place and getting in his way and constantly wandering off and looking at my phone. And the sound man who said I was a nuisance preventing people from doing their jobs. However, They don't know I took some pics of the idiocy which I think will speak volumes. And the director Joe will vouch for me surely.

Sat 17th Oct

Got a spam mail. From the States. To my zolaisgod address. It's flogging shares.

----- Original Message -----
From: "Craig Sampson" csbholdings@ttesdale.de
To: zolaisgod@yahoo.co.uk
Subject: Please read

Investors and traders:
Peanutle Group Limited, Inc. Announces Acquisition of AEROFIRM METALS INC, a leading structural technology company focused on the development & commercialization of foamed aluminum products.

In Today's market, AEROFIRM METALS INC has cutting edge technology and little competition.

    Current Price: 0.70
    Short Term Target Price: $2.25
    12 month Target Price: $5.25

Peanutle will acquire all of the issued and outstanding shares of Aerofirm for new Treasury Shares of Peanutle. The number of shares will be 3,500,000 common shares. ✶ Sincerely
✶ Craig Sampson

★ peanutle.de

My reply

Craig. And all the little Peanuts.
Lovely to hear from you. I hope Mrs Craig is well and recovered from her fall. We all prayed for her at St Swithin's. I hope she will be able to bear you more little Craigs in the future. There was a rumour that you pushed her down the stair as you were seeing Dirty Deeana at the Diner and wanted rid, but I defended you and told everyone that he who was innocent of sin should cast the first stone. And funnily enough no one said a word! Because they were all banging Deeana as well! So you got away with it you lucky cheating bastard because I KNOW you pushed her. You owe me Craig. You owe me big.
Hey. Sampson! Don't cut your hair! Bet you never heard that one before! Haaaaaaaa!
All the best
Cedric Trubshawe (Mrs)

Annoyingly no reply as yet

Sunday 18th

Got a dvd of "Road to Perdition" and Girly came over to watch it and eat Sushi. It was beautifully shot with great music and Hanks and Newman were excellent. Girly insisted on squeaking fearfully all the way through it as if all the plot developments were a big surprise. I mean it was obvious Jude Law's eccentric hit man had to come back and kill Tom Hanks coz he hadn't been in the film for about twenty minutes and he hadn't been killed earlier on, had he? (There was even a huge close up of his getting up alive but bloody) So he had to come back at the end and tie all the loose ends up. That's the formulaic way films are made. "They make 'em like that" I said. The girlfriend's response was not the admiring one I'd hoped for.

"For fuck's sake just watch the fucking film will you? Don't fucking analyse the fuck out of it? You're so fucking not fun and up yourself all the fucking time" she said.
Oops.

Monday 19th

Booked for two hours at SB Post studio in Chalcott Square for this corporate for a plastics firm, Awkle, who I'd never heard of, where I'm measured and succinct and serious coz business tones are required.

It was well weird. Firstly the producer blokie with an unlit roll up dangling from his lips running the session had somehow arrived without the film that I was supposed to be voicing. I mean derr. Which was slightly disastrous.

"Could you hang on till it arrives?" he asked.

"Of course" I replied. Luckily for him it arrived minutes later in a cab, delivered by a callow assistant.

"Well that's the budget fucked" he was heard to say.

So I started the job. And finished it in ten minutes. The script was about two pages. The film was ten minutes long. Was he expecting someone with dyslexia? Someone who would find it a trial?

"You've done it in ten minutes." He blurted accusingly. So I did it again. In ten minutes.

"Fucking hell I've booked you for two hours. How the fuck did you do the job so quickly?"

I complimented him, not sure of what to say.

"Well it was such a well written script and well made film, it was easy to read."

He just looked at me. For I was indeed talking bollocks.

The engineer sent me cheerily on my way.

"Thanks JK! Well done!"

Lynn phoned as I was on my way back.

"That c*nt you just worked for only wants to pay you for half an hour. Says we've cheated him by not telling him you could do the ten minute film in ten minutes. The fucker actually said "you never told me he was so good". He's offered £50. Which isn't even a quarter of an hour. I've suggested he pay the proper fee."

"That was restrained of you."

"Well actually I told him to fuck off and said if he wanted shit reads go to a shit voice agent."

"Yes of course you did."

"Let's see what occurs."

We'll never get the money.

Tuesday 20th

Zoologica Studio in the Mews. I love the well thought out design and decor here. Big wooden palm trees and sharp tree house stairs. It's Jumble's twin. Naturally they have "stolen from Zoologica" on their pens. A fistful of which I put in my rucksack. And as you'd expect top engineers and cooing surly-at-home receptionists.

Did a corporate for a MudStubidishi Stagbeetle or something. To be played in house to their staff? About this new all singing all farting vehicle.

The clients and producer were Japanese American and very fastidious in their direction which outlined the company's policy and demands from the VO. Inspiring, educational, serious, comprehensible, not patronising, welcoming, playful; several contradictory I thought eg playful and serious.

I have to say, it sort of went over my head really as they must have wanted me as they'd chosen me from my reel but as always with these things, you listen but then try out your usual corporate read to see what they think, expecting to do a variety of takes. In this instance I went through the 4 pages without making a mistake and they instantly turned off the talkback and spoke to each other animatedly. Several minutes later they reconnected.

"May we do another?"

We did.

"Thankyou so much. Good job. May I remind you how important your confidentiality is. Please sign this form before you leave. It has been a pleasure working with you. You are a top voice over."

Well that was nice.

I phoned Lynn. "Shall I sign the form Lynn?"

"What fucking form?"

"The confidentiality form".

"Oh yeah they sent me that. I was supposed to send it to you so you can sign it."

"Ah."

"I haven't have I?"

"No."
"Let me 'ave a look at it an' I'll get back to you."
"They want me to sign this one now."
"Don't trust 'em. It may say they can use what you've just done in their ads for nothin'. For ever. That's what these fuckers do. They're all c*nts."
"Ah yes of course. You read it first. I'll tell em we'll send it in tomorrow."
I did. They didn't object. Just reiterated "Great job". Nice.

Wed 21st Oct

It's the following day and I can't even remember what the bloody Stargazer or SlagButterer thing was called. Don't think I'm going to be blabbing to anyone about the product and breaching its confidentiality. It's not uppermost in my thoughts having a car chat.
ME: "Ooh Roop! MidshutSushi have got a new people carrier out. It's called the Starcatcher. It's top of the range! It's got five wheels and 270 seats!"
ROOP: "Fuck off JK. I don't give a flying fuck."
ME: "No Roop. Me neither."

Re Bitty Cake. Sent Lynn my account and the pics of the "no light" and the little autocue light. And the grinning thumbs up autocue man. And have asked for the assistant's name who said the show was shit. And mentioned my mate Joe.
"Ooh these are good. The c*unts." Said Lynn as you'd expect.

Went up for a gay perverted sadist today for an ep of a drama series called "Memorable". For ITV. So I put all three earrings in. All holes had closed up. The lobe was consequently very red. Was a bit self conscious about this all during the interview but no one mentioned it. Wasn't even Iain who told me about this job, but his assistant Jeanette.

    I never normally speak to her. Well "speak" is the wrong way of expressing it. She's always pleasant if a bit on the taciturn side. Taciturn is a nice way of putting it really. "Silent" is the reality. As the grave. Monosyllabic does her a favour. She mumbles a sentence and pauses. Stops completely in fact I wonder if it was her who got me the interview? If so how did she communicate with the casting director? Possibly by email? Definitely not by the spoken word.

    As usual for these telly things I'm up for, the character hardly has any lines. But at least he's not nerdy. Very butch in fact. And gay. Iain surely ought to be telling them I'm not, for authenticity? Mind you there's no reference to it.

    At the interview in a community centre in Hanwell, miles away from anywhere and really difficult to find, I experienced that weird frequent thing of having the director spend ages talking about the character and the motivation and the story, but it all seems so out of proportion to the small amount of time my role is actually in the piece. I mean it's very polite to keep me in the loop as it were but I'm in one scene where I enter late, grunt a line or two then shuffle off this mortal coil. In fact I'm just sitting there thinking he must have said this slightly tedious speech (he sounds as if he's boring himself and knows it) about fifteen times already and do I need to know all about the whole show's story line and what great lead actors he's already cast?

Naturally we did the whole of this long scene I'm in. Which I've already mugged up having been sent it. The casting director read all the other characters. Really dreadfully. I mean hopelessly. In exactly the same voice. Men, women, killers, victims, everyone. Embarrassingly crappily. I mean can she not hear herself? It's like a test of some sort. Will your patience snap? You are itching to shout out

"What is this self indulgent masturbatory shite. Can you hear yourself? You're fucking terrible. Schtopppppp!"

And I'm right at the end of the scene. And not in nearly all of it. So how do you decide on whether I'm any good or not when all I've said is "Yes" and "Of course. I'm on your side" before I'm stabbed. I mean they might as well have just looked at my photo and made a decision. Or even looked at my visual showreel? Wasn't it a complete waste of their time to rabbit on about the show when my character had naff all to do?

And….am I now up for either nerdy or butch gay parts through Iain? Hmmm.

Thinking about it, I probably shouldn't have screeched and gurgled loudly after I'd been stabbed. Or slumped headfirst onto the table. Or talked about Henry Hedgehog when they asked me what I'd been doing.

Thursday 22nd

Iain phoned. They'd liked me for "Memorable" but thought I was "too nice" to play the butch psycho who gets murdered. That'll learn me to be pleasant for these violent drama thingies. Need to go in with a snit on don't I. And also he said that they'd seen I had a very red ear and they hoped I was ok. I told him about the ear rings. "Oh well if it gets you into character." But he seemed quite pleasant for a change. I suppose he sees an avenue of potential casting for me. Which means dosh of course. For him. As well as me. But more importantly for him.

Worked at the BBC in town. The security is bizarre. Can't gain access to reception from the street unless you swipe by the revolving doors. I obviously haven't got a swipe card so have to get the attention of the burly man inside standing by the Underground type turnstile by tapping on the window. He ignores me. There are other doors. I try them. All locked. The burly security man finally hears/sees me and shakes his head. He beckons me back to the revolving door which jerks into action. It revolves so quickly I have to dance in, doing the twist. Or is it the Watusi? He points me to a receptionist. He never speaks, he just points. It's quite un-nerving.

"JK. Doing a voice for TV Licensing for Neil Drell. Studio 1T." I say.

"It's 1R" says the receptionist snottily, scowling at me from above her specs.

"Ok. 1R it is."

"You'll have to wait to be escorted".

"But of course. You're the BBC. I would expect nothing less", I say slightly facetiously. She hands me a pre-prepared pass on a lanyard. They're expecting me. I wait. There is nowhere to sit. I feel a bit exposed. I lean on a rail. It's not a rail. It's some tape. I fall over.

The receptionist stifles a laugh. As does burly man. Finally my escort arrives after five minutes: A huge woman bursting out of her BBC uniform with a very merry face.

"Ah you're both guide and guard aren't you. Where are we going?" I utter.

"The first floor." She replies, grinning friendlyly as if I'm the funniest thing she's seen all year.

We get in the silver lift. And instantly out. We turn left and there's a small flight of stairs down to an armoured door with a tiny pane of reinforced glass in it. Just before the small flight of stairs is a phone. You have to lift the receiver to say you're coming in. My "guard" phones through. I am let in. The guard chuckles at me as if sharing the ludicrousness of the situation. I mean ffs. I am merely here to do a voice on TV licensing and I'm being treated as if I'm delivering plutonium, or am entering a top security prison. Or am there to have a secret meeting with an alien life form. I expect to be at least greeted by a man carrying an Uzi machine gun but am disappointed.

Straight ahead of me in a badly lit open plan room with no windows, is a receptionist. I say the magic words "Studio 1R" with a question mark on the end. She says "TV licensing. JK." and ushers me into a cubicle with a circular desk and a microphone and with tiny headphones that slide off your head plugged into the table and a script laid out. I exit briefly to make myself a coffee with one of those cartridge machines where the tea/coffee is actually ok and enquire if I shall be meeting anyone or is it "down the line"? (ie there's someone on the end of the mike somewhere in Britain.)

"Yes down the line" she says with all the personality of a whicker chair. And a voice comes through my cans and I speak to Neil who's in Swindon.

"Hello JK! It's Neil. Love your work!" (Aw that's nice).

I do the job quickly - "You don't want a big fine do you? Remember to get your TV licence."

"Great stuff JK!" - and am directed down a flight of ancient stairs and having put my lanyard in a box and exited a sturdy door, find myself annoyingly in the street. I'd have liked as much secrecy for my exit. It was fun.

Fri 23rd Oct

Lynn has heard back from Bitty Cake. They're not paying. Despite the pics which they say reveal nothing about my behaviour. And neither Joe nor the other bloke have corroborated my story. I bet they never even asked them. Lynn is taking them to court.

Sat 24th October

Emailed Damian as Cedric Trubshawe to find out how much I owed him for the "party" in the pub in Yorkshire:

From: JK<oohbanana72@yahoo.co.uk>
To: "damian mackenzie" <damianmackenzie@hotmail.com >
Subject: Regular Birching

Bruce
Despite the unbelievably rude reception my short statured wife Clarissa and I received from your so called friends (was it really necessary to refer to her as "that dwarf?) I am willing to put the reception down

to "high jinks" and forgive all (though the incident with the goldfish will be a source of dismay to her for years to come. Thank goodness your Laura was forced to endure the same humiliating experience. She will never look at a sink plunger with detachment ever again). Yet even though we have been subjected to the most bizarre behaviour on your part there is something weirdly alluring about the event (is it the wobbly jelly hurling competition which Clarissa excelled at?) and we shall both likely be back for the next reunion. As long as the more rascally members of your entourage can be prevented from constantly encouraging Clarissa to "get her tits oot for the lads", something that even I have great difficulty getting her to do since her mastectomy.
All love
Cedric Trubshawe (Mrs)

ps how much do I owe you for the evening?

Damian's response:

"damian mackenzie"<damianmackenzie@hotmail.com>
To: JK<oohbanana72@yahoo.co.uk>
Subject: Falling down briefs!

Hello Cedric

Sorry about the goldfish - I don't know what came over me! Or Laura for that matter. Boom boom!
Pity about your "injury"......we won, by the way. More details later.
Yes, I'll let you know about costs.

Damian

Sunday 25th October

    Mother phoned. Apparently she's had some dentures fitted that don't fit.

"They're too tight. I can't get them out. We had a tug of war in the surgery yesterday."

"Are they out now?" I ventured.

"Of course they are. Brute force won the day."

"Good."

"Well not really because I don't want to have someone have to come over to help me get the bloody things out every time I put them in."

"Good point."

"The dentist has suggested some sort of lever."

"A lever?"

"Yes. To lever the teeth out. Apparently it's more likely to remove them than my finger."

"Or anyone else's finger I suppose."

"Yes.

"Yes. Is the lever the only way?"

"He's worried that if he reduces the dentures in size they'll fall out when I'm on the bus."

"Why the bus? Why not in front of the telly?"

"Darling I suppose it might be because of the lurching."

"The lurching?"

"The jiggling and lurching. On the bus. Some of these drivers can't wait to get back to the depot for their tea."

"Yes I see. The bus might be a perfect environment for "teeth expulsion"."

"Are you taking the mickey?"

"A bit."

"Well don't. It's not nice. No wonder you find it difficult to make friends."

And she puts the phone down.

Monday 26th October

Henry Hedgehog today. Henry went to "Badgerville." Cliff not there for these eps as he's away filming, but we're going to catch up with him next time apparently. Henry is fast becoming a sort of animal Sherlock Holmes. Today he solved the case of someone stealing all the Dew wine from the storage area under the oak tree in Badgerville. Barry Badger the Policebadger beautifully played by Ian Sengle who has a strange click thing whenever he delivers his lines which no one mentions.

The wine's been nicked and drunk by Satchel Skunk (you know where the writer was coming from: Drunk as a skunk. This is unfair to skunks as they're not constantly rat-arsed but they're destined to be forever inebriated in the nation's psyche by having a name that rhymes with "drunk".)

Willy Worm is now Henry's "Watson." Fucking Jack Taylor is in practically every scene with me. He greets me with

"How's your new mate Cliff then? Been to any showbiz parties?"

It is a long four hours as he ribs me constantly and I take it all with great humour whilst secretly wanting to deck him. He has an infuriating habit of saying

"You're not going to say that line like that are you?" when we read through a scene to rehearse it. And then reading it the way he would do it.

"I'm fine thanks." I reply. And "Well in fact I am going to say it like that. Actually."

He has laughed and shaken his head a couple of times at the end of scenes. This cannot go on and won't. I shall tell Nick. He will ignore me. Nick is happy with everyone and everything.

"Very good today. You're developing a marvellous relationship with Jack Taylor. Such a nice man and such a good actor, don't you think?"

"No I think he's a c u next Tuesday actually" is obviously what I think. I say:

"Ooh yes. Very good. Yes."

"I've suggested we pair him with you as much as possible" adds Nick.

Oh dear God no.

Tuesday 27th

Mama phoned and calmly informed me that she'd been out in the garden attempting to block a hole up where the neighbour's dog gets in and leaps about the garden as if he owns it, and when she returned to the kitchen, there was a man standing in it.

"Darling. Guess what I said?"
"What?"
"What did I say?"
"God knows. I'd've freaked out."
"Guess."
"Oh bloody hell. I dunno. Um. 'Do I know you?'"
"Nope."
"Oh Mother for fuck's sake. Don't make it a quiz. What happened? Are you ok?"
"I'm fine. Guess what I said."
"Bloody hell….er…"Get the fuck out"…er…"I've got a gun…"Help, police"…I dunno."
"What are you doing in my kitchen."
"That's what you said?"
"Yes."
"And what did he say?"
"Nothing."
"What he didn't say anything? Or he said "Nothing."
"The former. So I continued "I think you'd better leave don't you?"
"What did he say to that?"
"He agreed and said he was lost and did I know the way to the Post Office?"
"For fuck's sake."
"I then said "You know some people might think you were a burglar."
"What did he say to that?"
"Yes I suppose they would. But I'm not."
And then I showed him out through the garden door. He rather politely moved the flower pot I use as an extra barrier. He told me he'd climbed over the fence next door."
"What did the police say?"
"Oh I haven't called them yet."

"What?" Steam blew out of my ears.

"I haven't called them. I was very calm. I rather surprised myself!"

She certainly surprised me.

"Yes that's as maybe but you've got to call the police because he may do this again and someone else might not have your diplomatic skills and he might assault them."

"Oh do you think so?"

"Yes I bloody well do!"

"What's their number?"

"9 fucking 99."

"Don't swear darling. Who do I ask for?"

"The police of course!" I am aghast and exasperated. "I'll drive over."

And I do. When I get there there is a van outside and a cheery policeman is on the radio to someone.

"Ah hello. Son and heir. Is she ok?" I communicate efficiently.

"Yeah she's fine. My colleague's speaking to her."

"He sounded a bit touched the bloke who got in." I said.

"Your Mother was the fourth. He's apparently walking up by Putney Bridge at the moment. He's got a thing about kitchens."

I wandered in and my Mother was complaining to the poor policewoman about how many people were living next door and the terrible smells emanating from their kitchen.

"Hello mama" I blurted out, taken aback by how much it had upset me.

"She's fine. She's been very brave" said the policewoman rising before I could ask how she was.

"Thankyou so much for your prompt response" I said rather pompously. I ushered her out. I gave Mother a big hug and a kiss.

"He was rather large you know," she said.

"Was he?"

"Yes."

She burst out of my grasp.

"Pooh. Your breath is rank. You must do something about it. No wonder you can't maintain relationships. It smells like a sewer. I'm surprised you have any friends at all you poor thing. People won't tell you you know. But I can tell you. Go and buy some mouth wash and keep some with you at all times. Or chew some coffee beans. Will you do that for me? That'll take the appalling odour away. You have no idea what it smells like. It's as if something dead is rotting in both your teeth and stomach. Have you eaten enough today? I'm sure you haven't. You're too thin anyway. Get some meat on those bones. Hmmm?"

Ah how lovely that nothing horrible happened to her. I do love her. All back to normal. I volunteered to tidy the flower bed that she'd pointed out needed a bit of work last time I was there. She gave me a cup of tea and a slice of carrot cake. Thank goodness she's alright. Phew.

Wednesday 28th October

One line Film 4. With the wonderful Ian Chrottam at Station.

"Lonely Boy. Thursday at 9.00. (Pause) On Film 4."

One take. Thrown away. Husky. A don't give a monkey's read. He's happy.

"That's the gobstopper. No need for any more. Bliss."

Iain phoned. Audition tomorrow. Oratorium 2.00. Meg Crippen casting.
"You're playing "an English nerdy balding man" darling. It's you! It's a Sci Fi where you get eaten by a "canibalistic symbiote". I'm reading this darling not making it up! Ha ha! Do you know what that is as I haven't a clue?"
Blimey. Iain's joshing with me. This is rare! He must be blootered. But "it's you"? The bastard.
"Er I do know what that is actually." I replied as if answering a question on University Challenge.
"The symbiote is usually a parasitic aspect of the super hero that has become detached from him taking corporeal form and rampages about before a final showdown between the two of them".
"Ha ha I knew you'd know darling. Ha ha! Get the job please" ha ha ha gurgle ha ha ha. Ho Ho Ho. Hee hee fucking hee". Prat.
Still a patronising bastard but he sounded vaguely as if he liked me today. He must've received a huge cheque from an A list client and was rolling around in the commission like a Hippo defecating in his own watery shit then snorting it up through his ample nostrils. I looked at the role I have to audition for. I have one line. It's set in a library.
"Could you pass me that book over therrrrrrrrrrrre."

THE CHARACTER IS SUCKED OFF INTO THE SYMBIOTE'S THROAT.

Ooh er. I think they mean he's swallowed whole. That'll be an interesting special effect.

No voices tomorrow. Booked myself out with Lynn. But the audition is in town so if anything comes up eg her forgetting I'm booked out, I'm there already.

Thursday 29th Oct

Casting. Usual bollocks. Hanging around for fucking ages. No sign of Meg. Her pneumatic assistant is there in teeth braces and introduces me to a gleaming cap-toothed shiny besuited American who says curtly
"I want three versions one after the other" and just says "Action". I am wearing a white shirt and a vivid purple kipper tie and comedy specs. I do the three versions. All big. The second even bigger. The third is an appalling primal scream and ululations as I'm bitten. The "there" of "could you pass me that book over…" is immense and becomes a roaring falsetto.
"Wow" says the Yank. And claps. Sarcastically? I have no idea. And I'm outta there.

Friday 30th October

Phoned Henry Hedgehog Director/Producer Nick about Jack Taylor. Told him of my problems with him.
"Oh really? Well we'll have to let him go then. Can't have our Henry having trouble with one of the actors. He's fired."
"Thanks Nick. See you soon."

This above is of course a dream sequence. I have yet to speak to Nick but I shall and must. Not today but next week. I haven't phoned Nick because he'll tell me to "Get over it." I know he will. He's like that. Oh bloody hell.

Did really interesting job today. Voiced a staff film for London Underground at Clearcat, explaining all their safety precautions. Did you know that all that stone debris on the track is called the "cess"? A plot of land six feet wide by the track is called the six foot. A plot of land four feet wide is called the four foot! And that they have to put small explosive detonators on the line in order to warn workers that a train is coming so they can get away from the track? I will now travel on the Central line that little bit more well informed, so should I be called upon by ITN to give an eye witness report of an incident, I can say. "Yes. The alien lifeform grabbed the robot with its tractor beam on the six foot, tore his leg off with its beak on the cess, dropped his severed head in the four foot, and sat on a detonator whereupon it blew up." Perfect.

Iain phoned. I have been pencilled for the nerd eaten by the symbiote. He is over the moon.

Sat 31st October

More spam to my jklovegod email address

Dear Sir/Madam,
The National Lottery
P O Box 1010
Liverpool, L70 1NL

UNITED KINGDOM
                WINNING NOTIFICATION:
We happily announce to you the draw (#1009) of the
UK NATIONAL LOTTERY.
        You drew the lucky numbers:
01-40-43-44-48-49 which subsequently
won you the lottery. You have therefore been approved
to claim a total sum of £778,226 in cash.
(For security reasons, you are advised to keep your
winning information confidential)
To file for your claim, please
contact our claims agent:
MRS.JULIET JONES
Email:
            uklottowinninginfo@gmail.com

        Yours faithfully,
Richard K. Lloyd.
UK NATIONAL LOTTERY

My reply:

        Richard. Wow. I've won something at last! And here was me thinking I was the unluckiest man in the world and universe etc. Four divorces, an earthquake, a plane crash, a bizarre tropical disease where I lost control of my arms and bladder, at least 27 accidents where I've fallen down flights of stairs and been bitten by dogs, my most recent wife went off with Clint my best friend, my cat Woofer was disfigured in a car crash, my children taken away from me in an encounter with a yeti, several stints in prison for things I didn't do, countless GBH and drug convictions none of which were my fault, and all of a sudden you send me this.

You've made my day. Possibly my life. It's weird how things go eh? Since the latest drug fuelled incident (I lost my memory for a bit and thought I was King Scrotyitt the third of Humplbegonia) I've been convinced fate was joshing with me. But this is fantastic. What do I have to do to claim my magnificent life changing prize? Do I collect it with a showbiz celebrity to hand over the cheque? Could it be Christopher Biggins? I have to warn you that I've broken both my legs in a brawl in a pub and have both arms in slings since the incidents with the crossbows. Will the prize giving place have a bar? And naked dancing girls? Oh this is to good to be true. Tell me what do I do now? You've saved me Julia. I owe you everything. I'm filling up here. I'm the happiest man in Frinton.
All the best
Cedric (Trubshawe) Mrs

Awaiting a reply

Sunday 1st November

　　Faffed all day. Gymmed. Faffed. Slept. Ate. Binged on telly.

Ooh oh oh. Got a reply. A threatening one! Telling me to tell them why I won't accept the money or face legal action!!!

Dear Sir/Madam,
The National Lottery
P O Box 1010
Liverpool, L70 1NL
UNITED KINGDOM

fileyourlottowinningsclaim@gmail.com

ATTENTION: Cedric Trubshawe (Mrs)

LETTER OF FORFEITURE/FINAL NOTICE
Due to your inability to claim your cheque deposited in Geotrus Insurance/Security company you are hereby ordered to forward a letter of forfieture stating reasons why you have decided to forfiet your £778, 226.00 won by you from the SWEEPSTAKES Lottery organized by the UK NATIONAL LOTTERY.
This request is to protect you and Geotrus Insurance/Security company from facing legal actions in future concerning this lottery winnings.

When you make your claim you are required to make a payment of $650 for the courier delivery of your winnings/cheque immediately. This payment should be made through westernunion money transfer in the name of our accounts officer:
ALBERT PRINCE
27 ABBOT ROAD,
SE4 1EZ LONDON.

Thanks for your anticipated coperation,
Mrs.JULIET JONES,
FIDUCIARY AGENT,
UK NATIONAL LOTTERY.

I replied "wittily"

Dear Juliet.

Tis I, your canine loving pal Cedric.

Thanx for letter. I'm glad you like dogs. I shall of course comply and send you a donation for your dogs' home. I am a big fan of dogs and their offspring (known as "puppies") and have four myself, a Pitbull, a Wolf a Rotweiller, a Tosa and a Siamese. They have great teeth. I let them roam in the fields playing joyfully with the sheep. If you send me your date of birth, credit card and passport details I will send you a cheque for ten dollars. With people like you to look after them, our four footed friends will never go wanting!
Woof!
Cedric Trubshawe (Mrs)
Must dash. The shed's on fire
ps I've attached a picture of a goat

Not really expecting a reply but you never know

Mon 2nd Nov

    Lynn phoned to say could I get down to Sky to do a promo as fast as I possibly could as someone was uncontactable (probably lying in someone else's bath "stoned out of their gourd" knowing actors) and could I step in as my voice was similar.

    "With joy!" I said and sprang onto the scooter.

    Had never worked with this bloke before who was producing it who asked me to try and sound like this other bloke who had an annoying young person's DJ type voice. I got pretty near it I thought, but the producer, a softly spoken chap with one of those weird "tuft" bits of hair grown just below his lip that makes me think he's just forgotten to shave there or is a member of a religious cult, got me to do it over and over again without any direction whatsoever.

"One more" he kept saying. "One more."

"Do you want me to do it differently at all?" I asked.

"No. Just one more," he whispered. His mobile phone went and he exited to have a loud conversation just outside the studio. With him out of the room, the engineer said

"You got it on Take One. He's been wanking about for the last fifteen minutes. He's new. He does this. He's just trying to justify his job. We'll do another ten I'm afraid."

And we did. And he just said.

"Yeah. Ok. Thanks."

And that was that. Odd. I will probably never see him again.

Pencil taken off the symbiote. Iain didn't even phone. Just a mail. "Symbiote pencil off" it said. No reason. Just that. Ye Gods, small fishes, an aspidistra and a series of farts. Aaaargh. I'd have liked that. It'd have been fun.

Got a call from Lynn to redo the Argot ad at Octopus. Had no idea why. Thought that was finished long ago. A few tweaks perhaps or they'd had a problem somewhere. Client suddenly didn't like the script and the celeb/star wasn't available for the mo? Greeted by Leon.

"The client likes your voice very much." He said.

"Oh thanks." I said. Well I mean that was good to know but I hadn't got the gig had I? The ad was great. The little boy was brilliantly cast. Some actors and the little boy became cartoons and then back again. The little boy as per the sketchy stick animation now completed, flew to magical lands, to other planets, gazing at the wonders of the Argot range. The bespoke music - Mick Casso I believe - not a pop track of yore, swirled and beeped and gurgled and took off gloriously into the stratosphere. I added my storyteller's tone and it blasted off to infinity. Everyone in the studio glowed.

"Brilliant JK" said Leon.

"Can we go again a little warmer on the family scene and more excited on the football scene but magical and gushingly sc-fi on the planets and video games?"

"Aye aye Capitaine. I'll beam you one up" I trilled, not really quite understanding what they wanted but guessing a tone change. This was sounding as if I might possibly have the gig. But don't get your hopes up. ie. I asked nothing.

"Great job JK. Thanks." Was the overall view. I left puffed up like a chuffin puffin who was chucklin'.

Tuesday 3rd November

Back again at Octopus. Client present. Redid a fridge. And a radio controlled car thing. Client loved it. Did 30 second and 10 second versions. In fact they've emphasised the soft story telling aspect and the whole voice's journey from soft to epic and then back to the softness of the joy of Christmas.

"Am I doing the voice then Leon? Is it me?"
"Of course it's you. It's on air tonight. ITV!"
"Wow. Thanks brilliant."

Possibly one of the best series of reads I've ever done. Such enormous colour and highs and lows and tone changes. Wow. On in the break at seven forty five so Leon said. Whoop. Told Lynn. She was ecstatic.

"Fuckin' hell JK. Brilliant. Fuckin' brilliant. Several grand for this lot!"

Evening

Watched the Argot premier on ITV. It wasn't me. It was Patrick Stewart. Patrick Stewart was the voice. You can imagine the scenario can't you. All the floating and space imagery and suddenly someone from the advertising agency sees it and thinks "Star Trek" and finds out he's in the country and available and tells the client who wets himself and Picard wanders into Ostrich and does them all quickly in the hour and they don't tell him how to do them as minutely forensically as they told me as he's Patrick Stewart and you don't give stars much direction as you don't wish to offend and you let him do "him" and ok he's good as he's Patrick Stewart but there's not much of a vocal journey or soft whispering or each situation having a different subtle vocal intonation and I'm sorry Patrick but it's a bit Picard on the bridge "making it so" on the Enterprise. Which is clearly what they decided they wanted I presume. FOR FUCK'S SAKE.

Phoned Lynn on her mobile. She picked up.
I told her it was Picard.
"The c*nts." She said. "The fucking c*nts. You ok?"
"Yes of course. That's the biz isn't it."
"Good. Fuck "em."

Wed 4th Nov

    Had to get a new photo for the Spotlight actors' directory. So phoned up Alan Thorpe, the "Photographer to the Stars" (that's my name for him) who fitted me in for tomorrow.

    He'd had a cancellation which was lucky as he's very popular and busy and it normally takes an eternity to get seen by him. He's a bit up himself and name drops for England but takes very good slightly elongated photos which I like and I look slimmer in the face. Iain thinks I need some new ones anyway. He'd phoned.

    "The others are too old and you look balder now than you did, what with your shaven head and I've had several enquiries for bald headed men that I've put you up for and they liked you the other day for "Memorable" so I think you need to exploit it and I've got too many photos of you with a sort of head of hair so get some done. Ok?"

    He said that without breathing. It's impressive if slightly scary.

    Got a mail from Damian.

damian mackenzie<damianmackenzie@hotmail.com>
To: JK<oohbanana72@yahoo.co.uk>
Subject: Soiled strides

You poove! We've done all the calculations and everyone's paying £150. Here are my bank details.
20 15 27 9215578901

Up yer bum!
Damian

WTF? 150 quid? Gold plated vols aux vents? That I never had? Or saw?

Thursday 5th Nov

Morning

    Three hour NatGeo Shark doco "Are Sharks Now Preying on Humans?" with a young producer I'd never worked with before who alarmingly said " Wow you don't make many mistakes do you?" Bewildering. Does she work with people who do?

Afternoon

    Had me photies done. With spaghetti thin short shaven back and sides poodle hair on top of head multi tattooed Alan who wears a singlet with that bloke from Talking Heads on it and tells me the moment I arrive he's got some incredibly important soap star who'd just been on Strictly who was booted out in week two coming in next who he's "had" to fit in, so we'd better hurry up or would I like to come back in six weeks time when he knows he has a window and we could spend the full hour? I said no let's do as much as we can as I know he's a busy man and thanks for squeezing me in etc. etc. fawn fawn grin grin lick lick, when I'd like to say for fuck's sake why didn't you mail/text me if you had a problem you aaaaaarse! (Sorry mother).

Took the denim jacket (well I was wearing it) and the short leather one and a dark suit option. Some black tees, round and vee neck, and a white one and a white shirt. And a check blazer. A couple of ties. All in a wheelie suitcase. No need to bother about the trousers as it's all waist up stuff. So wore the black jeans for the whole session. Considering we did it all in about ten minutes it went ok. We never made it to the leather jacket or black tees or otherwise. Or white shirt. Or dark suit. Or check jacket. Or ties. Or anything at all other than the white tee. With the denim jacket. Or just the white tee. He snapped 80 pics as if his genitals were exploding. Never once suggested a discount.
    So a somewhat pressurised session. But I conjured up a lot of different looks. Large numbers of which of course were unusable. As they're all a bit too "comedic". And I was never quite ready for most of them. A positive amidst the negatives is that all the photographs are up on Alan's site by the end of the day.
    Did a couple with my top off at his suggestion at the very end. Looked ok! All that gymming works! Not quite a six pack. A four and three quarter pack! Not a 2-PAC either. Hee hee! The pecs look fantastic! Not man boobs at all despite that NZ bird in the gym who I chatted up saying so. I think she's left.

    Showed Iain the pictures. Well, mailed him where they were on the photographer's site and gave him the password. He phoned. Not a mention of the symbiote. He was dismayed by the lack of outfits.
    "Did you only take a white tee shirt and a denim jacket? And why do you always have to pull so many

silly faces? And you didn't appear to be ready for most of them!"

God he's such hard work. Fortunately he liked two of them, a denim and a tee, but said the pec pictures were ridiculous and I was wasting the photographer's and his time by having them taken and he had better things to do than look at my chest and when was I going to grow up but the one gazing slightly to the left of camera in the white tee near the beginning was ok...number 3?....and he could use it. With the denim smiley one? Number 65? And oh yes casting tomorrow afternoon at the Couch for business solutions ad for Italy.

"I'll phone in the morning with details. Get it please!"

He said, interrupting himself by ringing off.

Friday 6th Nov

Last minute Fix promo about Opal Diggers in Oz as an old crusty Ozzie and then up for the business solutions casting.

"It's a very small man" Iain had said. "Before you start, I know you're not very small, but the casting director knows you can act small, so they're getting you in, in case they cast bigger people around you."

Act small? He talks complete and utter bollocks doesn't he? Do you think he ever listens to himself?

In fact when I arrive it says on the script "very small thirty something man who can't reach the ceiling with his paint brush". So guess what this "solutions" company suggest. He gets a trampoline and bounces on it! (Rather than the obvious ladder).

The trampoline is a metaphor you see. For their fab ideas.

"We want comedy" says the casting youngster with the very short leather skirt and tattoos of a galleon on her calves and bright red lipstick and the video camera. She asks me whether I've ever done comedy. Or anything at all in fact. She has never heard of me and has no CV to refer to.

"Do you do physical theatre?" She asks.

"Oh yes. Always leaping about when I could be walking" is my slightly flip response."Directors have to prevent me from flipping and twirling for a joke when it's easy just to enter normally. I'm always inventing banana skins me ha ha ha." (useless attempt at ingratiating myself). She says nothing other than "action". I duly bounce on the make believe trampoline. Not very funnily, thrusting a non-existent paintbrush. Though I get fed up and do a series of high kicks and pirouettes and spins and turn grinning towards her.

"Avoid looking at camera please" she growls, as if I'm a novice.

The second half of the ad is the same "small middle aged man" with the description "puny" added, as in small "puny" middle aged man, being surrounded by files and paper. His solution is to order a large box which you think he's going to put the paper in. But no! He puts himself in it and hides from his secretary! Haaaaaa. I did the hiding well, but acted the box badly apparently.

"You've completely forgotten the box" the youngster with attitude, moans. "Create the box". It's as if she added "dickbrain" at the end of the sentence she is so withering.

"But I stepped into the box" I retorted.

"But you didn't create the box did you? Create the box."

I wanted to shout "But I won't have to fucking create the box if I get the ad will I, coz there'll be a fucking real box there won't there. Not a fake mimed box."

I don't shout though. Coz I want the job. I create the box. Rather well I thought. Those mime lessons have come in handy. But I spend far too long "creating" it, sharpening edges and smoothing the sides down and turning it over rather expertly. I even mime the huge roll of sellotape. And the scissors. I've overdone it. I've taken the piss. She knows I've taken the piss. We both know. I couldn't help myself.

She says "Thank you very much" indifferently, bringing the audition abruptly to a close the moment I've stepped into the newly created top class box and curled up in a ball to hide and she avoids eye contact and "busies herself" with something meaningless.

I am left to grab my coat and jacket and keys and loose change (left in a pile so's to avoid it jumping out whilst I am trampolining and box creating) and it's embarrassing as I am now a non-person. My turn is over and I am out-staying my welcome and surplus to requirements. I slink off and recover in the ante room. The job assumes homunculus shape, cackles at me, and leaps down the corridor, throwing its clothes off, and waggling its finger disdainfully before dissolving. I look in the bag of talent at my feet. Empty. No fairy dust. Nothing. Oh the shame. But then again. What a box.

I know it's not the 5th but Girly out at "girls fireworks night". I've never heard of this before.

Being at a loose end, I thought I'd let a few fireworks off that I'd kept in the cupboard from last year. Sought some company to do it. Rang round. Roop ill. Others not going out anywhere. Some doing it tomorrow. I went to Mother's and let off three large bomb things and scared next door's dog Blooper.
Opened an ancient strange Turkish champagne bottle I found deep in the sitting room cupboard. Ate a lot of Garibaldis and felt a bit sick. Checked the water tank in the loft and tried to find out what the funny smell was in the airing cupboard. Mother is worried as my eczema has flared on my face.
"Oh you poor thing. Apply your ointment."
"Will do."
"You'd be perfect casting for a Sioux" she adds insensitively.

Sat 7th Nov

Girly running. Stoke or somewhere. Faffed and fannied. Watched some Star Trek Voyager. Great ep where the ship and crew get duplicated in some freak space thingie anomaly accident. And then one ship has to self destruct as it's been boarded by homicidal aliens. And Harry Kim dies on one but is replaced by his duplicate from the ship that blows itself up. Wow. I'd like a duplicate. But I think it would make me lazier than I already am. I'd be lying around saying "JK.

Can't you do that?" We'd quarrel and he'd walk out. (Sorry. I'D walk out) I know it. We'd fail to work as a team. We'd compete. Ah well.

Sunday 8th Nov

    Went to the gym. Took a selfie of me training to Tweet but I looked too red in the face so deleted it and didn't. Watched a bit of footy. Went on Facebook. Liked a few vids. A mate had a pic of him made up as the Grinch. As usual everyone had just put "wow" or "don't come near me this Christmas" or "oh Dave you are so funny" or the typical "lol". I put "are you wearing any trousers?" To which he amusingly and refreshingly posted a pic of a man from the waist down wearing surgical stockings.

Maria phoned.
  "Whacha doin'? She asked.
  "Watchin' telly."
  "Do you want to come over and have sex with me?"
  "What?"
  "Do you want to come over and have sex with me?"
  "I heard. I was just a bit taken aback."
  "Well do you?"
  "Yes."
  "Well you can't." And she puts the phone down. I phone back and it's voice mail.
  You've got to laugh really.

Mon 9th Nov

    No work.

    Went to newsagent to get "New Scientist" and the "Stage". I like New Scientist coz it gives you handy bits of info you can throw in at voice sessions.
    "Did you know that an earthworm has five hearts?" was one I learnt today.
    And the Stage to see where some of my actor friends are plying their trade. It gives me great joy to see that some nasty little shit or old devious upstager is working in some dingy rep somewhere in some small part.

    Iain phoned.
    "Got you an interview for a low budget film. That means there won't be much money. That's why it's called "low budget"".
    "Yes I know thanks."
    "I have to say that because you actors get in all of a lather when they get the job and they're told they're only earning twenty five quid."
    "Twenty five quid?"
    "No it won't be twenty five quid, but it's an example. Now it's casting at Flynn Films, 371 Beak Street. Five o'clock Wednesday. Got that? Good. We need the money this end so do do your best not to get up anyone's nose with your farting about and please get it. It's a comedy by the way. Part is "Axel" an American oil magnate. Bye bye."
    And he's off. I don't like him. I really don't.

Decided to have a dinner party on Saturday and phoned several people and left messages. Some will be unable to come as always but I'll get a nice crew together. What shall I have? Italian evening's easy. As is a fish stew. Yes. Fish stew I think. I'll have a ponder on't it.

Tuesday 10th

Went onto Facebook. Friend request from a young Thai woman showing me her bottom who has 6 friends none of whom are mine, all of them tattooed blokes with what look like guns.

Showing of the short film "Rough Soup" (what a weird title) which I shot last May directed by Paul Kamera (I'd done it for expenses so Iain wasn't involved. He knew about it though) whose wife was in that harmony barber shop band with me, "The Hootheads". I was Snod Hoothead. She was Wilhemina Hoothead. Everyone was a Hoothead.
I was in the short with that actor out of "Pigs" cop show who I got on really well with, Garth Mangan. It's a two hander all about a secret elixir that allows you to be totally aware of all your memories from your previous life when you reincarnate. And Garth was playing a dying teacher who'd belittled me at school. But it was a film with a twist in its tail. He nicks the elixir off me - which I'd wanted - but comes back as a dog. Revenge!
The almost naked flash back scenes where my character had learnt his magic went quite well I thought. Looked pretty fit! The clever designers made a load of small sand bumps in a titchy film studio in

Southwark look like Australian mountains. For the semi-naked scenes (other than a mask shaped like a dog's face over me goolies) I had to be caked with mud to play the character in a flashback who's become a "Shaman".

One of the make up girls got carried away with my bottom, and drew large white targets on it. The costume designer, Sylvie, got far too close to my balls applying the mask straps and there was an embarrassing moment but we survived.

When I appeared in all my "as nature intended" glory, there were huge laughs from all and sundry. Happily they were laughing at the dog mask. The stomach was as flat as a pancake.

Film was shown at the Screening Rooms in D'Arble Street in Soho and various bods from the business were invited, including a couple of casting people, Kate Lindbury of Lindbury's and Jim Huber of the Hubers. Even Lynn from Diggerty came to support me!

However, Iain my agent, whose office is two minutes round the fucking corner, couldn't be arsed. (Sorry mother) When I phoned him at 6.00 to ask him if he was coming, which he'd promised he would do, he pleaded pressure of work.

"I've been seeing young up and coming hopefuls at drama school all week and have soo much paperwork. I'll try and see what I can do."

At 6.25 I rang to tell him the film was about to start and where was he? He said

"No. Not looking too good."
"What?" I spluttered
"Well I warned you. I'm very very busy."

I could stand it no longer. The worm turned. The biter was bit. The piggy blew the woluf's house down. The tiny man in the mac turned round and shat all over the sitting room etc. etc. blah etc..
I told him:

"Look. (I said "look". I meant business) The short film which I'm in from the beginning to the end which is really good, is about to be screened two fucking minutes walk from your fucking office. I know you didn't earn any commission from it as there was no money and I got it myself, but the casting director Jim Huber who you toady to all the fucking time is here. As is Kate Lindbury. Yes. Her. You may think my career is a fucking waste of space but do me this favour and spend twenty five minutes of your fucking obsequious life looking at my film would you? Ok?"

As with previous entries in this diary it should be

"This is what I thought. What I said was….."

But no. That was actually what I said. There is no alternative. I gave it to him exactly like that. And you know what? He said

"Oh well you clearly feel very strongly about it" ….and came. And said "How about that then?" at the end. Which could mean anything, couldn't it. He might have absolutely fucking hated it. But "How about that then?" is sufficiently enigmatic to make you not know. As long as a hug follows there is a kind of feeling of approval. Of course my agent wouldn't hug me. But still. "How about that then?" is well thought out. The steaming turd.

Everyone else really liked it and told me so. It is a very good little short. Well constructed and beautifully shot. Half hour long. And I'm the lead.

Speaking a lot. In FBCU (fucking big close up) a lot of the time. Jim Huber was very impressed.

"Well done mate. Very good performance", he uttered. I'll get you in for something!"

Even if he lied it was nice to hear. Kate Lindbury said "well done" and both chatted extensively to Iain.

It's out on Channel 4 in March. I shall have a party! But Iain. What a fucker. He is history. I shall bin him tomorrow.

Wed 11th Nov

Text from Iain. He has dumped me. Felt the time had come for a parting of the ways. Didn't think he could do much more for me. Felt our mutual respect had "lessened" somewhere along the line. I was to get my pictures and show reel out of his office as soon as possible. A text? Not even a fucking email? A TEXT? I am so annoyed. I am not annoyed I am furious. I am "eyes staring out of their sockets" furious. And what is more galling is that he beat me to it. But I am well out of this aren't I? Yes I am! I shall get down to writing to new theatrical agents tonight. I'll show him. But a text? Not even a fucking email. What is the world coming to? Or even a phone call? All I did was abuse him a bit. Correctly for his lack of support. This is really not fair. Is it? Am seeing Roop today to discuss. The absolute bastard.

Saw Roop at the Carnaby Street Preta as I was doing a narrative at Grand Theft for IronBrew playing a dolphin for Bill and Y agency just after. And he was in town for a casting for a new play at the Donmar. Despite his being a doctor type for commercials he's taken very seriously indeed by some casting directors. I'm fucking not. I told him my story.

"Well no wonder if you spoke to him like that. The man may be a git with the squeaky attitude of a pusillanimous mouse but a wounded git with the attitude of a pusillanimous mouse. Anyway he's got that bloke who's doing films in LA who used to be in Spooks who earns about three quarters of a million a year who's his major earner. 20% of that? You're laughing. No wonder he never bothered with you. Probably really doesn't bother with anyone much.

"Not sure. I think the Spooks bloke may have left."

"Oh well anyway, fuck him. Apply to my agent, WAG. I'll put in a good word for you."

"Ta me old mucker!"

"No prob. That's what friends are for".

Film interview still on despite my having "left" Iain. I got a mail. "The casting is still on" it said. Is all it said. Beak Street. A wonderfully plush beautifully styled wooden walled office in a tiny bit of a Dickensian building that you can find only in Soho. Objets d'art and film awards everywhere: silver and gold arrows and bronze masks, lumps of metal that were either awards or objets d'art I couldn't tell. Huge vibrant sofas with technicolour "throws" on 'em and several industrious 19th century haircut haired types (all short back and razor sides and hair piled up on top, some with top knots with massive beards and swirly tattoos clearly all from Shoreditch) crouched intensely behind computers.

I was plonked in a side room with a desk and a table by an annoyingly lovely girl as usual. These companies always employ 'em. Or more likely they're attracted to this business and those who inhabit it. It is mega on-trend after all. A boy came in.

Hi. I'm Stone Oliver."

"Oh. Hi!" I said enthusiastically.

Stone Oliver? He's taking the piss! That's Oliver Stone the film director, backwards. I tried not to giggle.

You're up for…..?" he continued.

"Axel."

"Axel? You're too young looking. He's about sixty five. Can you play older? And fatter? We could pad you out but it wouldn't look real. And you don't appear to be American."

"Well I'm not. But I can do the accent."

"Ah well we wanted genuine Americans. Are you genuine?"

"Yup my mother's from Maryland." I said, slightly pushing my accent towards the mid Atlantic.

"Ah!"

Where did that come from? My mother's from New Malden. The only time I've been in the States was playing a pirate in a low fat crisps commercial where we spent most of the time at sea in a replica of "The Bounty" that had an engine, and several weeks in New York as a student when I had a crush on an American girl I'd met in London and followed her over there until my money ran out (and she went back to her husband). But I was undone. I chose Maryland. He knew Maryland.

"I know Maryland well. Whereabouts?"

Or was he bluffing?

"Well she was born near Lafitte Square" I seamlessly replied, remembering there'd been some bloke called Lafitte in the American War of Independence. I think. Or was it Lafayette?

"I don't know it."

"I haven't been there for a while," I drawled in my now becoming even more American non Mid Atlantic accent and possibly old southern gennelman.

"But I've got an Uncle in Pittsburg" I said deciding to change the location.

"Ah" he said. And followed it up with "Thanks very much!" The dreaded "Thanks very much" signalling the end of the proceedings.

"But I…"

"Thanks very much". He repeated. And he looked down and buried his head in a document. And that was that. No chance to read, no further discussion of the role, nothing. Dismissed. Elbowed. Because I was nothing like the part at all. Was this Iain's final dismissive act sending me to a casting knowing I would be humiliated? It smacked of that. I couldn't bear it. As I left the room the gremlin of piqued ego got the better of me.

"What's your real name?" I asked him.

"What?"

"What's your real name? Your name's Oliver Stone backwards. It's a device to attract attention to yourself."

"Yeah. You're right. It is. My real name's Dave. Dave Cheeseman. Thanks for pointing it out. It's silly isn't it?"

"Yes. And you're a dick."

"I know. Thanks."

Of course I didn't do any of that because I am an actor. Eager to please. Avoiding conflict in case it causes a problem so you get a reputation. I merely toddled off and exited without saying a word other than a hearty cheerio to the totty by the door, who oblivious to what had gone on smiled and said "Oh bye!"

Thursday 12th November

Girded my loins. Expected a confrontation. Got into a bit of a state. Didn't get one. Not that I wanted one. Made a special trip to go into town. Didn't have any work. So…..Took a deep breath. Went into Iain's office in Wardour Street. He was on the phone and threw me the showreels in an envelope and waved at me before ushering me off the premises all the time speaking to some casting director or other.

"Sorry it didn't work out" I heard him say as he closed the door, but he could have been talking to the casting director.

Henry Hedgehog fanmail! From someone spookily in Shepherd's Bush who has sent a letter to the production company that makes Henry H.

Dear Henry, (I'M THE FUCKING HEDGEHOG AGAIN)
I'm Alex. I love you. Could we meet?
(WHAT DOES THIS MEAN? DOES SHE WANT TO MEET ME OR THE HEDGEHOG? SHE CAN'T MEET THE HEDGEHOG COZ IT'S A FUCKING CARTOON)
Have you got any animals Henry?

(ONCE MORE IS THIS ME OR THE HEDGEHOG? THE HEDGEHOG WOULDN'T HAVE ANY ANIMALS WOULD HE? I MEAN ALL HIS CHUMS ARE ANIMALS SO THIS MUST BE TO ME AS JK)
I've got a black cavalier King Charles, a Scottie called Ping, a cat called Pong, a hamster called Pong-Ping… And a bat called Ping-Pong. (Not really this is a joke!) (HA BLOODY HA!) It's lucky for Mum Dad and I (ME, SURELY?) that they don't fight. (MARVELLOUS INFO BUT WHO GIVES A MONKEY'S?)
I only live round the corner from you and my Mum has seen you in Tesco. She remembers you from that Windy the Witch series on the telly!"
(OOPS. SPOTTED. IT'S DEFINITELY FOR ME, JK)
Hope to here (DOHH) from you soon.
Love
Alex.

Oh fuck some pre pubescent is going to bound up to me in Tesco asking me to do the Hedgehog.

 Emailed a whole series of top agents today (9) with CV and the "butch" photo that Iain liked. Have not sent my video showreel on a CD but have said they can have access to it on the net on a link on my little website Jk.tv if they're interested.
 Well, to use the metaphor of the football divisions, I've sent mails to five Premier league agents, three Championship looking for promotion and one Division one who would have a good League Cup run, just in case. Well actually to make sure I get at least one reply! Ha ha ha. And I've sent 'em all letters with all this info repeated.

I told Lynn what Iain had done. She was aghast and got ludicrously more and more irate after a slow start.

"But that's a fucking disgrace! What a complete and utter wankpod! (!) What is the fucking matter with him! I mean a letter is obligatory. I mean I know these are modern times, but a text? I would never do that. I'd invite someone in to talk about it and then possibly a letter if things didn't pick up. But a text! And how much money have you earned him over the four years you were with him? (ER NOT A GREAT DEAL TO BE FRANK) And coz you got annoyed he wasn't coming and he's just round the fucking corner and you gave him what for? No no no. An absolute arsewipe. You're well shot of him. I didn't think there were people like that in the business. But you live and learn, don't you. Bloody hell. (SHE'S COOKING NOW) Fuck him. He's a complete c*nt. (THAT'S MORE LIKE IT) That's the kind of fucking c*ntish behaviour that gives c*nting agents a bad name. How dare he c*unt you off like that? (BLIMEY!) What a total c*nt. I remember I met him at the screening of your little film. What a weak wussy c*nty man he was. With a feeble limp fucking girly handshake. Yeeuch. Well, well out of that. Fuck him. The c*nt. Plenty of good agents will be champing at the bit to have a talent like you on their books. Fuck him. What an arseholing c*nt."

Phew! She's on my side then! Just! Even if there were several c*nts too far. She's suggested I write to her agent friend Sean Major who she can highly recommend.

"I'll put in a good word for you sweetheart. Drop 'em a line and mention me. They're not c*nts."

They're good! I will.
"Job for you at two"
"Goodo!"

This was it: A "pitch". This is when the advertising agency normally call the session "Brand X" or "Project Mysterious" because they want to maintain secrecy so none of their ideas for the ailing product get nicked by another agency who could then use 'em and win the business themselves (apparently). Coz they're attempting to bid for huge amounts of wonga aren't they. Getting an account is worth large piles of dosherama. So they do this pitch in the hope of "winning the business". Though quite frankly some of the ideas in these "ads" are so pitiful that God only knows what the client would see in 'em.

This was for Mineral Water (Hush hush) and I had to play a Bulgarian singing fish. Which I have to say I was quite good at! Bit of falsetto with an accent never hurt anyone. Nice thing about doing voices is that you don't have to go through the pain of being interviewed. They cast you through your reel. When you go the studio, you've got the gig! And the money.

"Great fish!"

They said. Although in reality it was me doing a nerdy Eastern European falsetto.

Spent most of the night on the loo. Must've been that roll mop herring.

Friday 13th Nov

Henry Hedgehog at Il Punto studio. Before we started, went to the loo to puke. Seemed to do the trick!

"You poor poor chap" said Nick.

"But you are being such a trooper. Henry is sounding a touch feeble, but much squeakier, which I like. Could you be ill every time we do this? Aha aha aha aha!"

All the actors very very supportive. Especially Billie Thrubdon who is the young Tanya Tortoise with the crush on Henry who put her arm round me and said

"You're being very very courageous. Well done."

Clearly fancies me. Hem hem.

"Henry and the Trampoline" was the theme for this one. Trampolines are clearly synchronicitous at the moment. Once again Cliff not there. I thought this was where we did the catch ups with Cliff we'd missed last time. But no. He's asked to be re-cast. Jack Taylor greeted me with

"Well your pal's fucked off. No more Cliff fucking Jones. He couldn't stand working with you and asked to be taken off. So we've got your other pal Lee Trinn doing an impression of him. You'll love that!"

Jack knew he wasn't my favourite person. Nick had told him. The bastard.

We started. Trinn and I ignored each other. But really I was feeling so ill I was past caring. Trinn pontificated for all four hours between takes and discussed the Labour Party, Muslim Fundamentalism, his cock, why we should all become more right wing, film stars he had worked with (Pierce Brossun was a darling) horse racing (he has a horse) how stupid sport was, and how much better everything is in America. Billie said "What about the guns? What about the racism?" But Trinn ignored her. No one else wanted a political chat. And Nick said "Can we get on please?"

Trinn then actually, actually, ACTUALLY said

"Since JK's feeling ill, if you want I'll do Henry and you can let him go home."

"Yes, but you'd be talking to yourself on several occasions" said Nick.

"So?" said Trinn.

He needs a smack doesn't he.

Although ill, I made sure I got through everything. Jack as insufferable as ever. Ian Sengle clicking non stop.

The plot for all four eps: Henry built a trampoline from an old plastic bag that he stretched over four acorns and twigs stuck in the ground. He then arranged a competition. But Fred Fox asked to enter. No one likes Fred Fox, (Fred Fox is the excellent Bob Grover) especially Tricia Termite who Fred once deliberately trod on. Willy Worm is equally not in love with Fred who in a previous ep used him as a lasso. So Barry Badger the Police Badger is called in. He now has an assistant played by Bella Conwit who is a rather cute tall twenty something with an annoyingly superior attitude who I think I shall ask out some time and she will say no. But of course won't.

Henry is useless at trampolining as his spines get caught in the plastic bag, but the competition is not what the episode is about at all. It's about everyone "getting on" and ultimately getting an apology out of Fred Fox who, having seen the error of his ways, and saying sorry, is unfortunately squashed on the motorway, trying to get Tanya Tortoise to hurry up.

The subplot was Vicky Vole and Mick Mole spooning in the countryside and actually never having any scenes with us. And Mick Mole goes off to become a film star! So we'll be seeing no more of Trinn then! Werhay!

Felt slightly better by the end of the cartoon which was just as well as I had more work. Went back home then scootered to Sky and parked in Tesco Osterley. Was a bit street cred and shouty at the same time for "Stones."

"Wednesday at 8.00 …Stones" and the actors do their bit of dialogue and I do my bit. "Wednesday at 8.00. Sky Drama."

"Now you need to speak when the actors have finished speaking and it's your turn" said the producer teaching me to suck eggs.

"Oh ok," I replied.

As I've said, this is the way I deal with crassness. "Oh ok," I say, when I'd love to say "No really? I was under the impression I should speak when they're speaking so you can't hear a word they or I am saying you ARSE (sorry Mother)."

But I don't, because as you would expect, I like working and to play "weak and low status man" gets you employed more often. They don't go away thinking "rude man, I'm not using him again". They go away thinking "Ah yes. He listened to my directions and did what he was told. Good." But they don't know that when I'm going "Oh ok" I am thinking "ARSE"! (Sorry again Mother).

On the way out I bump into Stavros Green, a fruity voiced old actor who's with the Dawgs who's just done Sky Movies and just doesn't seem to understand the VO business at all despite success as an actor having been in various seminal sci-fi series and the National. He's always bewildered when the voice overs don't flow in. He still thinks he's the bees knees though. He doesn't work much, partly because he has one voice and it's a fruity one. I'm not sure fruit is particularly tasty at the moment. If ever. (Unless you're Tom Curley). He's very old school and told me previously he sends flowers to female producers after jobs which personally I find a bit sleazy. And I'm sure other people do too.

"Ah. Congratulations on all the work."

He fruitily drools at me. He's always over the top charming.

"Thanks Stav! How's business?" I enthuse, slightly looking as if I can't stay. I know he won't be doing much. He never does. And he'll ask for advice.

"Sparse. Very sparse. Just done this one but first for weeks. Any tips?"

Ye Gods I dunno. Why would I know?

"Redo the reel? Do some lighter stuff? Some charity stuff? Could ingratiate you with an agency doing some free stuff?" I suggest.

"Free? Oh I don't like that."

I do agree. I don't know why I said it.

"Or at a reduced fee?" I suggested.

"Oh yes. Good idea. Thanks!"

"No prob."

"It must be lovely to reach the stage when you can walk out of a session whenever you feel like it." He slips in as I was about to leave.

"What?" What is he talking about?

"If you don't like the job or the producer. Just walk out. I do it all the time."

"Oh I don't!"

And I wouldn't ever. You wouldn't be paid for a start. And you'd get a reputation for being difficult. If he does this no wonder he doesn't work very much.

"Well you should. It must be lovely to know you've reached that stage!" He continues.

"Er yes!" I think it's a kind of status thing. He means I've become as well known as him. But he's not well known. And neither am I. Actors can be so up themselves. And weird.

As predicted some pre-pubescent, egged on by her mother, bounded up to me in Tesco's asking me to do the Hedgehog. I pretended she'd made a mistake and it wasn't me. She didn't believe me and after she'd kicked me in the shins for the third time I caved in and was forced to do the "Her her her Henry Hedgehog" song.

"It doesn't sound like Henry. You're not him." she sneered and ran away, aiming another kick, but I was too swift for her. I failed to notice her right hander though which would have been fine had it merely been her fist. As it contained a pencil it was quite painful. The mother apologised and thanked me profusely of course, while I was bleeding.

Sat 14th Nov

Soir: (I'm being French coz I'm in chef mode now) Dins chez moi. I chose an Italian theme knowing I could knock it up in a few mins. But still be praised for my efforts. Oh the cunning. Buffalo Mozarella in the Insalate Tricolore to start with and then linguini, with seafood, a bit of fruity bread with olive oil and several cheeses and fruit salad. All Tesco fare. Al Fresco Tesco! Haw haw haw haw!

Invited some luvvies over. Bazza who was Steve Stoat in the first series of Henry Hedgehog and his wife Pearl. (Steve Stoat died of old age which was all done rather beautifully to keep children aware of death).

Graeme Smith from "Windy the Witch", and his partner Theo (who is the most pierced man I have ever met).

Harry Soskin who produces BBC radio comedy stuff with whom I did "The Velvet Triangle" and his partner Caleb.

Luke Toser, who directed me in my Edinburgh one-man-show 6 years ago "Tiger in Pyjamas" and his fiancee Tabitha, (with the shaven head!).

My old acting chum Tony, who I worked with at Chichester in "Much Ado".

And Roop and his girlfriend Tish.

And the Girly.

The evening started dreadfully, with the Girly appearing on my bike in her sports gear and getting completely pissed on Pinot Grigio before anyone turned up, and then five minutes before they were supposed to be there, leaving the house "looking for sparkling water". She returned well into pudding,

("Where's your girlfriend JK?")

"Well she went out for San Pellegrino".

"All the way to Italy? You cruel man!")
stood at the end of the table calling everyone loudly a "load of fucking weirdos" grabbed another bottle of vino and staggered to my bedroom where she crashed out asleep on the bed.

I explained she'd been under a lot of pressure lately coz of the studying and training and competing she does, so everyone should be understanding and not criticise her too much. Though this was slightly unforgivable. Roop said

"Ha ha ha she is well peculiar. But we know that. What's going on there? I mean that was crap wasn't it?"

I agreed. Sort of the end really.

"I mean bloody hell…." Said Roop.

Tabitha said we were being unfair and she obviously felt intimidated. She went to see her and returned immediately saying she had conked out and had at some stage puked along the wall.

Apart from this hiccough, the evening was a great success. Though Theo made a rather obvious pass at me, and showed everyone his tattooed nipples at the death. Tony was very amusing and got on very very well with Tabitha. Luke was getting on very well with Caleb (!) and didn't seem to notice. Roop's a bit keen on Tish and hugged her a lot. Good selection of highly amusing people who all got on very well. Vairy vairy well done me. The Girly is history after this behaviour.

The Girly, having woken up with fumes of sick breath emanating from her has just smashed me repeatedly about the head with the pillow, screaming "I hate you I hate you," and left to get the police on me because I shouted at her somewhat vehemently to get her to explain her somewhat antagonistic behaviour of the night before. I admit I waved a copy of New Scientist at her, the one with the info about the earthworm, in a provocative manner but that was only because she kicked me. She said it was all my fault, and we were finished, and stormed out. I hastily put on a black Nike running top. And some black running joggers that were at the foot of the bed and shouted at her as she was cycling off on my mountain bike,

"Oi come back with my bike you thief! Thief! Thief!"

Far too theatrically as is my wont. Of course Sod's Law had it that a police car was cruising past the flat at that exact moment I was at the front door and stopped dead outside.

"Is everything alright sir?" asked the copper in his usual dead pan voice. For some bizarre reason only known to my psyche, I replied as "frog and toad, apples and pears" caricature cockney geezer.

"Yes all pukka thanks mate ta. All is kosher." ("Kosher?" For fuck's sake where did that come from?) I said, instantly arousing all the suspicion in the world. I mean I was suspicious of me so the police certainly were.

"Is this your property sir?" said the nasty aggressive policeman, ignoring me completely and shining a brilliant torch right at me. I mean it was like a small sun.

"Er. Yes officer. Well the ground floor flat. " I said blinking shiftily, now in ludicrously posh mode almost with a lisp.

"Been here long have we sir?"

"What. Schtanding at the door?" I ventured completely unfunnily and lispily.

"No sir. Resident in this property," he persisted manfully.

"Er yesh. I know you meant that. Er about five yearsh."

I was totally unconvincing. It was as if I was impersonating me very badly. I was actually a burglar. And although I didn't know it yet, a murderer. This policeman was making me feel I should confess to having buried my grannie under the patio, despite the fact she'd been cremated at Mortlake Crematorium. Another policeman appeared with another torch. It was super nova bright.

"What's your name sir?"

I had great difficulty remembering who I was I was feeling so guilty and was so effectively blinded.

"Er er um Jay Kay" I stuttered. "JK! "That's me. Yes. J to the er K". I was now in rapper mode.

"Can you prove that sir?" he persisted ignoring my funky moves.

"Why certainly officer. I've got my name on this envelope here."

I grabbed at an unopened circular on the communal hall table.

"There. You see?"

"That actually doesn't prove anything sir. Does it. Your picking up a letter. You could just read the name couldn't you. And pretend to be whoever's name you read."

"Er..yes..I mean no. (Help!) I suppose it doesn't. (?) Er....ha ha ha. Yes. That was a bit daft of me wasn't it. Haw!"

I was now a Hooray Henry with a peculiar high pitched giggle. Haw! I felt arrest was imminent. At that moment a van went over one of the sleeping policeman speed bumps near the flat and crashed down the other side rattling its exhaust pipe. I chattered nervously

"Doh. They do that all the time. It's so noisy in this street. A few months ago a taxi came up here so fast he took off from a speed bump and smashed into three cars and overturned."

"Ah yes sir. I was the first policeman on the scene for that. About ten months ago wasn't it?"

"I don't think so officer. About six I think."

"Yes I think you're right sir. And we spoke didn't we."

"Oh did we? Sorry. Memory like a sieve."

"Yes we did. You came over and we had a conversation."

"Oh."

"Well I won't trouble you any longer. Goodnight Mr Ray."

"It's Kay, officer. Kay."

"Yes sir. That's what I said." He hadn't. I didn't pursue it.

Oh the drama of it all.

Sunday 15th

Played footie for Roop's friend Dick's Veterans team, Vopipu FC, Very Old Past It Players United, or something, on an artificial pitch in Holloway. Was sub. Calf seems to be alright. It was naturally much colder than it ought to have been (it always is when you're standing about), and I didn't really want to play but thought I'd have a go in the determined midfielder role (when required) - expecting to be sub of course. Took every track suit I possess in case I spent the whole game subbing and watching.

    As it turned out today the oppo only had ten players, so I guested for them against Dick's team! It all went surprisingly well. I was hugely influential. Ran around like a blue arsed fly (this is one of my Dad"s expressions. Do blue arsed flies which are clearly blue bottles have anything going for them particularly well in the swiftness department as opposed to other flies?) super unluckily hit the bar three times with headers and a volley, and provided the pass for the winning goal (much to Dick's bemusement). Was surprisingly much fitter than I thought, being overweight and nerdy as I am. Though, to be frank, everyone is a bit ancient and paunchy, but they've still got all the old slogans, giving a hint of the annoying competitive wotsits they must have been in their youth.

    I've never been able to take the whole thing seriously, and avoid shouting out football cliches like:

    "Up his arse" (sorry mother) which is said to you when you should be marking someone very closely and you're not.

    "Back door" which means "Come back this way and try a different route".

    "Switch it" which means move it to the left when you're on the right and vercy viccer.

    "Get it in the mixer" which is put the ball into the six yard box (the box is the mixer).

    "Man on, man on" when someone is upon you and you haven't noticed. And

"I'm going to break your legs you c*nt" which is when a member of the opposition informs you that he doesn't like the cut of your gib.

I tend to be a bit more unaggressive about it all. I always rely on dialogue like

"Go on" and

"Watch it" and

"Me me me me me. Give it to me"

And

"Quick over there. To him to him" (I never remember anyone's name).

And

"Oh don't be ridiculous".

And

"Oh what are you doing. Why did you foul me? What do you do for a living? You're far too aggressive? I think you need counselling" (Much too long winded I know).

And I have been known to say "Your soul is black" if someone has kicked me.

This naturally tends to make the opposition think you're a bit of a nance. Or as some bloke from the team from the Royal Mail I was once playing against said,

"'Ere mate, for a posh c*nt poof, you're quite a good player."

I think that to feel complimented was the right reaction. Though I did say

"I'm not gay actually. Though I am very much in touch with my feminine side." (Though as Roop says, "You're so in touch with your feminine side you'd take it out and shag it.")

On reflection I'm surprised I didn't get punched. Regularly.

Anyway, there was all this aggressive guttural footie-speak. Not having played for two years, it was strangely refreshing to hear it all again. The opposition who I played for, Tooting Streatham Thing Rovers, or something like that on the way to Croydon, have asked me to turn out for them regularly, which has amused Dick a bit. However I think I've aggravated the piles. Obviously too much twisting and turning.

Mon 16th

Morning.

No work. Had a pencil for a car commercial at Slick. Pencil taken off. Was then asked by the Dawgs if I could get in at short notice to do a commercial for bathroom furniture. Hung about expectantly in the Deli and had scrambled eggs and smoked salmon. And three chai lattes. But heard nothing so phoned Lynn.
"Oh that's gone. Ages ago. Didn't I tell you?"
Ffs.

Played squash. Felt very faint. Perhaps Mother was right. Perhaps I am too delicate for all that twisting and turning. I think perhaps the main problem was that I wasn't fit enough. This really old bloke..and I mean old….in his seventies or something...he'd just performed in an ironman or triathlon or something unbelievably hair-raisingly energetic and was the British champ for his age...(I think because there'd only been two entries in the whole of England and the other one had died, so he was English champ by default) anyway I played this bronzed fitness monster with black dyed hair, (what little he had) and was run around the court as if I was a total beginner. I was reduced to a red faced pillock. It is unrepeatable how knackered I was. No. I can say it. I was so knackered that my willie disappeared.

    This is clearly what happened to the body in prehistoric times when it was under attack by a lion or something when we were hunter/gatherers. The body goes "oops, great stress, protect the meat and two veg for use when the danger has gone" so what happens is that the old boy shrinks back up itself. It's called "penis foldback" apparently. Actually it's not. I just made that up. Anyway, after several cups of tea and a long lie down, the old chap reappeared refreshed. Isn't that nice to know?

Evening

    Girly update: Dinner at "Dan Dan" Japanese. The trip in the car was stonily silenced. Once sat down in the restaurant she goes for me! Apparently I was ignoring her. And she doesn't like any of my "theatrical" friends who also ignore her. I've amazingly agreed next time to invite some of her acquaintances so she can have people she feels at home with. I have apologised for my behaviour and she has accepted my apology. I have "lent" her four hundred pounds for her motorbike. We went to a hole in the wall! What the fuck was I doing?

    And after I've given her the money which she folds neatly and puts it into a small purse, she bursts into tears. And chucks me. Ffs.

I mean actually it's a good thing as I was going to chuck her. Wasn't I. But bloody hell. And hang on! She's got my bike. And four hundred quid. Ffs.

Oh well. Plenty of Fish. Plenty of sea. You don't make an omelette without breaking eggs (not sure what relevance that has but it sounds good) Ee aye addio I haven't won the cup.

Tuesday 17th

Did a voice over ad for a travel company playing a very high pitched fashion designer at Sparse. Well I wouldn't say they thought

"Hmm. We need a high pitched fashion designer. Who shall we get? I know JK!"

No. They said we've got a fashion designer we want you to play, and we've heard your reel and you're very versatile so what do you suggest and I immediately said

"Well how about high pitched and a bit designery?" and they said

"Yes good idea."

I also made him Austrian, which hey, was very original (well possibly not). But then it's down to the timing and comedy skill. The first time I read it, it being a 60 second commercial so I thought, it came out at 46 seconds to which I said

"Ah well I've got 14 seconds to play with then. I'll spread it over the read".

This is an old one, "I'll spread it over the read" and although true, gets a bit of a chuckle from the assembled crew. But no. It was in fact a 30 second commercial so I had to read like a hyena with its fur on fire looking for a puddle to cool off, to get it in. Which I did. Though the rather lovely Irish producer said

"You're gabbling. Can we go again?"

Now gabbling is a word I'm not keen on. "Going so quickly it's difficult to understand" is what I like, which I agree with. "Gabbling" implies I'm shit. But I don't tell her that. She's gorgeous. I'm that shallow. No. I merely go

"Oh ok. I'll try to make it more comprehensible."

Which I try to do. And succeed. But it's back to being long again.

"You'll have to knock off three seconds," she states obviously.

"Yes. I will. But I suspect I'll have to "Gabble" to fit it in."

"Well don't."

She smiles. Hmmm. This could be tricky. But the engineer bless him, interferes beautifully.

"To be fair to JK, there's too much copy. He can fit it in because he's that good (I love him) but it's going to sound rushed. Or too flat. I suggest we look for a few cuts."

"I think we should just get him to go again."

"Ok we can try. But it'll sound too quick."

"JK....." , says the really gorgeous producer whose annoying use of the word "Gabble" still hasn't stopped me from appreciating her beauty and wit,

"....Go again please and make it quicker but slower. Faster but sound slower."

You can do it. By putting less expression into it. By being flat as a pancake. But he's a high pitched Austrian fashion designer for fuck's sake. There's a lot of fey expression. You can't do fey flatly. But she's top banana drop dead lovely so I don't communicate my disquiet.

"Ok" I say. And fit it in easily.

"I knew you could do it" says gorge bird. I crinkle. "Well done everyone."

I mean there's no one else involved, it's just me but she's congratulating the group as it were. The engineer beams. The creative beams. Another person I've no idea what their role is, beams. The tension leaves the room. Job done. I stand up to leave the booth. But hang on. The creative says

"Can I listen to it one more time?"

Whoops. He wasn't paying attention was he? Everyone settles down. I stay in the booth. The last take is played again. He utters his assessment.

"But look it's dull and not as funny as the other one" says the creative.

"Which one? The gabbled one?" says gorge bird.

"No. The three second over one".

"We can't use that one, it's too long."

"Well yes obviously."

"Then what are you saying?"

"I'm saying that it's funnier when JK has more time and more room to play with it."

That's true of course. I like that.

"Let's cut it then."

"Well that's difficult because the client has approved the script."

"Well let's phone him."

They do. He's not around. Of course he's not. The microphone is turned off so I can't hear them. They exchange info. I'm turned back on again.

"We're happy JK. Thankyou."

"I can try a quicker one without gabbling and being dull if you like." I say quickly, eagerly over-trying to be accommodating sensing the job tip-toeing out of the building.

"No that's fine thanks."

I exit the booth and shake everyone's hand and exit. I should be back soon, possibly tomorrow with a shorter script. But then they might find someone else. You never know. I think I'll be back. I suspect I'll be back. I hope I'll be back. Yes I should be back. The fandabbydozy producer I have discovered is called Siobahn.

Lynn phoned. Pencilled tomorrow for an ad for a feminine hygiene product for twelve for Lemon.

Wednesday 18th Nov

No call about the Lemon job. I faffed and read the paper. I phoned Lynn at eleven.

"Is the Lemon job on?" I asked, fearing I might have to go through what I went through the other day when she cocked up. I continued.

"The Hygiene Thingie you told me about yesterday for Lemon?"

"Lemon? Lemon? (She says "Lemon" in a strange accent as if pronouncing a word from a dead language). Oh 'ang on...(rustle of paper as she looks me up on a job sheet).. Ooh still on a pencil. I'll chase 'em. Toodleoo."

She didn't ring back so at twelve o'clock I rang again, wary this time after the last ridiculous experience. No going off running this time. Half an hour to get into town.

"I presume they don't want me. The feminine hygiene thingie."

"Oh yeah the thrush stuff. (She can be so indelicate) Narr they never phoned back. I left a message on the producer's mobile. I'll try again. But it's looking unlikely isn't it."

By 12.35, despite the experience of the other day, I'd given up and was in Westfield looking for a new pair of jeans. The mobile rang. It was Lynn. It was deja vu.

"Where are you?"

"Shopping."

"Where? In town?"

"No. I'm in the Bush."

It was the running scenario all over again.

"Whose?"

"No. Shepherd's Bush".

"Oh fuck. They need you now for that Lemon job....They just phoned to say where were you"

"But they hadn't phoned back."

"They did. I forgot to tell you. Sorry. I'm on my own in the office. How long will it take to get in?"

"Half an hour."

"Double fuck! I'll tell 'em twenty minutes. Tell 'em there's a problem with the tube."

"But I'm cycling! I'm not on the scooter!"

"Tell 'em that's why you're cyclin'."

"Can't I tell them it's your fault? Coz it is you know!"

"No fuckin' way. Go go go!"

I cycled like the wind and it was only when I was in Soho that I realised I'd no idea what studio I was supposed to go to. I phoned Lynn whilst cycling.

"Diggerty Dawg, can you hold?"

"No no no I'm not holding. It's JK. Where is it?" I pant, trying to cycle and phone at the same time which is always dodgy.

"Where's what?"

"Where's the ad taking place?"

"The minge ad?"

(As we've established, she can be so delightful).

"Yes."

"Oh 'ang on…. You ok?"

"I'm cycling."

"You sound as if you're 'avin' a wank …er here we are…Angle Sound in Wardour Street! Quick quick quick!"

I got there completely awash with sweat having beaten the twenty minute barrier, crossed several traffic signals totally illegally and driven through an old lady with a stick who had a swish at me and almost crashed into a bloke who shouted "Do you like blue lights" which I thought was surreal until I realised he was making a reference to a police car. I was almost squashed by a reversing lorry and evaded a community policeman who was chasing after me for riding on the pavement. Quickly locked the bike to a signpost. It's five flights of stairs and the lift was out of order so I bounded up and got to reception drenched with perspiration, clutching my rucksack and helmet and breathing like a bagpipe and managed to squeak

"Hello…… I'm doing….. a voice…. for Lemon."

"What?"

"……Doing a voice for Lemon." (I used a bit more breath)

"Lemon.. Lemon.. Lemon," says the girl as if there can't possibly be any agency with such a silly name. (She scans her computer screen) "Lemon, Lemon, Lemon."

I mean you'd think she'd be aware that the voice hasn't turned up for the Lemon session and would whoosh you in with a knowing "ah yes you're late" look. But no. She's all aloof and I could be someone come to collect a package.

"Ah yes studio 4 with Vince."

Oh she's found it!

"I'll tell them you're here. Would you like a drink at all?"

"Tea please…. and an apple juice….. Not in the same glass…. obviously!"

"What?"

No sense of fun or humour. Clearly not a receptionist who's an actress .

"What's your name?"

Ye Gods I'm not even down on a list. What is going on?

"JK"

She rings the studio.

"Hello I have a JK here voicing?…………….. They're not quite ready for you."

Not quite ready for me? I'm 30 minutes late!

The producer comes to see me with the script. She is as usual rather beautiful and young.

"JK, you were doing the shop assistant in the chemist. We've done the MVO1 with Lee Trinn. But we waited for you and as you weren't here he suggested he play your part, (The fucking bastard!) which he did and the copywriter likes it, so we don't need you."

She bewilderingly shows me the script of what I was playing but now I'm not.

"You see?"

What am I seeing? The part I didn't play. Wtf?

"Lynn told us you'd had a problem with the tube. Have you cycled?"

"No I'm a tad dishevelled and sweaty because I'm been sodomising a chicken and this helmet I'm clutching is a handbag" I would like to have answered. But I merely said "Yes." somewhat gobsmacked.

"Sorry about this. But we weren't sure you were going to get here. We're happy with how it is now. "

I sat down. She left. I correctly presumed Trinn hadn't left yet. Gabbing away no doubt. I went downstairs and waited for him. He exited the building. I confronted him.

"So you do fellow actors out of work do you you slimy turd?"

It was a radio ad. He'd denied me my studio fee and the network fee which is the fee to play it on every radio station. No shame from him though.

"If you'd been on time there wouldn't have been a problem. I was the solution to the problem. That's the way it works! Cheerio!" he said.

As he went past I kicked him very hard on the right leg and he fell over. A trainers-kick but nonetheless painful. The look of disbelief on his face was priceless. I really really did this. I phoned Lynn and told her what happened. She was very sympathetic.

"The c*nt. The total c*nt. You do not do that. What a c*nt! And not only has he done you out of your repeat fee I've lost my c*nting commission! If I ever see him I'll punch his c*nting lights out. Fuck me wot a c*nt!" etc.

27 c*nts later she rang off. She had completely cocked up though hadn't she. Again. I mean actually it was completely her fault and Trinn was justified in doing my part wasn't he. And I shouldn't have kicked him really. I enjoyed it though. I fear I ought to leave Lynn and the Dawgs, oughtn't I? (Does anyone ever say "oughtn't I" anymore?)

Thursday 19th Nov

Mother decided she wanted a mobile phone, which was odd after the warning about the microwaves and the cooked brain. Ah but this was different. She wanted a mobile to phone with, when out. In case of emergencies. That was progress! So I got her a cheap "pay as you go". And delivered it to her. But now the phone was in her hot little hand, she began to waiver. She informed me that they weren't as good as people said they were as you couldn't phone a mobile phone from a mobile phone.

I suggested this was rubbish.

"But I heard it somewhere" she said.

"From whom?" I retorted.

"From er someone" she said faltering. "Somewhere".

"It's utter bollocks. I phone mobiles all the time. That's part of the deal. Not being able to phone a mobile would be absurd. I mean completely ridiculous. It would muck about with their revenues for a kick off. They make masses phoning mobiles. Phones phone phones. Look. My friend Roop has a mobile. I'm phoning it now."

I did so. Roop who would understand when I got through to him that this was a good cause. Naturally it didn't go through and said "call failed".

"You see! You see!" She cackled triumphantly .

"No no. (Ffs) The reception isn't very good". I tried again.

"It's ringing. I said." I handed it to her. She glued it to her ear.

"Aargh what's happened?" She threw the phone at me. It had clicked onto his voicemail where he was pretending to be a Dalek.

"It's his voicemail. Fret not!" I said soothingly.

"I thought we'd been invaded". She shrieked. And continued shrilly,

"Anyway this mobile. The knob is too little. I can't turn it on".

"Well obviously Mother it's difficult wearing those gardening gloves." I said, bemused by her desire to invent reasons to avoid using it. She ignored me.

"Look. I won't be able to cope. It's far too much for me to take in. It's just like a mini computer and you know about computers because you're the younger generation. I know nothing."

(To be fair, she can't even work out how to use the washing machine. And all you do to make it start is turn the knob to the correct programme which is a large symbol, and pull it out. She even has difficulty holding her Oyster Card over the reader and regularly inserts it.) There was a pause. I persisted.

"I've put my number into the phone for you."

"Where is it?" she panicked.

"Well you press this icon here to access it. Well obviously you will find that difficult once again whilst wearing the gardening gloves."

"Ohoh. You've used the words "icon" and "access". That's computer speak. I can't understand that at all. I don't like the sound of any of this. I'm very worried this isn't for me."

She puts the phone on the work surface and covers it with a piece of kitchen towel. This is actually a good sign. Had she put it in the drawer I would be worried if we would ever have seen it again.

I feel there are a few adventures to come with this phone idea.

Friday 20th

A foursome of jobs today. The first at that small basement cupboard studio just off Carnaby Street, Metronome. Lots of swirly art on their walls. The designer had a field day. "I want colour. Get me colour" being the obvious over the top theme. You need to wear your shades. And you are perched on a stool to voice. What the fark is that all about? What sadist thought of that? My legs dangle. How is that comfortable? Ffs.

Had to be top testosteroned for a Superb Bikes end of show tag. These are the sponsorship moments just before the ads.

"Superb Bikes is <u>sponsored</u> by Delm" in best deep thrusting tones. Or is it "<u>Superb Bikes</u> is sponsored by Delm". Or even "Superb Bikes <u>is</u> Sponsored etc. etc.." You could go on and on.

And a warm soupy voice naturally for a soup TV commercial "test" (ie they may give the job to someone else) at Factotum.

Then some promos for National Geographic at Fix.

"The Rat. Though vermin, this creature is considered a God in India where it is worshipped and fed. But...They are feeding and worshipping something whose diseases can kill them"….

And another one:

"This dog has the sharpest teeth in the Northern hemisphere. Yet it is a household pet. The killer on your hearth rug. Thursday at 9. On National Geographic."

Then off to Minute Sound in Great Marlborough Street for a Golf tournament promo. I had only just sat down in the session, had just put my cans on and was about to put my phone into airplane mode… (never have your phone on in a session) when my phone started vibrating on the desk - I always turn the "ring" off and "Unknown" came up. Barney the shaven headed producer with the scar on his nose was on the phone to some client so I flicked a headphone off and answered it.

"Hello".

"Ohhhhhhhhhh. I"m naked and on the bed. I'm inserting two fingers up my...."

Just at that moment Barney spoke.

"Let's do it".

"Take 1" said the engineer. I poked at the red button feverishly to banish her and energetically lurched into it.

"It's the Kasumikaseki Trophy where last year Leigh Mears struck a course record 9 under par 58. That'll take some beating this time, but Sanapachi Vagina is up and coming and is out to get him after his success in the Hyundai Trouville Masters."

There was a pause.

"Can you do that again?" asked Barney. "You sound strangely out of breath. Flustered even. And you said "Vagina" instead of Vin Van Sing. It's Sanapachi Vin Van Sing."

"Oh ok. Did I? Sorry. Ha ha ha."

Blast. How unbelievably embarrassing. I thought I was dealing with it. What is she doing? I know very well what she's doing. She's playing with my mind. She turns me on like a tap. Bloody hell. I must ring her back as soon as poss. In my newly chucked state I'll be like a rampant beast. But then she'll fart about. Aaaargh!

Phoned her up at the end of the session. Voicemail. Of course. It's always the fucking same with her. And me. She's got me stitched up like a kipper.

Damian is actually getting shirty

damian mackenzie"<damianmackenzie@hotmail.com>

To: JK<oohbanana72@yahoo.co.uk>
Subject: Money

Put the money in my account please. You are the last one. Everyone else has paid up
20 15 27
9215578901

Didn't even sign it. And ordering me about. Don't like that.

Sat 21st Nov

    Replied to Damian. Thought I'd be non confrontational. I wrote as my manservant Dobbin

JK<oohbanana72@yahoo.co.uk>
To: damian mackenzie"<damianmackenzie@hotmail.com>

Subject: Testes

Mr McBollock! My boss is of the opinion you should put the money where the sun don't shine. He was only there for a night.
And his snogging your missus is certainly only worth a couple of quid!
Pooh!
Dobbin. Manservant to Mr K

Sun 22nd Nov

    This morning far too bright and early I was phoned up by Clem, from Tooting Thornton Heath

Thingies who I'd guested for the other day, (What is their real name?) asking me if I was free to play for them, as he'd had a drop out.

"We need someone with your skill to play for us" is what he said. "We've got a tough cup game:"

"My skill!" How nice! How flattering! I of course said yes after such fawning despite still being in bed. I'd have to play as a "ringer" as I wasn't registered for the club and you needed to be. So Clem told me I was Danny Postlethwaite. However when I turned up Danny was playing so I was told I was now Aaron Godfrey. But he was there too and rightly objected so I was now Max Tremlett. Max was in Ibiza. So if I was booked by the ref I'd have to give that name. But the problem was that Clem the manager hadn't told the club captain, Dave that I was going to play. Dave had been injured when I'd played the other day and he had no idea about me as a player and didn't want me to play instead of his mate Jimmy who I would oust if picked in midfield.

"But JK's good. He almost scored for us the other day. Hit the bar twice!" said Clem. (And the post actually. Really unlucky).

"And he set up a couple!" (In fact, one.)

"Well I'm sorry but I'm the club captain and I think he should be sub as I've no fucking idea what he's like".

Firm but truthful.

"But I've got him out of bed" said Clem. Which to be frank didn't strike me as a good argument for my selection. But after a chat (they shouted and swore quite a bit actually, Dave complaining that he hadn't been told and he should have been) Dave agreed with Clem that he'd bring me on at some stage which was a compromise I suppose. Clem apologised to me profusely. I therefore bowed down to Dave's decision and froze to death on the side lines waiting to be brought on as sub. I presumed I'd get on at half time, but despite the team being four nil up, Dave faithfully refrained from subbing anyone. Well he subbed a player from the defence. At 5-0. But not a midfielder. Where I was playing. As they were playing 424 the midfielders were him and his mate Jimmy. Clem kept shouting from the sidelines "sub Jimmy, Dave" but Dave doggedly refused. He was clearly making a rather feeble point. With about a minute to go Dave let me get on. At fullback. At 6-0. Slightly unwarmed up I slid in for the ball and played the man quite deliberately and the ref got his yellow card out. I had to give my name. I of course had forgotten who I was, Max somebody or other. So I gave him the name of someone who had been the original Henry Higgins in George Bernard Shaw's "Pygmalion", (later the musical "My Fair Lady"),……. Max Beerbohm Tree, an actor manager of the 1900s who ran His Majesty's Theatre in the West End.

    The local Football Association would find no such name, and the club would be fined for playing an unregistered player and possibly thrown out of the competition.

    The referee blew his whistle for the end of the game soon after. I had utterly wasted my time and had almost got hypothermia but had gained some revenge for being treated so badly. As I trudged back the quarter mile to the changing room, Clem apologised once more saying he would have a word and would I please play again? I of course said yes meaning no. Coz after that demeaning fuckwittery I will never ever return O Tooting Thornton Chocolate Caramel Centres. Or ever know your name.

Evening

    Pub with old twinkly actor chum Oliver and his girlfriend Claudine. We did a brief telly ages ago playing delivery men who got splashed by a truck and had a comedy drenched moment together - expletive acting - and I've since played cricket with him. Very amusing and good fun. Has a very good googly.
    Claudine, sneering over her distracting facial mole (surely these things are easily removed) was so snobbish about her being at the RSC.
    "Of course you're not a proper actor" she tells me. "All this advertising and voices and cartoons and TV. You've sold out completely. Theatre is the art. That's where you truly extend and stretch as an actor."
    "And make fuck all money."
    "What?"
    I asked her what car she drove.
    "A Fiat. Why?"
    "How old?"
    "Ten years I think. Why?"
    "With a coat hanger aerial?"
    "No".
    "And do you live in rented accommodation?"
    "Yes. Why?"
    "And do you work as a secretary or waitress or call centre person part time?"
    "When I'm not working, yes. In fact I have a very understanding boss who allows me to go off and

audition whenever I get one. Why all these questions?".

"Because I live in a flat I pay a mortgage for, drive a two year old Mini and never ever have to do anything other than be an actor, which is still what all the voicing and Tellying and cartooning and advertising is, regardless of whether theatre is art or not. Forgive me for not dwelling in a garret and living off bread and water. Forgive me for not suffering from consumption. Forgive me for not signing on. Forgive me for not waiting on tables. Forgive me for not being a Barclays Mortgage adviser reading off a card, sounding sincere. Forgive me for making a living in a world where hardly anyone makes a living."

"Ooh who rattled your cage?" she replies.

"You fucking did".

I bought a round and defused the situation.

Mon 23rd November

Night

Bloody dreams. In this one I have long jet black hair that I keep flicking backwards every time it dangles into my face. Which is all the time. Flick flick flick I go. I gyrate wildly in a skirt and white blouse to no music at all. I slink slinkily. I hoist my skirt up. I flick. My legs are very hairy. I am wearing stilettos. A photographer is taking pictures in a harshly lit studio. I am squinting into the lens the lights are so bright. I can't see him.

"Show us a bit of cleavage darling" he goes.

I am now wearing a long black dress. I lean over revealing my mahoosive pecs.

"Yes that's it sweetheart. More of that." He drawls lasciviously.

I look into a mirror. I am flicking my hair. I have bright red lipstick on. Botox lips. And somebody else's nose. I like it. I stretch luxuriously like a cat. I purr loudly. I look into the mirror again. I am not me. I am Frank Lampard. I volley a football coming towards me at an impossible angle ludicrously competently into a goal despite my pencil thin skirt hampering me. The referee in a white coat signals six. The crowd invade the pitch and carry me on their shoulders. I am holding hands with Wayne Rooney. I am flicking my hair. The crowd throw me into the air and I float down onto the grass. I sprint with Wayne joyously and we slide speedily on our knees towards the corner flag which I grab and strum like a guitar. I sing "Chiquitita" by ABBA. My mother is there in Chelsea kit, sings harmony with me, and handing me a strimmer, orders me to mow the pitch.

"Mow it. Mow it NOW" she barks.

"Do you like my hair like this?" I ask her in a small Welsh voice. I flick it.

"Well you've always wanted to be an actress haven't you cariad?"

She simpers and hands me a tiny tiny script from her patent leather handbag. It's an ad for shampoo but with minuscule writing.

"20 seconds! Fit it in in 20 seconds!" She suddenly demands angrily.

"But I can't see the words. I can't see the words!" I cry in despair. "Give me some light!"

"When you're ready JK" says the engineer into my headphones.

Wayne screams "Fit it in. Fit…. it…. in!"

And shakes me. My head bobs from side to side like a teddy bear with a wobbly head. My hair falls out and lies at my feet. I am bald. My legs spontaneously combust. I am in agony. I scream like a Munch painting.

I wake up instantly with terrible cramp in my left calf, throw the duvet off and stand by the side of the bed hopping like a one footed ferret. Ffs

Morning

Did a session for Sky at Sky again. Rather attractive producer Adrana with cheeky grin. Did a promo for "Airplane". Did posh nerdy voice.

"Like you do for that fruitbat ad" she added.

"Ah yes. Of course ha ha!"

Ffs. Who is that? Is it me? Did I do the job and I've had a brain fart and forgotten?

On the way back from Sky I popped into the Tesco just behind the biscuit factory just up the road from the studios for a protein bar and a prawn sandwich. A bloke dressed as a Jaffa cake leapt up to me and greeted me very lugubriously. It was of course Derek Fazakerley fresh from the huge hem hem success of "Closet Partitions" which apparently never got on

"The vagaries of the fucking fringe old love. Got one actor - said he knew you, you'd been mice together? - and he got a fucking part in a fucking sci-fi series playing an alien with a fuck off mask and very few lines, but a lot of scenes apparently, so I had to let him go and do it. Then I sacked the director for being shit. Well actually for not being there at all. He had a job in Curry's which he clearly felt was preferable. So I took over the directing. Then the stage manager broke her leg slipping on a milk shake, and then two of the actors got meningitis. Knocked it on the head love. But not daunted. Am doing an hour long version of Hamlet, "Hamlet Revisited", with me as the Great Dane himself and the Ghost and Polonius, and my new girlfriend as Gertrude, Ophelia, Horatio, Claudius and the Gravedigger. Doing some interesting re-interpretive re-writes! Cast of five. Lots of doubling and trebling. (No really?) I think you know her? Mandy Fard?"

Mandy Fard? Know her? I've hidden behind Renault Vans for her.

"How long have you been seeing her?"

"Oh about six weeks."

Six weeks? God she's two timing Derek with Jeff. And what about Derek's wife Fleur? For fuck's sake.

"What about the Jean Genet project?" I asked him.

"Oh my God oh my God oh my God…." he said as if he'd caught his foreskin in his zip.

"What? What? What?" I said, worried for him. But at the same time hoping he had.

"Love…I forgot I asked you to audition for that. Yes you were unavailable weren't you. Bad calf or something you said. How is it?"

"Still bad." I said massaging it and wincing convincingly. I'd have suddenly limped heavily if we were walking, and pretended to feel a twinge.

"Oh poor you. Anyway….we were unfuckingbelieveably unlucky. It's a terrible story. The bloke I cast got bitten by a dog the evening after the first day of rehearsals and it went septic. He was perfect. The thinnest bloke we auditioned. Looked like Gollum from the Hobbit. Shaven head. Great knowledge of French, being French as he was…and even knew all about Genet, the lot. He'd studied him. And Antonin Artaud. Great knowledge of the Theatre of Cruelty. Thierry Pantalon was his name. Had done a lot of French theatre. Theatre Des Bouffes apparently. Even been in prison. Like Genet. Something unhinged about him too. And gay of course! Would have been marvellous. We did one day of rehearsal where the atmosphere had been electric and he'd even threatened me...in character of course…with a knife …so realistic…and he'd just borrowed 600 quid off me to pay his rent as he had his wallet stolen at the weekend - well he threatened me in character with the knife. And accompanied me to the building society cash machine, still in character - and then he phones - angrily, so good - to say that this nasty little canine has gone for him and he doesn't think he can come in for the week. And then a friend of his phoned me to tell me he'd died. Septicaemia or something. Unbloodybelievable. Bloody Dachshund. They can be very mean spirited for such a little dog. I think they've got inferiority complexes. My mother had one and it got run over. Driver couldn't see it. Thought it was a stick. Bloody unfuckingbelievable."

    Personally I don't believe a word of it. Thierry Pantalon? Which translates as Terry Trousers? The bloke's fine. He just worked with Derek for a day, saw what he was in for and buggered off back home to

France. Or Hackney. Probably Brian from Bethnal. With 600 smackers for his trouble.

Tuesday 24th

    No response from any of the agents I wrote to. Even the crap one. Nothing from WAG (thanks Roop) or Lynn's "Sean Major". I shall have to make a sodding effort. Dohh.

    Back at Sparce for the Austrian travel agent job with a much shorter script and annoyingly no sign at all of Irish gorge-bird. Instead the producer is a fella who I don't remember at all but has clearly worked with me as he asks me about the Girly. I say we are kaput. I have no recollection of him whatsoever. But I act as if he's my bosom buddy and discuss the prospects of his football team and don't ask about his girlfriend in case he's gay and I don't want to offend and just ask questions and seek subtle info as to where we worked together before.
    Then of course I realise he's seeing Kim, the girl I was seeing briefly last year (well for about a week… well I took her out twice) who wanted to get into voices but had a pronounced stutter when she got nervous. And was Roop's friend. And we'd met at that dinner party in Parson's Green where I got pissed and demolished the hall table with vase and flowers all over the place on leaving, with my umbrella. Oops. But all remorse vanished as we concentrated on the shortened script which slots in easily at 22 seconds plus 7 seconds for the end line and we're all sorted, which is what the engineer says.
    "Well done JK. Sorted mate."

"You're done" says Colin (for that is who he is) "
"Fab job. See you soon."
Nice when they like it.

Got a mail from Damian

damian mackenzie"<damianmackenzie@hotmail.com>
To: JK<oohbanana72@yahoo.co.uk>
Subject: Money

I do not wish to have to repeatedly send you requests for your contribution to the weekend. Pay up now. Here again are my bank details. I'm beginning to take a dim view of this.
MacKenzie

20 15 27
9215578901

Ooh er. Sense of humour failure and it's appallingly unfair of course.

Wed 25th Nov

    Have asked out the girl who works behind the counter at the comic shop just behind the British Museum. I go in there and pose questions about past editions of Marvel and DC comics and we flirt a tad. Her name is Edwina. She's cute. She has a multi coloured tattoo of a Chinese dragon just above her backside crack which she shows to all and sundry. We're meeting in the Slug in Fulham on Sunday.

Voiced another video game at Suede. I die a lot from a series of sharp instruments.

"Now a spike pierces your abdomen".

"Arrrgh!" I go.

"Yeah, good. But can you go sharper".

"Eeeeeee." I go.

"Yes that's it. Now louder and more horrible."

"Aaaaaaaaeeeeeeeeerrrrrr."

"Good yes. Now you're flung through the air…"

"Pierced first?"

"Oh yes."

"Loud horrible piercing?"

"Yes."

"Ok…Are we still recording?"

"Yes we are."

"Ok then………………………

….."Aaaaaaaaeeeeeerr….wohhhhhhhhhh. Er. Ooof errrrrrr."

(The "Wohh" bit is me flying through the air and the "Er. Ooof errrrrr" is me landing and dying.)

"Perfect."

What a a way to make a living.

"You give very good death you know?" says Justin the producer

"Oh thanks!"

Finally. A response from an agent. Ffs. It was from the girl who used to be an actress who I worked with on that fringe show and she was sleeping with one of the cast members (Karl Meadowbright) with whom I was sharing a dressing room (the size of a mouse hole) while she was engaged to the lead bloke in the play Miles Cuttle. She then married Miles the lead bloke the following month, after we'd finished.

When she came back from the honeymoon, she started up the affair with Karl again! Which she kept going for two years. Miles was away a lot with the RSC! Karl told me all about it when I saw him again at a casting last year. She was Jane Dinkley.

Anyway she was now an agent and I'd written to her coz apparently she was quite good, asking if she recalled our "stage sharing" (I camply wrote "Do you remember us "on the green" with me in a dreadful wig") and she sent me the following note:

"JK. I remember you. It must be twenty years. (FFS IT WAS ABOUT TEN. I'M NOT THAT OLD) "Childrens' Parties" was a rich piece and I enjoyed working with you immensely. Whenever I go to the Tron in Glasgow I always think of the many fond memories we had there. It was a lovely company. (AS WE WERE IN SCHILLER'S "WILHELM TELL" AT THAT PUB IN HACKNEY I DON'T KNOW WHAT THE FUCK SHE'S ON).

You played Captain Dean, the children's entertainer who was put away for molesting the young son if my memory serves me right? (WELL IT FUCKING DOESN'T COZ I PLAYED ULRICK VON RUDENZ AND SEPPI THE HERDSBOY AMONGST OTHERS. WE WERE A CAST OF 7 IN THIS USELESS PROFIT SHARE PRODUCTION AND SHE WAS TELL'S WIFE GERTRUND OR SOMEONE AND HEDWIG SOME PEASANT WOMAN, AND OTHER SUNDRY

WOMEN – IN FACT I REMEMBER HER RUSHING ABOUT IN THE CRAMPED CONDITIONS OF THESE ROOMS ABOVE THE PUB IN A "WENCH'S OUTFIT" AND KARL MANAGING REGULARLY TO HAVE SEX WITH HER IN THE LOO IN THE EIGHT PAGE GAP IN ACT ONE WHEN NEITHER OF THEM WAS ON, AND NO ONE CAME TO SEE IT AS IT HAD DREADFUL REVIEWS AND ON SEVERAL OCCASIONS I REFUSED TO GO ON BECAUSE WE OUTNUMBERED THE AUDIENCE AND WAS CRITICISED BY THE DIRECTOR, JEZZ LEVY, FOR MY ATTITUDE. I REMEMBER SAYING

"I'M NOT PERFORMING IN FRONT OF ONE PERSON FOR NO MONEY OK?"

AND HE SHOOK HIS HEAD AND SAID I'D NEVER DO WELL IN THE BUSINESS IF I TOOK THAT APPROACH AND I TOLD HIM I COULDN'T SEE HOW NOT DOING THE SHOW FOR ONE PERSON WOULD BLIGHT MY CAREER?

"AH BUT THAT PERSON MIGHT BE A CASTING DIRECTOR OR PRODUCER. YOU NEVER KNOW. YOUR CAREER COULD BE MADE."

"WELL IN THIS INSTANCE IT ISN'T LIKELY TO BE BECAUSE IT'S KARL MEADOWBRIGHT'S FUCKING GIRLFRIEND STRIDDY WHO'S SEEN IT SEVEN TIMES ALREADY AND IS ONLY HERE BECAUSE SHE THINKS HE'S AFTER JANE DINKLEY, WHICH HE ISN'T AS HE'S ALREADY GOT HER"

I also wanted to say that if anyone important did see the show they'd never cast any of us coz the show was total shite but managed to restrain myself.

Anyway, she continued. "Unfortunately I have someone like you on my books, Alan G MacDee (WHAT THE FUCK? HE'S A BURLY SCOTSMAN OF SIX FOOT TWO WITH A THICK MANE OF BUSHY HAIR AND A FACE LIKE THE BACK OF A SKODA WHO DOES MUSICALS! HE'S A FRIEND OF ROOP'S!) and you would clash. (FFS HOW?)

How lovely to know you're still in this business of show! (PATRONISING OLD BAT)
Good luck with your career. (WHICH MEANS "DON'T EVER WRITE TO ME AGAIN ASKING FOR REPRESENTATION YOU LOSER")
Jane
Ps I see from your CV you're in Henry Hedgehog. (I'M NOT JUST IN IT. I AM THE FUCKING HEDGEHOG) Give Jack Taylor my love. He's with us. He's a sweet man.
(AAAAAAAAAAAAAAARGH)

Thursday 26th

Mailed Damian

JK <oohbanana87@yahoo.co.uk>
To: damian mackenzie"<damianmackenzie@hotmail.com>
Subject: Money

Bloody hell I suppose I'm going to have to take this seriously as you seem to have lost your sense of humour. Not once did you tell me I was paying for the whole weekend. I was there for the evening. I didn't gobble down any grub on the sunday or gargle any booze so don't feel I should contribute to your

breakfast lunch or tea or supper AS I WASN'T THERE. Also not once did you mention any money in any of your prior emails, which on reflection was silly, as of course I will contribute to the food and drinks on the Saturday evening as that is only fair. But the Sunday? The food and drink and for some the Hotel? No! I will put £60 into your account. And I think that's generous as I drank fizzy water.
Best
JK

Managed to persuade mother that the mobile phone is a good thing for her well being. And she's agreed. Which is a result. However I phoned it today and it automatically went onto voicemail (recorded by me!)

"Hello. This is Tiggy's phone. Please leave a message for her after the beep".

I phoned her all afternoon. Always to voicemail. I even phoned it when I knew she was out as she had a doctor's appointment for the mole on her hip. It still clicked onto messaging.

I got worried. I phoned home later on to see if she'd not gone out and was in and ill. Possibly. Or something. Possibly lying in a heap at the bottom of the stairs! But phew. She picked up the home phone.

"Hullo?" she whooped in that strong well modulated belt of hers.

"Oh you're there!" I said somewhat taken aback that she appeared to be fine.

"Yes I'm back from the doctor's. Nothing to worry about. Mole, he is fine. Mole, he is benign. Ah that rhymes!"

"You didn't switch your mobile on" I told her.

"Didn't take it with me darling."

"Why not?"

"Too precious. Might get stolen. I've put it in a sock"

"In a sock? Why?"

"So no one will think it's a phone"

"They'll think it's a sock with a phone shaped centre" I replied unhelpfully.

"Anyway they won't see it in the basket," she added.

"It's in the basket as well?"

"Oh yes."

"So you did take it with you although it was in the sock in the basket but you didn't turn it on."

"No no. It is in the sock in the basket and I didn't turn it on and I didn't take it with me coz I put the basket in the larder".

"Why?"

"In case a thief happened to open the kitchen door looking for spoils and spotted it lying expensively on the kitchen table, I thought I'd fool him by putting it in the sock then into the basket and then into the larder."

"This anti theft thought is all very commendable but has nothing to do with actually using the phone does it? I mean the temptation to steal has been taken away from the hypothetical burglar completely."

"Yes indeed!"

"But you're stymied because no one is using the phone. You have a mobile that is never used. You have managed to deter the would-be burglar, yes, but have rendered the phone meaningless as regards for what is was invented, viz, to be a phone. You are treating it as a precious object, which it is, but are thus depriving yourself of using it as a technological device. It has assumed the status of artefact."

"Pardon?"

"Do you want me to repeat all that?"

"Not really….. you're saying I could use it if I took it out of the bag."

"Yes but you'd be at home which is defeating the object. You could use one of the other home phones."

"I do."

"Yes I know you do….You need to use it when you're out when it's turned on and out of its sock and basket."

"Yes."

There was a long pause which spoke volumes. The pause was in fact undeniably loquacious.

"This isn't going to work is it Mother." I said firmly.

"No not really," she replied equally tersely.

We quickly made a deal. I would collect the phone tomorrow. This was a telepathic moment between Mother and son. She would never use a mobile and I would never act opposite Tom Cruise.

Friday 27th Nov

Lynn has caved in over the Bitty Cake fiasco. She left a voice mail message.

"They've offered half the fee. I can't be fucked to argue. It's taking up too much time with all these emails pinging all over the place and we couldn't prove much from your photos and everyone had the same story about you just ignoring the cues and making a fuss all the time. And the director wouldn't comment. And anyway I don't want to offend the production company who may never offer us any work ever again. Sorry JK they're clearly all c*nts. Laters".

Ffs.

Did a peculiar job today. Had to pretend to be a jogger for a radio ad. Except I was jogging in the studio on the spot on a slab of paving. The slab was mic'd up.(there was a mic at shoe level). The idea was that my fellow runner and I would be jogging and whilst jogging I would mention the financial advantages of the product TBL Health Insurance (as you do when out for a little jog with a mate) including the phone number and web address and how much the Health Insurance had cost me. And what good value it was.

My fellow jogger would react with approving inquisitive noises and a few responses along the lines of "yes" and "oh really?" And "where can I get the info?" Finally shouting out the name of the product as I sped off into the distance.

Here's the script:

TWO JOGGERS. RUNNER ONE, A FITTER BETTER RUNNER THAN THE OTHER, IS RUNNING WITH HIS MATE, RUNNER TWO, AND TALKS TO HIM ABOUT TBL HEALTH INSURANCE

AND THEN RUNS OFF. RUNNER TWO HAS DIFFICULTY TALKING WHILE RUNNING AND IS SLOWLY MORE OUT OF BREATH AS THE ADVERT PROGRESSES.

RUNNER ONE: (RUNNING EASILY) Jim…..do you know that TBL Health Insurance?
RUNNER TWO: (SLIGHTLY OUT OF BREATH) Yes!
RUNNER ONE: (CRUISING) Well they've come up with a great deal!
RUNNER TWO: (MORE OUT OF BREATH) Oh!
RUNNER ONE: (STILL CRUISING) It's great! From as little as £1 a day.
RUNNER TWO: (FINDING IT DIFFICULT TO REPLY) Interesting!
RUNNER ONE: (GETTING A BIT QUICKER) It can help you gain speedy access to private treatment and covers the costs!
RUNNER TWO: (PANTING) Yes of course.
RUNNER ONE: (SPRINTING) They've got info on their website. www.tblhi.com
RUNNER TWO: (STILL PANTING) I didn't quite catch that.
RUNNER ONE:(SPRINTING AWAY) www.tblhi.com Or you can phone them on 3235085379
RUNNER TWO: (SHOUTING OUT AS HIS FRIEND RUNS OFF) T.B.L.H.I. eh?
RUNNER ONE: (IN DISTANCE) And there's a discount if you're a member of a fitness club! See you later!

    It was a 40 second commercial so each "take" meant 40 seconds of jogging and gabbing. Well about 36 seconds to be pedantic as there was a warm assuring female voiceover - Kim Roberts doing her thang - at the end to sum it all up lasting about 4 seconds. ("TBL Health Insurance. Looking after you") She'd already done her bit before us so we didn't meet. And there were 4 seconds of swift Ts&Cs (terms and conditions). Me or the other voice doing that I presumed. So actually 32 seconds in fact. As I started jogging before my cue, and always went on running swiftly after my dialogue had finished, each jog took me approx 34, so as you can imagine, as no one had informed me that I would be running, I was slightly taken aback and not pleased. Though I was wearing trainers of course. Coz I do anyway. I'd just eaten a baked potato with avocado and prawns and some salad (no coleslaw) plus two cappuccinos and a Mars Bar which wasn't great preparation.

    When we started I thought we'd do about five takes and that would be that. I hadn't bargained for the other actor playing my jogging pal. Because he'd been doing some voice over work for another ad for the Insurance Company, TBL, where he'd been the straight VO, he was employed as the other jogger. It can happen. The producer takes a shine to you and employs you again. Or even the client. But in this instance there were two problems.

A) He was in a studio in Chelmsford and not with us and we were doing it "down the line"

B) He's about 60 and had clearly never been jogging (or I suspect had any exercise at all) in his entire life. Thus his understanding of being out of breath and having me jog away into the distance leaving him behind, calling out after me breathlessly, was way beyond him.

    I mean you'd think that being an actor, he might have the ability to imagine what it might be like to see your jogging friend run off into the distance as you fail miserably to keep pace with him, and this consequently render you speechless through lack of puff; and it was coherently described in the script by the copywriter; but the concept proved very difficult for him.

    I meanwhile had foolishly created a rod for my own back by actually sprinting on the spot as I delivered the website address and phone number leaving him in my wake. I mean it made it "realer". And this would have been fine if we'd done a few takes, but after fifty minutes I think we'd done 35.

    Seymour Simon, the other actor, was so lacking in understanding of how to build his character's "journey ", his getting more and more out of breath as I accelerated, that he started off the whole thing every time gasping like someone having an asthma attack, and by the time I'd sped off (on the spot) was having a minor seizure, which although funny was not actually the kind of funny that was required at all.

    From the first take Seymour was sounding like a foghorn. "Yes?" He bellowed raspily to my first line. His "oh" was almost demonic. His "interesting" was a writhing monster. His "yes of course" was a dog chasing a rabbit. His "I didn't quite catch that" was an unintelligible sea creature. The copywriter interrupted him.

    "Seymour sorry to interrupt as we've just started" said the copywriter.

    "Yes?" said Seymour from the studio in Chelmsford with slight echo.

    "That's great. Just a few ideas."

    Very tactful copywriter. It was in no way great. It was as far away from great as trousers are from a thong. But you don't want to ruin the artist's confidence.

"But could you build the character's reactions up a bit? As it says in the script? Make him a bit out of breath but attentive at the beginning and a bit more gaspy as the run progresses and by the time JK speeds off, slightly even more so and you project after him the "TBLHI" because that's the product and that's what he's been talking about?"

"Okay!" says Seymour, slightly with the actor's tone that says "I'm listening, but I'm not quite sure what you mean but I'll get on with it."

We do another one and he is less loud but this time sounds as if he's having a coronary.

"Er Seymour."

"Yes?"

"Er that's great…(liar again) but er you were sounding er…exhausted. Unwell even"

"Oh. You don't want me to be exhausted?"

"Well out of breath yes. But you need to build it."

"Ok," says Seymour again quite firmly. But I'm not convinced. I don't think he's grasped this at all. I am proven correct instantly. My first line is "Do you know that TBL Health Insurance?" to which he is supposed to say yes, bemused we're about to have a chat whilst running but he'll listen. It's a sort of inquisitive "yes." He goes "Harrrrrrrraaargh."

"Er Seymour."

"Yes?"

"Harrrrrraaargh" is weird."

"Oh is it?"

"Yes. I want a "yes" rather than a "Harrrrraaargh." Do you hear what I mean? It's less out of breath. I mean he's a bit out of breath, but not as much as "harrrrraaargh" is conveying. Do you understand?"

"I think so" says Seymour.

"And we need to hear him say "yes"."

Once again I know from experience this means Seymour hasn't got a fucking clue and wishes he was elsewhere having a gin and tonic. I am proved correct by our next pass through. I start jogging on the spot again – the engineer has sprinkled salt on the stone slab to give a sort of scratchy effect – and deliver my first line again:

"Oh hello Jim…do you know that TBL Health Insurance?"

Seymour does a reasonably straight delivery but says "No!" which isn't in the script at all. The producer doesn't stop us. We carry on. We go through the whole thing and far from being out of breath and jogging it's as if Seymour is ensconced in an armchair having a cup of tea and a Hobnob. And then finally when he's supposed to be pooped at the effort of keeping up with me, delivering the "TBLHI" line to me as I disappear into the wild blue yonder, he says the line not only as if it's a secret word to be heard by no one else but him and his pet spider, but also in a bizarre cockney accent.

"Er Seymour." Says the copywriter.

"Yes?"

"That's great."

"Uhuh."

"But you said "No" at the beginning when JK said "Do you know that TBLHI?" That's not in the script. The client would go mad if you denied you knew the product. It just isn't good advertising. Please make a positive noise and don't say "No".

"Ok."

"And secondly, when you're gutted at the end because JK's running too fast for you, don't whisper the TBLHI name which is the product, shout it out at him because he's running away into the distance."

"Ok."

"And thirdly."

"Uhuh."

"You seem to have affected a strange cockney accent."

"Oh have I?"

"Yes. JK is being sort of neutral but your character is coming from somewhere in Theydon Bois."

"Ah."

"I don't think it should."

"Oh ok."

"Ok?"

"Ok."

We started another take.

"Oh hello Jim….do you know that TBL Health Insurance?" I ventured again

"No!" said Seymour slightly hysterically.

"Stop stop stop" said the copywriter. You said "No" again."

"Oh did I? Sorry."

"Yes. Don't. Ok?"

"Yes."

There was a silence.

"Are you alright?"

"Er yes." Said Seymour.

"Good. Let's do another one then. Oh hang on!"

The copywriter had an idea.

"I think you should stand up."

"What?" said Seymour somewhat startled.

"You're sitting down aren't you?"

We couldn't see him as he's in Chelmsford.

"Well yes!"

"Well I think you should stand up. Would open the diaphragm. You are supposed to be running after all."

"Yes I am."

"Well you wouldn't run sitting down would you? I mean you couldn't! Ha ha ha! It's physically impossible!"

"Well yes."

"Right then. And you could move a bit then couldn't you as if you're running."

There's a pause.

"I'll have to find the engineer. To move the microphone. He's gone off to have a fag and left me here," said Seymour sounding as if he wished he was in a rocket on the way to Venus rather than here doing this ad or having to stand up which was an unbelievable inconvenience. We heard him go off mic and shout out slightly weedily

"Hello. Hello. Brian? Brian?"

"It's going very well" said the copywriter, lying.

Several minutes passed in which we heard a lot of scrabbling about as Seymour's mic was readjusted for him to stand up.

"Ready Seymour?" Said the copywriter.

"All set up here". Said a deep voice. The engineer in Chelmsford.

"So Seymour…" said the copywriter.

"He's just gone to the loo…" said the engineer.

I asked for another coffee. It appeared.

"He's back" said the deep voice.

"Hello." Said Seymour.

We recommenced.

"Now remember Seymour, to build it up. Ok?"

"Ok."

We started again and Seymour said "No" again.

"Seymour."

"Yes."

"You keep saying "No."

"Oh sorry." He said a tad sullenly.

"It's not in the script."

"No."

"Listen."

"Yes?"

"Let's try these noises with your lines." And he provided Seymour with a "herr" and a "haaa" and a "eeugh" and a "hoooo" that even I found a bit confusing and possibly desperate. For Seymour it was like offering a frog a piece of frog to eat.

"Yup. Got it." Said Seymour in the slightly strangled voice of the actor who has absofuckinglutely no fucking idea at fucking all.

And he ignored the creative completely and did it in exactly the same way as he'd done take one. And added some forbidden "Harrrrrraaarghs" Except he was obviously bouncing about a bit. From one leg to another.

"Seymour can you take your keys out of your pocket, it's picking up on the mic" asked our engineer.

I did that thing I don't like doing but I was getting fed up running for 30 odd seconds and speeding up and worrying about the calf possibly pinging and the spud and prawns and salad making an appearance. I gave him notes.

"Seymour. Excuse the notes love, but I've been in this position coz I used to go out with an elite runner who would frequently motor on and leave me hundreds of yards away."

Silence from the other end. Nothing. He doesn't want notes from me. I won't give up though.

"She'd also attempt to have conversations with me when the only thing I could do was keep up with her. Conversation was totally beyond me. She'd be completely unpuffed of course and finally accelerate away into the distance having got merely a series of grunts out of me."

Still silence.

"It's a bit like that."

"I get it."

He's sneering. He hates me but I can't bear this. I commit the awfullest sin. I read the script all the way through telling him how to do it. In fact I play him. I am Lee Trinn. I suppose I did it out of a desire to help but I was also frustrated that he didn't have a clue.

In the studio area next to the mixing desk the copywriter is nodding admiringly in agreement at me.

"Ok Seymour?" I add.

"I get a "Yup" back. A "Yup" of evil.

But it's in one ear and out of the other. In fact I don't think it ever made contact with his thought processes.

"Ok then let's do one," says the copywriter.

"Take fifteen" or something says the engineer. We do another ten all the way through and some progress is made in that Seymour actually doesn't say "No" and manages a lot of squeaks that have a progression to them. But nar he hasn't got it. We continue. It's awful. We finally do one that could pass muster. It's not great but the copywriter seems satisfied. However the Producer Eloise who's been on the phone for the whole of the session, has come off the phone and decides to direct me. I haven't had a single direction in the fifty minutes and suddenly she's in like Flynn. It's deflecting. She doesn't really want to direct me. It's just taking the focus off Seymour. Well, that's what it looks like.

"JK?"

"Yup?"

"You're not sounding as if you're having a conversation. You're just providing facts and figures. Can you make it more conversational? As if you're in the pub? (Running in the pub? Why are advertisers obsessed with all conversations taking place in the pub? We're running ffs!) And also you need to run faster at the end."

No I don't.

"Oh ok then."

We do another one much more conversational (in as much as it's possible to make an ad that's talking about websites and telephone numbers and amounts of money that policies cost, conversational, whilst running) and of course I'm fine but Seymour is making bronchitic fart noises so we do another ten takes and Eloise whispers to the copywriter but I hear it:

"We've run out of time for the two actors. We need to finish now. Or they'll cost us another half hour which we can't afford."

The copywriter knows it must come to an end. And neither of us has done the Ts&Cs.

"Ok! That's great Seymour. Let me listen to takes 36 and 42."

And he does. We all do. They're both ridiculous. Gasps and "no's" and "arghs" as if Seymour is being attacked by a seagull.

"Thankyou Seymour very much! Good session. See you soon!"

"Byee" says Seymour. "Thankyou". He says this with as much enthusiasm as a dog having its gonads removed.

"JK. Thankyou! Great!"

He can't be happy. The engineer remembers we've only got one set of foot steps.

"Oops quickly before you go…JK. You need to be Seymour running. And also can we have some passes of you just running at various speeds. Wild. Sorry to get you to run again."

"No prob." I lie. And we do five more takes while I try to sound as if I'm having difficulty running. And several more of me running steadily and then more quickly and then sprinting, with no dialogue. And of course all on the spot. And I do a pass through of all my lines without me running. And I do something I am ashamed of. I ask to play Seymour's part and get them to record it. And I do. And they do. And I am completely Lee Trinn doing a fellow VO out of work were they to use it.

    I leave somewhat sweaty, pecked on the cheek by Eloise who is perturbed I am a bit damp, my hand heartily shaken by the copywriter, but convinced we'll be back again to do this - especially as we haven't done the "Ts&Cs" - which is confirmed by my having been pencilled for it again for Monday.

But no. Running commercial pencil is then off.

    "It's off! That pencil for Monday." Said Lynn. "And I spoke to Seymour who thinks you're a c*nt. He phoned me in a state. You told him how to do it."

    Seymour is represented by Diggerty Dawg as well as me.

    "But I just directed him a bit Lynn. He was shit. He's never jogged or clearly had any exercise in his life" I said.

    "Yeah possibly but he can act. He's been in the West End. "No Sex Please We're British". Ages ago I know but he has been there. He phoned me to tell you that he thought you bullied him and he's a man of 70 (60 surely) and couldn't jog and what was wrong with acting and he's pulled a muscle and he blames you. The upshot is that they're doing it again with him because the client loves his voice and he's done all the previous campaigns and they're replacing you. So you've been too smart arsed and lost all the repeats and we've lost your commission. So next time don't be so fucking keen on impressing with all this jogging stuff. I know that Seymour's an old c*nt but you should have treated him with more respect. Gotta go. I'm on me own in the office. Laters!"

   Ye Gods. And I bet they use my running. I deserved it though. I'd done a Trinn.

Late afternoon.

     Another ad with Tom Curley. This time at Jumble.
     "Ah my favourite voice over, the mellifluous JK. Are we working together?" He trots out. "You have me at a disadvantage if so. I can't compete with your various velvety voices. What will you be giving us today o inspirational one?"
     "Well as you know Tom it's a mortgage company commercial."
     "Is it?" He says feigning astonishment and no knowledge. "Is it really?" He says knowing exactly what it is.
     "Yes. And I've been told I'm the Ts&Cs. (Terms and Conditions)".
     "Well you would be. You are the fastest Ts&Cs-er in the business. Women quiver at your Ts&Cs. Their knickers descend automatically. Some have been known to faint at the speed your inner clock speaks to you. Fit it in in 6 seconds they say, despite it being a mouthful of mouthfuls, enough words to kill a cat, more sentences than a bicycle botherer on a barge, and you do. What skill, what articulation, what focus. If only I was like you."

So much of Tom's spiel is of course taking the piss or indeed just meaningless flim flam but I indeed go like the clappers if required and am understood, whereas so many slur it all. Which is not allowed. It has to be comprehensible or the ad won't go out. As I say, this is a 30 second ad for a mortgage company. And I was employed just to do the legal bit on the end, which I had to do very quickly (actually "very" is the wrong word. Unbelievably quickly. Stupidly quickly) not helped by Tom taking an eternity to do the MVO smoothly and laconically. He had to say

"Choosing a mortgage is difficult. Why choose one company over another? We at Simon Woodburn get it. Next time you need a new mortgage consider us. We treat each applicant individually. We prefer to meet you in person to understand exactly what it is you require. Call 4395824162 to make an appointment. That's 439....582....4162. Simon Woodburn.

No one asked him to change parts or not do the main body of the read so he was happy. They did cut the repeat of the phone number to give me a bit more space. But he had no need to blow raspberries all over me this time. It was all him. With me Ts&Cing. But he didn't make it any easier for me. He eased through it. Dawdled and drawled it. And coz he's a star they refused to tell him to do it quicker which was pathetic really but inevitable. Well they had one go, but his read was longer so they gave up. So he got it in at about a leisurely 19. With breaths and pauses cut out about 17 and a half.

I had to say:
"Your home is at risk if you do not keep up repayments on a mortgage or other loan secured on

it. Written quotations available on request. Insurance may be required. Credit broker fees of up to point 5% may be charged depending on the type of product. Simon Woodburn is an appointed representative of the Simon Woodburn Partnership Ltd which is regulated by the Personal Investment Authority. The PIA does not regulate mortgage business."

13 seconds I had for that. I did it. Like this: "YourhomeisatriskifyoudonotkeepuprepaymentonamortgageorotherloansecuredonitWrittenquotationsavailableonrequest.InsurancemayberequiredCreditbrokerfeesofuptopoint5%maybechargeddependingonthetypeofproductJohnWoodburnisanappointedrepresentativeoftheJohnWoodburnPartnershipLtdwhichisregulatedbythePersonalInvestmentAuthorityThePIAdoesnotregulatemortgagebusiness."

As you can imagine it was as if my trousers were aflame and a cheetah was wearing them while being chased by a mutant wasp in go faster stripes. Blimey. Do people actually pay any attention to this gobbledeegook? I suspect not. And the engineer has software that can make it even faster if he wants!

"Your————-weeeeeeeeebrrrrrm————-business."

The listener blanks it out. But "tees and cees" as they're known are essential to make the ad legal with the advertising authorities. And I'm not blowing my own trumpet here but I actually made it work! Tom doodled a large primitive picture of balls and a penis whilst humming quite loudly whilst I was doing it and had to be asked to be quiet but other than that was well behaved. Until the end.

"Well done JK! Audible! Clear! And in!" Said Graham the engineer. "I've only had to speed it up a smidge".

"Well done you two" said Kasia the producer. "Nice work".

We both exited the booth. I stuffed my script in my rucksack. I keep them all of course. Proof to my ego I'm working.

The client, a beaming suited baldy who had basked in the occasion, downing an excessive number of cappuccinos and stuffing more almond croissants in his chops than he'd ever had in his life, was in seventh heaven meeting a hero from the telly, and leaping up from behind the long fitted desk where he'd been seated, echoed this sentiment, with Tom obviously as the focus.

"Brilliant job. Great to meet you! Fantastic!" And proffered his hand. Tom ignored it and boomed

"What an appalling experience that was. 25 minutes of my life I'll never get back. You should all be ashamed of yourselves. None of you has any critical facility at all. The script was utter horse shite." And pirouetted out. What a delight he is. You know it's coming. You just don't know when.

Evening

Went to a huge do featuring a bunch of up their backsides ad people and their arse licking attendants, a group of voice overs. Actually the collective noun for voice overs shouldn't be "group". It's a "wank of actors. So it should be a "node" of voice overs. No, worse than that. "An "ego"? Narr. A "resonance"? Possibly. A "waveform" of voice overs? Still not got it. A "self obsessed self serving "read" of voice overs."

And a "totally up themselves horde" of advertisers. Oh make your own up.

    So…..to translate the above….The Adman's Ball at the Grosvenor Park Hotel took place this evening, where huge numbers of advertising persons all conjoin with a few actors in attendance (who hope they might remind someone they exist and thus get employed), some studio owners and engineers, and some post production bods, to drink mightily, toot possibly and get off probably.

  Being a cheapskate and not wishing to eat anything or speak to anyone during the charity auction where such things as "two hours at Birdhouse studios" with Josh (the speccy engineer) he'll record whatever you want. I'll start the bidding at two thousand pounds" are deemed attractive, I avoided the food and bought a half ticket and turned up at nine thirty and cruised from table to table, initially from voice agent table to voice agent table ("Larynx," "Emporium, "Minah", "Hoodoo" and "Alternative Mouth" were the ones in evidence. No "Dawg". "Too fucking expensive" said Lynn. "And anyway they're all c*nts") where I briefly pressed the flesh with some fellow artistes I'd worked with. The super talented Harry Gover. Impressions galore. He greeted me as The Queen. The myriad voices of Jan Riverly. Marvellous at politicians. And hugged a couple of VO agency owners. Eve from Larynx.

    "Join us JK. Join us! I'll only take 5%!"

    And Jessica from Minah.

    "Take a long holiday JK. Let some of my clients work ha ha ha!"

    Ah ha ha ha ha ha.

    And then once the bidding for things like "a meal with Clarky Goon, star of stage and screen, shall we start the bidding at one thousand five hundred?" had ended, I did my overall all over the place schmooze and encountered producer after producer who you just sort of acknowledge really. My conversations tend to go like this:

    "Hello!..(mwah mwah) Three kisses please!...ha ha… Yeah. Very continental!.... How are you?.... How's work!... Dance with you later?.... I'll be getting my badself on down like MJ!.... Yeah! Shamone! Wooh!"

    In fact the reality is that you'll never dance with this person. Or if you do, it'll be just in passing on the dancefloor.

       Oh what I forgot to mention is that everyone's in their ball gowns and tuxes (tho some coolly come in jeans and open necked shirt with a tux jacket. Like me) and the music is unbelievably loud. You are screaming in the ear for all these conversations, especially when the band's on. The band are usually a mite cabaret eg a Stones Tribute band. Though Lulu was on once. But tonight it was just a soul band who were good, but oh the din.

       During the band I was off chatting to a few engineers, or the odd producer. The best place to talk was by the loos upstairs as it wasn't so noisy and you could get someone's attention a bit better. I had a long chat with fellow artiste Jake Smoker, who was slightly pissed. We talked about the "business" and ads we'd done and how was Roop who he knew and then he let slip "You still with that Ozzie gym person?" he asked.

"Nope. All over."

He'd met her at the Poland Street Preta in Soho one afternoon after we'd both done an advert for Bababill cheese and the Girly was weirdly free. Oh I remember. I was buying her something.

"Thank fuck for that. She never said anything. 'Scuse my being so up front but I didn't know what you were up to. She must've been hell. She didn't like me. No no no!"

(She hadn't, I remember. He'd taken the piss out of her for being Australian. "Fair dinkum cobber" he'd said. And "Cor strewth" before every sentence he spoke, saying he had to preface each sentence with these phrases coz then she'd feel more at home. And ended every statement with an upward inflection.)
He continued.

"Cold as the fucking North Sea. Dress sense of a down and out. Must've been fucking good in bed for you to hang about with her. Yes. Sorry for being so personal, but she sucked your soul out of you she did."

He did have a point.
He continued

"Must get back. I'm going to try and find that Vanessa from QQQ&K You know her? The one with the great ….(he mimed a very large chest)…….."

"Good luck."

"Look. Kick me tomorrow if I've been a c*nt, but you're well out of that mate."

Producer James Moore from Red Cheese was next on the spot.

"JK! You look different! Less miserable! That's what it is! And you've shaven your head of course. Yes! You've not come out have you ha ha ha ha?" (Too many "ha has" for my liking) "You busy? Silly question. You're always busy! Busiest voice in the business. Along with Trinn. How's he? Do you see him? You must do. Is he here? He's imitating you in that Fruitbat ad isn't he the loon. Must go. The girlfriend's downstairs. See you later."

Soundbites. We all speak in soundbites. As you can imagine I didn't get a word in with this chap. And the Fruitbat is Trinn? Ffs. The fruitbat is fucking Trinn? Doing an impression of me? The info made sense of course. But it had rebounded on Trinn ha ha the whelk, as I'd got work from his "impression".

Soundbite city. Hundreds of meaningless "hello great to see yous!" And "Alrights?"

Masses of brief compliments and air kisses and confusing bottom pinches

A young bloke came up and said "Ooh hello excuse me you're JK aren't you. You're a hero of mine. You're a fabulous V.O."

I was taken aback I never thought anyone knew who anyone was. It's such an anonymous job.

"Oh that's really lovely of you. Thanks so much. I really appreciate it. We rarely get praised. What's your role? Are you an ad person or an actor? Or…" I gushed.

"I'm Pierce Sark. I stood in for you briefly on that Argot commercial. You did a wonderful job on that. And they used Patrick Stewart didn't they! He was still on the bridge on the Enterprise wasn't he. Ah well. Their loss. Well yours financially but you know what I mean. Artistically."

I was dumbstruck. What a sweet chap. How churlish I'd been. I was ashamed I'd been so rude about him. Having said that, he did sound weird, even in real life. Drawly and lispy and flat. Dull as a dullard who is the dullest dull person in Dull-land. But how nice of him. We shook hands and I said sincerely, "looking forward to working with you." He blew it completely by saying "By the way I love that fruitbat ad."

I went and danced for a few moments, dragged there by someone who I fancied but who once on the floor disappeared amongst the pulsating bodies.

I now dance like an incompetent I have to admit. I can't take it seriously any more and when dancing, swim and do gym exercises and pretend to be John Travolta and do ridiculous arm gestures, or bob on one foot. Dancing is ultimately a ludicrous exercise when in yer velvet tux or any constricting outfit and just gets you sweaty. And there was everyone sweating away like geysers. Bloody hell, the understains on that lot.

Someone familiar was getting himself badly on down near me. He spun round. It was fucking Leonard Dobbard. He clocked me.

"What the fuck are you doing here?" He cackled, gnome like. And was gone. I thought of asking him the same question, but it was too late. And he was with Chietty Chisholm ffs. Fabulous or what. And he's a dick. Bloody hell. But a well connected TV director dick.

And fuck me rigid with a large piece of industrial cable but also there was the woman from the crem.

The celebrant. The one I'd snootily given advice to. And got rid of with a flea up her schnozzola. Dressed in a huge tent like outfit. It was like something out of a dreadful novel with all the loose ends being tied up. All it needed was a leering Maria to emerge from a cake waggling a dildo, to make it the stuff of nightmares. The celebrant (well an ex celebrant by now if she was at this auspicious event) roared at me

"Oh hello Mr Fruitbat! (Wtf?) Thought I might see you here."

"Oh yes?" (Wtf again). We're both jiggling to the music of course.

"I made a reel as you suggested!"

"Good!"

"I'm with Hoodoo!"

"Glad I could be of assistance! Let's celebrate!" I bawled back. Not at the same pitch as her obviously. And not really meaning it.

"See you on the circuit!" She cackled.

Well she's got the jargon! The circuit! The video games and cartoon troll circuit! Well good luck to her. I wonder if she can wield a broad sword? Fucking hell. Any more loose ends? Any more people to fuck me over?

And yes! Trinn! Grooving like a gimp. With the lovely Nancy from Squidge agency! What on earth is she doing with him? I asked her out last year and she said she'd love to but had a boyfriend. I mean ffs they were all over each like measles. And she's a looker. And he looks as if he's had a severe fright and never got over it. Has she not realised he's a complete fuckwit?

And next to him, smug Chorley. The smuggest smugster from Smugvillle. With the moves of a giraffe hopping in a minefield. With another production company beauty. Liz from Melt. How do they do it? Surely they've been sussed. Run away JK! Run away!

The music by now was so loud it was physically excruciating. The bass resonated in everything, table legs, bottles, glasses. And above all in you. I felt decidedly uncomfortable and fled for the quieter environs of the huge interior.

And then, just as I was chatting to the very pretty Donna Jones from Lemming, (just chatting about football, no chance there, a nymphette with a spiky haired youth hanging desperately onto her hand, and a discussion about the FA Cup) the whole evening was turned upside down by Sarah being there.

Sarah Maltby-Singh. The firebrand ex. Of course she was..Sarah. The "don't go there" girl. The "argh hide she'll emasculate you with curling tongs" woman. Who was of course a producer at Felch who I'd gone out with for about a month just after splitting up with Naomi and I was shit to her. I admit it. I was rubbish. I didn't want to see anyone I was too miserable and so I just couldn't get it together at all with her. And she masked her inadequacies by drinking too much. And to my horror at the time my insouciance made her more keen on me. Which culminated in the naked knife incident when I'd suggested we stop seeing each other. And there she was, looking fabulous, with every appalling insecurity bubbling under the surface of that exotically structured black lace ball gown and those elegant fuck-me shoes.

"Hello you gorgeous man" she purred at me. Though she'd clearly had far too much to drink as usual and it was only eleven thirty.

"No don't be attracted by this JK" I counselled myself. "Leave it mate. Leave it. She's pissed out of her skull. As usual."

And I ignored myself and she drawled alluringly

"Are you not bored with all of this? Why not come back to my place and make love?"

Well. Something like that. A bit cruder obviously. And I slipped out with her and took her back to her place in Brondesbury….(I'd driven to the Ball and parked on a single yellow line round the corner) and she fell asleep en route absolutely plastered in the car, which of course she always was and was always the problem and was why we split up in the first place (as well as her dreadful insecurities that I tried to be sympathetic about but it frequently ended in her hitting me). Having rummaged in her bag for her keys, I carried her into her flat (well with her stumbling help. I'm not that butch!) and left her on her bed. Well done. Mother would have been very pleased.

I forgot to say. My main joy, on wandering off to the loo at the ball, was to see the rather lovely Irish girl Siobhan, who I'd worked with last month on the Austrian designer gabbly ad who worked for Bibble Bobble Berk and Smee.

I got her email address (as one does) asking ostensibly for a copy of the ad I'd done but hoping to ask her out. Getting the email is not like asking for a number. It's less aggressive and could possibly be just business. But it's a way in. She's a very good height with all the appropriate things I like in a girl: ie she appears to like me and laughs at all my jokes. And she's beautiful and bright and fun. And well proportioned…….and and and……

Sat 28th November

    Emailed Siobhan. Rather nicely I thought, in the form of a dialogue:

JKoohbanana72@yahoo.co.uk
to siobhan.mchinnie@bbb&s.org.uk

JK: (breathlessly sauntering into the studio) Hello. It's me. I wondered if you'd like to….
SIOBHAN: (interrupting) Who?
JK: (now a little desperate) JK. I did the Austrian read on that ad where….
SIOBHAN: No I have no recollection of you at all.
JK: (pathetic) But….but…surely….I er…
SIOBHAN: Wait a minute. I do remember you! You're the gabbling one with the unfortunate er…
JK: (desperately interrupting) Can we go out for a drink sometime?
SIOBHAN: (OTT) Oh yes! Oh yes! Oh yes!

I sent that. I got this back:

SIOBHAN: (VOTT) Oh yes! Oh yes! Oh yes! Thursday ok? I'll ring. What's your number?

I emailed it! Hooray! I really like her!

TO BE CONTINUED IN "CAN YOU BE HAPPY BUT SAD?" DECEMBER TO APRIL. PART TWO OF "AN ACTOR'S DIARY"